THE CUILLIN
& Other Skye Mountains

*The Cuillin Ridge & 100 select routes for
mountain climbers & hillwalkers*

mica

Tom Prentice first visited the Cuillin of Skye in 1976 and has been a regular visitor ever since. A journalist by profession he is former Editor of Climber and Assistant Editor of The Great Outdoors (TGO) magazines, author of Mica's two-volume Walkers' Guides to *Loch Lomond and The Trossachs National Park* and a joint-author of the SMC (Scottish Mountaineering Club) guide to *The Grahams & The Donalds*. Until 2017 he was Publisher for the SMC, overseeing the compilation and production of their climbing, scrambling and hillwalking guidebooks. A member of the SMC, and the Alpine Club, he lives in Glasgow with his wife Gerrie and has a daughter

THE CUILLIN
& Other Skye Mountains

*The Cuillin Ridge and 100 select routes for
mountain climbers & hillwalkers*

Tom Prentice

mica

ISBN: 978-1-9993728-0-4
A catalogue record for this book is available from the British Library

Front Cover: Am Bàsteir and Sgùrr a' Fionn Choire, Northern Cuillin

WARNING

The British Mountaineering Council and Mountaineering Scotland state that climbing and mountaineering are activities with a danger of personal injury or death.

Much of the Cuillin of Skye can be made safer with the use of a climbing rope and specialist climbing equipment, but this is not possible in all situations and there are few more dangerous activities in the mountains than climbing without a rope.

Rapidly changing weather and extensive areas of loose and unstable rock give the complex terrain of the Cuillin a level of seriousness out of proportion to their modest height. Wearing a climbing helmet is particularly recommended.

Mountain climbers and hillwalkers tackling the Cuillin and other Skye mountains should be aware of and accept these risks and be responsible for their own actions and involvement.

While every effort has been made to check the accuracy of the information contained within this book, neither Mica Publishing, nor the author accept liability for personal or third party injury or death, or damage to property, arising from its use.

Published by **Mica Publishing**, Glasgow & Edinburgh

Printed & bound through Latitude Press, Cumbria, England

Distributed by Cordee, 11 Jacknell Road, Dodwells Industrial Estate, Hinkley, LE10 3BS
(t) 01455 611185   (e) sales@cordee.co.uk   (w) www.cordee.co.uk

North from Blàbheinn over Srath na Crèitheach to Sgùrr nan Gillean and the Northern Cuillin, left, and Marsco, right

CONTENTS

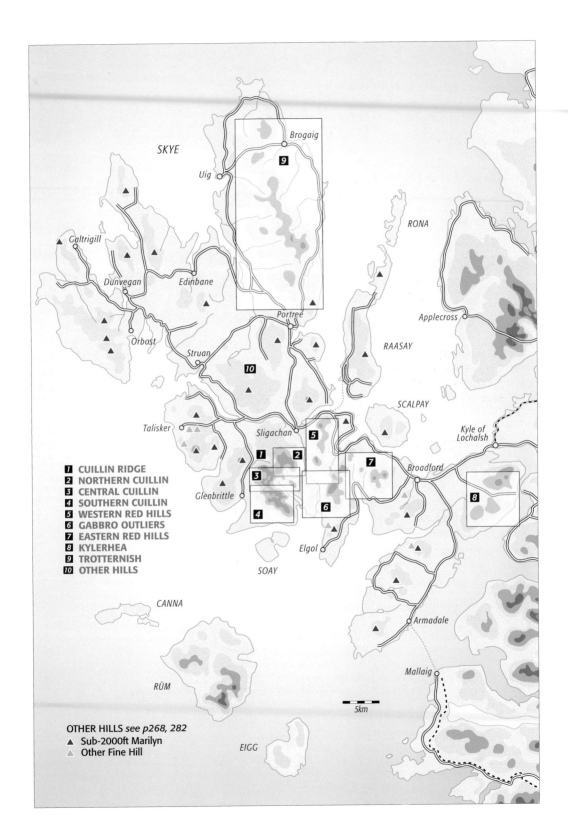

SKYE

Brogaig

9

Uig

RONA

Galtrigill

Dunvegan

Edinbane

Applecross

Portree

Orbost

Struan

RAASAY

10

SCALPAY

Talisker

Sligachan

Kyle of
Lochalsh

5

1 **2**

7

Broadford

3

6

8

Glenbrittle

4

Elgol

1 CUILLIN RIDGE
2 NORTHERN CUILLIN
3 CENTRAL CUILLIN
4 SOUTHERN CUILLIN
5 WESTERN RED HILLS
6 GABBRO OUTLIERS
7 EASTERN RED HILLS
8 KYLERHEA
9 TROTTERNISH
10 OTHER HILLS

SOAY

CANNA

Armadale

Mallaig

RÙM

5km

OTHER HILLS *see p268, 282*
▲ Sub-2000ft Marilyn
▲ Other Fine Hill

EIGG

Glamaig/Sgùrr Mhairi, granite scree giant of the Western Red Hills. To the right is the summit of Beinn Dearg Mhòr

Skye is a paradise for mountain climbers and hillwalkers. This guidebook describes more than 100 varied mountain routes from all over the island, ranging from some of the most challenging in Britain, to pleasant ascents of grassy summits.

The jewel in the island's crown is **The Cuillin**. This is the only mountain range in Britain that bears any sort of comparison with the Alps and Pyrenees and a summer traverse of the Cuillin Ridge, the 30 or so peaks and tops that form the Cuillin crest, is a major challenge to any mountain climber.

However, a full traverse isn't the only way to tackle these summits. In fact, most mountain climbers in the Cuillin aren't doing a full traverse at all. They are climbing one of the 11 Munros and eight Munro Tops (*see p10, 19–20, 286*). This can involve rock climbing up to Moderate grade and is a big enough challenge for many; no other British mountains require so much hands-on climbing.

Understandably, some hire Mountain Guides to help them succeed on these summits (*see p16*). However, others want to tackle them independently and these people are the main focus of this guidebook.

While up and down tick'em routes are possible on all of the peaks, they are just scratching the surface of what is possible. The Cuillin lends itself to some fabulous mountain days, enchaining multiple peaks round the corries to produce numerous rounds, which are among the finest mountain outings we have. In Britain, very little comes close to this level of quality, especially outside of Scotland.

For anyone actually attempting a full traverse of the **Cuillin Ridge**, prior knowledge can make a significant difference between success and failure. There is no better way to get this knowledge than by doing the Cuillin rounds in this book. They will reveal the greater potential of the area and some of the fine peaks off the main ridgeline, that don't get the attention of Munro-baggers or Ridge-traversers; peaks such as Sgùrr na h-Uamha, Sgùrr an Fheadain, Sgùrr Thuilm, Druim nan Ramh and Sgùrr Dubh Beag.

Skye also has masses to offer beyond the Cuillin. **Gabbro Outliers** Belig, Garbh-bheinn, Sgùrr nan Each, Clach Glas and Blàbheinn, are as fine as any Cuillin peak. Clach Glas and Blàbheinn offer one of the top traverses on the island, while diminutive Sgùrr na Stri, sandwiched between the Cuillin and the Gabbro Outliers, presents a panoramic view into the Coruisk basin; one of the great mountain views of the world.

And that's just the gabbro peaks. In total contrast to the spiky Cuillin ridges are the majestic granite domes of the **Western** and **Eastern Red Hills**, with their spectacular sea views. These Corbetts and Grahams offer less frequented hillwalking rounds and their lower altitude makes them good objectives in uncertain weather.

Two remaining mountain areas present yet more contrast. The Grahams and Marilyns (*see p10*) of the **Kylerhea** peaks are formed from Torridonian sandstone, in complete contrast to the basalt spine of **Trotternish**, which forms the island's northern arm. The traverse of this 22km upland ridge gives one of the island's great routes above massive lava cliffs peppered by gullies, tottering towers and lost valleys.

If that isn't enough, there are lots of comparatively low-level hills scattered around the island, some of which are **Sub-2000ft Marilyns** and some just **Other Fine Hills**. Despite their height, a few are among the best wee hills in Scotland. *See Mountain Index p286.*

USING THIS GUIDE
Grades

Hillwalks in this guide have not been graded. Hillwalks in **The Cuillin** and the **Gabbro Outliers** are among the highest mountains and on the roughest terrain, often with sections of easy scrambling. They are followed by the granite peaks of the **Western** and **Eastern Red Hills** where copious scree can be encountered. Aside from the peaks of **Trotternish**, the remaining areas offer less mountainous hillwalks, although poor visibility can still make them very challenging.

The Scottish Mountaineering Club (SMC) publishes definitive guides to Rock Climbing and Scrambling (*see p11*). The grades in this guide reflect SMC guidebooks. While an attempt has been made to take account of factors such as technical difficulty, exposure, steepness and style of climbing, grading is subjective and cannot take into account an individual's strengths, weaknesses or psychological approach on the day. In general though, moves feel harder in descent than ascent. All gradings are for dry conditions. If there is any doubt, always use a rope (*see p11, 15, 17*).

Scrambling Grades

Hillwalks gradually morph into scrambles, as rocky steps and ridges increase the need to use the hands.
• **Grade 1** – Much of the Cuillin is at this grade. There may be some exposure and the hands will be used on and off, but the mountaineering terrain is fairly straightforward and any climbing is unsustained or avoidable.
• **Grade 2** – Slightly more complicated mountaineering terrain, often with longer sections of climbing, requiring greater concentration, confidence and balance. Some may require the reassurance of a rope.
• **Grade 3** – Steep sections of climbing, needing greater confidence, experience and technical ability. The terrain may be very exposed and the climbing, while short, may be steep and intimidating to ascend or retreat from. Many will require the reassurance of a rope.

Rock Climbing Grades

As the rock steepens and becomes more technical, scrambles morph into rock climbs.
• **Moderate** – Move for move there can be little difference between this and Grade 3 scrambling. Moderate generally indicates more sustained sections of technical climbing where retreat may not be easy. Many will use climbing kit (*see p11, 17*) at this grade.
• **Difficult** – More technical terrain requiring rock climbing skill and experience. Most will use full climbing kit at this grade.
• **Severe** – Even more technical and serious terrain requiring rock climbing skill and experience. Almost all will use full climbing kit at this grade.

Timings

Time is subjective and influenced by many factors including fitness, terrain, vertical ascent, steepness, and the weather. As such, the timings in this guide are merely indicators of how long a route might take.

Time has been added for abseils where they occur, but no time has been added for stops, or for finding the best route. In the Cuillin and Gabbro Outliers, the route isn't always obvious and time spent finding the route, or following a sub-optimal route, can make a significant difference. All timings are for unroped climbing.

Needle Rock, left, and Old Man of Storr among the jumbled pinnacles of Coire Faoin, The Storr, Trotternish

Negotiating the rough granite boulderfield on Beinn na Caillich's East Face, Eastern Red Hills

Ascent, Descent, Distance & Grid References

Total ascent and descent is hard to calculate accurately. Counting contours is a start, but a long rocky ridge may involve significant ascent and descent between contours over its length, and this ascent and descent will not be represented in any calculation.

Reading ascent and descent directly from a GPS unit can be more reliable. However, digital OS mapping on mapping software applications is NOT accurate – you just need to run the cursor over a spot height on an imported digital map to see that. The height indicated will not be that on the map and different applications return different figures for ascent and descent over the same distance.

However, digital OS mapping does appear to record distance fairly accurately. Reading a GPS Track on different mapping applications gives the same figure, while tracing a GPS Track with an application's Route Tool, gives a similar figure to the original GPS Track.

Grid references have been taken from mapping software and in the field readings and are given to eight figures. They are **not** pin point accurate and should **only** be used as an approximate guide. They are useful for pre-planning using mapping software or online mapping, ie *www.osmaps.ordnancesurvey.co.uk*

Maps & Symbols

Route maps are drawn from out of copyright Ordnance Survey (OS) mapping, supplemented by in the field GPS tracks and personal observation. Route maps are only sketch maps and you are advised to purchase the up-to-date Ordnance Survey or Harvey maps (*see p17*). Coloured triangles on maps are as follows:

▲ Munros

282 peaks over 914.4m/3000ft. Originally compiled by Sir Hugh Munro in 1891.

▲ Munro Tops

226 lesser peaks over 914.4m/3000ft. Originally compiled by Sir Hugh Munro in 1891.

▲ Corbetts

222 peaks between 762m/2500ft and 914m/2999ft with a drop of at least 152.4m/500ft. Originally compiled by J Rooke Corbett in the 1930s.

▲ Grahams

219 peaks between 609.6m/2000ft and 762m/2500ft with a drop of at least 152.4m/500ft. Named after Fiona Graham.

▲ Sub-2000ft Marilyns

Marilyns are peaks throughout the British Isles with a prominence of above 150m/492.1ft. These include some Munros and all Corbetts and Grahams with the required prominence. The Sub-2000ft Marilyns fill the 'gap' below the Grahams. The list was created by Alan Dawson and named after ill-fated sex symbol Marilyn Monroe.

▲ Other Fine Hills

These are fine hills which do not appear on any of the above lists, although someone, somewhere is guaranteed to have put them on some height list or other. All are worth an ascent.

▲ Other Hills

These are generally small or unremarkable peaks.

—— Route	🅿 Car Park or Layby
—— Alternative Route	🅿 Other Parking
===== Track	
══ Road	
----- Other Path	

Map Names

The Ordnance Survey sporadically updates the names on its maps to currently accepted Gaelic spellings. Some maps show changes and some do not, while others have some instances changed but not all. The result is an odd mish-mash, where you have Sgùrr nan Banachdaich (new spelling) alongside the bealach, burn and corrie retaining the old spelling of Banachdich. Similarly, the OS have started changing Coir' to Coire. So Coire (Coir') a' Mhadaidh is now next door to Coir' a' Tairneilear and Coire (Coir') an Lochain lies alongside Coir' a' Chaoruinn. In an attempt to provide continuity, this guidebook adopts new OS spellings throughout.

Left & Right

In route descriptions, left and right are used looking up on ascent and looking down on descent, unless otherwise stated. In addition, a geographical indicator has often been included to reduce ambiguity.

GENERAL & FURTHER READING
Climbing Kit & Helmet

Carrying a rope, small rack, harness and belay device is recommended for all routes involving scrambling or technical climbing, but more climbing kit will be needed for a full traverse of the Cuillin Ridge (see p17). A 30m rope is probably adequate for ascending all the Munros except the Inaccessible Pinnacle, (see p129), where 40–50m is preferable. The Cuillin and Gabbro Outliers have a lot of loose rock and wearing a helmet is recommended.

Midges & Ticks

Skye is notorious for midges during late spring and summer and cleggs (horseflies) can also be trouble-some. Repellant will keep them away and there are lots of alternative brands available. Deet (diethel toluamide) is the most effective ingredient, although 'Smidge' does seem to keep work. A midge hood is a worthwhile investment if camping on Skye.

Sheep and deer ticks are present, although less so in the rocky Cuillin. It is worth taking precautions when moving through forestry, heather, or long grass (repellant on lower legs) and checking legs after a day out, as some ticks can carry the unpleasant Lyme Disease. www.lymediseaseaction.org.uk

Camping & Facilities

Skye has a lot of holiday accommodation although most is booked well in advance for spring and summer. There are a number of small campsites, but the two main ones are in Glenbrittle www.dunvegan castle.com/your-visit/glenbrittle-campsite-cafe/ glenbrittle-campsite/ and at Sligachan www.sligachan.co.uk/camping/

There are large supermarkets and petrol stations in Portree and Broadford. The latter station is open 24hrs.

Access

The Land Reform (Scotland) Act 2003 grants everyone the right to be on most land and inland water for recreation, providing they act responsibly.

These rights and responsibilities are explained in the Scottish Outdoor Access Code www.outdooraccess-scotland.scot

Weather Forecasts

www.mwis.org.uk, www.metoffice.gov.uk www.bbc.co.uk/weather (see also p15)

Further Reading

Skye Scrambles, Noel Williams, SMC (Scottish Moun-taineering Club) 2017. The scramblers' bible and a must for anyone venturing off the beaten track in the Cuillin.

Skye The Cuillin, Mike Lates, SMC 2011. The comprehensive guide to rock climbing in the Cuillin.

The Islands of Scotland Including Skye, Derek Fabian, Graham Little & Noel Williams, SMC 1989. Good general coverage of Skye's main mountains, but looking a bit dated.

The Cuillin, Gordon Stainforth, Constable 2002. A photo exploration of the Cuillin. Out of print.

Skye Walking, Scrambling and Exploring, Ralph Storer, David & Charles 1989. A useful, general overview of outdoor Skye. Out of print.

50 Best Routes on Skye and Raasay, Ralph Storer, Berlinn 2012. Interesting if limited selection (some 30 routes in the mountains), marred by vague descriptions. First published in 1996 and looking a bit dated.

The Isle of Skye, Terry Marsh, Cicerone, 2015. First published in 1996, the recent revision has extended many routes onto the high tops of the Cuillin. The result is not a success, producing a confused and confusing guidebook.

The Cuillin of Skye, Ben Humble, Ernest Press 1986. Ben Humble's history of exploration in the Cuillin was first published in 1952. An excellent read, although recent detailed research by Stuart Pedlar updates and corrects many aspects of the text.

Acknowledgements

I am grateful to my many companions for memorable days among the mountains of Skye; Rab Anderson, Dave Broadhead, Ian Brown, Calum Fraser, Gerrie Fellows, Maggie Fellows, James Hotchkis, Kevin Howett, Nick Kempe, Peter Macdonald, Freya Prentice, Richard Prentice, Simon Richardson, Raymond Simpson, Alan Smith, Duncan Tannerhill, Duncan Tunstall, Noel Williams & Peter Wilson.

Thanks to Rab Anderson for checking the manuscript.

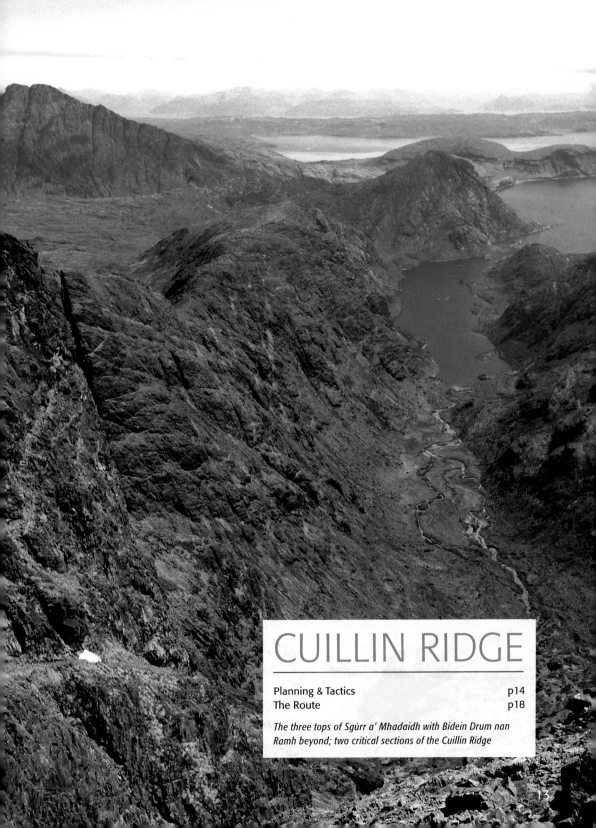

CUILLIN RIDGE

The three tops of Sgùrr a' Mhadaidh with Bidein Drum nan Ramh beyond; two critical sections of the Cuillin Ridge

13

Cuillin Ridge – Planning & Tactics

*P*lanning, safety, speed, good judgement and route-finding, are critical for success, as is a spell of settled weather. Prior knowledge will speed any ascent and bring the chances of success that little bit closer

Crossing Sgùrr Theàrlaich en route to Sgùrr MhicChoinnich on the Round of Coire Làgan

At 25km/15.5 miles, some 3000m/9850ft of ascent and descent, nearly 30 named summits including 11 Munros (if Sgùrr Dubh Mòr is included – see Short-cuts & Bypasses p16) and seven Munro Tops, continuous scrambling with sections of Moderate to Severe rock climbing and the likelihood of at least four abseils, completing the Cuillin Ridge on-sight in a single day is a massive challenge to any mountaineer.

The first traverse from Gars-bheinn to Sgùrr nan Gillean was made on 10th June 1911 by Leslie Shadbolt and Alastair McLaren, in 12hrs 18mins. Leaving Glen Brittle at about 4am, they reached Gillean at 6.25pm and were probably down at Sligachan 2hrs later; a total round trip of about 16 hours. Both were rock climbers with Skye first ascents to their credit and were familiar with most of the Ridge, although some linking sections were new. 100 years later, their **total** time of 16–17 hours is still a good aiming point.

By way of comparison, in October 2013 Finlay Wild traversed from Gars-bheinn to Sgùrr nan Gillean in 2hrs 59mins 22secs. Not surprisingly, his time reflected his intimate knowledge of the Ridge gained from many, many visits.

Most suitors fail on their first attempt. Skill, ability and fitness, planning and tactics, and a helpful weather forecast, are all essential ingredients for success, whether you try for a one day traverse, or spread your attempt over two days. Prior knowledge of the Ridge is also critical and the routes in this guidebook offer the opportunity to become familiar with the tougher sections, before committing to a full traverse.

GENERAL
Effort

So how tough is it? Physically and mentally demanding is the answer. The frequently complex terrain can be loose and rough underfoot and the rock steep and exposed. Mountaineering skills such as good planning, route-finding ability, teamwork and efficient ropework, will make the difference between success and failure.

Physical fitness gained among the mountains of Scotland, the Lake District, Snowdonia or Ireland, is likely to be sufficient, but this is only part of the story. Only those used to multi-peak rounds or routes of Alpine proportions, can imagine how deep you will need to dig, physically and mentally. Add some poor weather making navigation difficult, a sharp wind or blazing sunshine and the pressure will be on.

Climbing Ability

The Ridge is a mountaineering expedition. If you have the confidence to move quickly, safely and efficiently, on often loose and exposed terrain, wearing a rucksack and boots, then you'll be primed for success. A Ridge traverse isn't the place to learn rope management and how to abseil. You should already have practical experience in the equipment you'll be using.

Technical rock-climbing ability is important, as rock-climbing up to Severe will be encountered at some half dozen places, often on steep and polished rock, that feels closer to VS after hours on your feet. So, the general advice for attempting a Ridge traverse is, the more climbing experience you have the better. This isn't somewhere to climb at the limit of your grade, nor do you want to fail with the end in sight.

Speed vs Safety

The classic Mountaineering conundrum. Specific details of all the techniques below can be found on the internet. The British Mountaineering Council (BMC) has a series of useful videos on scrambling techniques.

Large sections of the Ridge offer relatively straight-forward ground and many people will solo this (*see Grades p9*). However, once the exposure, angle and technicality increase, the following can be used at different points, depending on experience and whether you are attempting a one or two-day traverse.

• **Pitching as a Rock Climb** – If you pitch everything you will take forever. This doesn't matter so much providing you have food, are prepared to bivouac and the weather holds. But the route will be never ending and you'll need stamina and luck to make it to the end.

• **Moving Together** – Alpine Mountaineers use this technique to provide a balance between speed and safety where the terrain demands. Pairs are roped some 15m apart and move together, the lead climber carrying a small 'rack' (*see p17*), placing protection and using natural features as running belays when required. The second climber limits slack rope in the system by varying speed, collects the protection in passing and hands it back to the leader when required. Both climbers can take a static belay at any point if a particularly hard section is encountered. This technique requires prac-tise. It will not prevent a fall, but providing there are running belays in place, it can limit the distance fallen.

• **Short Roping** – This technique aims to prevent a slip becoming a fall and can be used on less technical ground. Pairs are roped some 3m apart and move together, stopping at strategic points to brace them-selves and the rope, while the other climber negotiates a tricky or exposed section. The rope provides confi-dence and security, but may not stop a catastrophic fall when the braced climber is unable to absorb all the energy generated. This technique requires practise.

• **Soloing** – The fastest method is also the most dangerous. If you want to traverse the Ridge in a single day then you will have no option but to solo much of it and that will involve downclimbing steep technical ground as well as ascending it. Needless to say, safe soloing requires levels of skill, confidence and 'risk awareness' that only come from experience. For example, the knowledge that if you are soloing and there is a party above, then being hit by a small stone they dislodge, could have disastrous consequences.

• **Abseiling** – Nothing on the Ridge has to be abseiled, that is, everything can be avoided or down-climbed at a 'reasonable' standard, given ability and

good conditions. However, downclimbing is intimidating and some of these sections are steep, awkward and worryingly exposed. Accordingly, on a South to North traverse, most will opt to abseil three tricky sections.

• **Into the T-D (Theàrlaich-Dubh) Gap** – although the Gap can be avoided altogether via the West Face of Sgùrr Alasdair (*see p148, 157*).

• **Inaccessible Pinnacle** – although the confident solo scrambler can reverse back down the East Ridge.

• **Bidein Druim nan Ramh** – although the two abseils down the Central Peak can be avoided by utilising South Gap Gully and North Gap Gully (*see p80–3*).

Many of the other tricky descents are short and can be downclimbed either solo or with the security of a rope. While most of them can be abseiled, this is time-consuming and always requires good ropework. The last thing you want is to get the ropes stuck.

Commitment

It is possible to escape from the Ridge at many places, although it will require care and good route-finding in poor visibility. Knowledge that you can easily bail from the Ridge can be a life saver, but the option of being able to give up without dire conse-quences, can also provide an easy incentive to fail.

Weather

Conditions can make or break a mountaineering expedition and Skye's weather is notoriously fickle. Rain is one thing, but wind, mist and sun, can also play havoc with carefully laid plans. In recent years May to June have given some stable weeks, although mist and wind can still be limiting factors. Northerly to south-easterly winds usually offer the best conditions, but wet westerlies only mean one thing...

Gabbro gives reasonable grip in the wet. However, many holds have been polished by generations of climbers and much of the route is on fine-grained basalt and other lavas, which have the frictional properties of wet ice. The Ridge is best avoided completely in the wet.

TACTICS
Prior Knowledge

Making an on-sight attempt on the Ridge is a risky tactic, as the odds are significantly improved by researching critical, complex sections. Some of these are easily checked on the ground, but others may be too time-consuming and require guidebook study instead. Almost all of the Ridge is covered by the rounds and routes in this book, any of which will build the neces-sary knowledge. Reconnoitring sections of the Ridge in good weather, recording GPS tracks and waymarking significant points, will give you a route to follow should you encounter poor visibility (*see GPS p17*).

Short-cuts & Bypasses

Sections of the route can be bypassed to save time and energy. The Ridge is a mountaineering route, requiring mountain tactics; the ultimate goal is a successful end to end traverse and that may require compromise.

• **Sgùrr Dubh Mòr** – Although most now include this Munro in a traverse, it isn't actually on the ridgeline and you'll save time and energy that you may need later by missing it out.

• **T-D Gap** – Avoid this bottleneck by traversing west below the cliffs of Sgùrr Theàrlaich in upper Coire a' Ghrunnda and climbing Sgùrr Alasdair (*see p148, 157*).

• **Sgùrr Alasdair** – You can't miss out the highest peak on Skye and it's only a short diversion (*see p139–41*).

• **King's Chimney** – Collie's Ledge (Hart's Ledge in some guides) on Sgùrr MhicChoinnich is quicker than roping-up for King's Chimney and a highlight in itself (*see p149 & 151*).

• **An Stac** – Can be climbed direct, although most avoid it via stony ledges on the left (*see p126, 150*).

• **Sgùrr na Banachdaich Centre Top** – Probably quicker to go round than over, but not by much (*see p114–5*).

• **Three Teeth** – Probably quicker to go round than over, but again not by much (*see p118*).

• **Bidein Druim nan Ramh** – This time-consuming section requires scrambling and usually two abseils. However, the whole peak can be bypassed via scree on the west (Coire a' Tairneilear) side (*see p80–3*).

• **Sgùrr na Bàirnich** – This summit is easily avoided on its west side, but it doesn't save much (*see p95*).

• **Basteir Tooth** – Avoid completely via scree on its west (Coire a' Bhàsteir) side, ascend to Bealach a' Bhàsteir and climb up and down Am Bàsteir's East Ridge (*see p54*).

South to North, or North to South?

In summer, almost everyone traverses the ridge South to North, but that means some of the most sustained sections of climbing (the Tops of Mhadaidh and Bidein Druim nan Ramh) come in the second half, followed by the Basteir Tooth, Am Bàsteir and Sgùrr nan Gillean at the very end. Other disadvantages are the long slog to reach and climb Gars-bheinn (if this is your desired approach) and the potential log-jam at the T-D Gap.

It also feels there are more descents with tricky route-finding (Theàrlaich to MhicChoinnich, Banachdaich to Thormaid, An Dorus, Sgùrr a' Mhadaidh to its Tops, Bidein Druim nan Ramh West and Central Peaks, An Caisteal) and some tricky unavoidable ascents (T-D Gap or Sgùrr Alastair, Basteir Tooth – Am Bàsteir Link, Sgùrr nan Gillean's West Ridge).

On a North to South approach some steeper bits of climbing can be abseiled (base of Gillean's West Ridge, Am Bàsteir – Basteir Tooth Link and Basteir Tooth, Sgùrr a' Mhadaidh Second and Third Tops, T-D

Gap). However, there's still some tricky and unavoidable ascents, such as An Caisteal, Bidein Druim nan Ramh's Central Peak (although North Gap and South Gap gullies can be utilised) and some tricky descents such as Sgùrr Thormaid to Sgùrr na Banachdaich and Sgùrr Theàrlaich to Sgùrr Alasdair.

Route-finding

The best line is often indicated by a path, rock that's been worn to a lighter colour, or obvious marks such as crampon scratches from increasingly popular winter traverses. But be warned, some worn paths, such as that leading east from Banachdaich on the descent to Bealach Thormaid, below and beyond Mhadaidh's Third Top and on the east side of An Caisteal's summit are dead ends, worn by people going down them, only to come back up again! Meantime, crampon scratches can be misleading and the lighter colour of a worn route is easy to see in the dry, but everything turns black in the wet.

Mountain Guides

Employing a professional Mountain Guide will increase your chances of success. Few will match their knowledge of the route, the tricks of the trade, their insight into weather and conditions and what might or might not be possible. A number operate in the Cuillin.

Bivouac

While one-day traverses are common, doing the route over two days with a bivouac, is probably the most popular approach. It removes the manic element from a traverse and gives leeway for unexpected delays. Given good weather, a night out on the Ridge and seeing the dawn break, is an unforgettable experience.

An Dorus between Sgùrr a' Ghreadaidh and Sgùrr a' Mhadaidh, is about half-way in terms of time. There are reasonable bivvi sites at NG 4430 2275 on the Bealach a' Coire Ghreadaidh (not named on maps) between the Three Teeth and the South Ridge of Sgùrr a' Ghreadaidh (*see p118*) and some 100m below the summit on the West Face of Sgùrr a' Mhadaidh at NG 4461 2348 (no water, but spring snow possible). But bivouacking has it's downside. Spending two or more days requires more food and equipment and the more weight on your back, the tougher the route will be – see Equipment.

Pre-stashing

One approach to keeping rucksack weight to a minimum is to stash food, water and bivvi gear in advance. But make sure you mark the spot well, with a GPS for example. However, if you fall short of your gear or have to abandon the route, then you have further complications to deal with.

EQUIPMENT
Climbing Kit
Carrying a rope, small rack, harness and belay device is recommended for all routes in the Cuillin involving scrambling or short technical sections, such as on Sgùrr a' Ghreadaidh via An Dorus. Unless making a lightweight one-day solo, a full traverse will require more.
• **Full Rack**; 4-5 quickdraws (doubled up 60cm slings with krabs, not fixed krab 'sport climbing' style), 3-4 single (120cm) slings, 4-5 double (240cm) slings, 4-5 wires, 1-2 cams, 6 krabs including 3 screw gate, prussik loop for abseil back-up, 4-6m abseil tape, knife, helmet, harness, belay device and a 40–50m rope.

Ice Axe, Crampons & Walking Poles
Snowslopes high on east and north-facing slopes can last until spring. Chances are you'll not need crampons, but an axe could prove useful. Poles might be useful on the approach and descent, or on snow, but will be little use on much of the Ridge, as well as being cumbersome and adding weight.

Footwear & Clothing
Footwear might range from technical running shoes, to mid or ankle height crag approach shoes, to modern lightweight mountain boots. Fit and comfort over long distance mountain terrain is critical. Rock boots could be taken for the T-D Gap and Naismith's Route, but are a lot of weight for just a few sections. Better to use one set of versatile, broken-in footwear for all situations. New socks make a big difference to comfort and blister prevention.

Clothing layers and weights will depend on prevailing weather. Waterproofs are essential, but beware the gabbro which eats lightweight fabrics for breakfast. A sun hat or a warm hat/buff and lightweight gloves should also be packed. Some like to protect their hands by wearing cheap gardening gloves – others prefer to feel the rock under their fingers. Skye can deliver weather that's sunny and dry but windy too, so bear that in mind when choosing top layers.

Bivvi Kit
This will largely depend on the weather and if you plan to pre-stash this gear and leave it for later collection, or carry it on the traverse. The minimum is probably a Gore-Tex bivvi bag, mat, extra thermal top and long-johns and possibly a light sleeping bag or light insulated jacket. If you're pre-stashing and leaving gear for later collection, then you could expand it to a 2–3 season fibre sleeping bag, gas cooker, billies, mug, 'spork' and lighter.

General Kit
An alpine-style (no pockets) 35 litre rucksack, head-torch (lithium batteries?), water bottle or bladder (Source hydration tubes fit most bottles), sun lotion, lip salve, midge repellent, simple first aid (plasters, Compeed, ibuprofen/paracetamol) and guidebook (photocopy pages and put them in sealable plastic bag).

Map, Compass, GPS & Mobile
• **Maps** – The best maps to the Ridge are the Ordnance Survey Explorer 411 *Skye-Cuillin Hills* 1:25k and Harvey *The Cuillin* 1:25k. This latter map has more topographical detail, an enlargement for the Ridge at 1:12.5k and some useful labelling. The Harvey map uses 15m and 75m index contours.
• **Compass** – The Cuillin Ridge has a reputation for sending a compass haywire. In reality, these problems are localised and forewarned is forearmed. For all the weight involved this essential item should always be carried in the mountains.
• **GPS** – Maps are fantastic in good visibility but once that is lost, the complex nature of Cuillin terrain makes identifying your position very difficult. A GPS will give an exact grid reference and higher spec models will also offer a compass and (calibrateable) altimeter. OS 1:25k or 1:50k maps pre-loaded on the device, will add another layer of navigational assistance. GPS units are heavy, but navigation is critical to safety and speed on the Ridge. Most GPSs offer 16hrs coverage and more with spare lithium batteries. Like all electronic items, a GPS can break down or fail, so it can't replace a map, compass and prior knowledge of the terrain, but it can save the day.
• **Mobile** – Well worth taking in case of accident and as a fill-in GPS, but the later function is probably best performed by a dedicated unit with replaceable batteries.

Food & Drink
• **Food** – This is largely personal choice. Carbs are good, but it's important to take tasty food you want to eat. Cereal bars, nuts, chocolate, dried apricots or mango and some treats. If you plan to stash food in advance then your choice will be wider.
• **Drink** – Avoiding dehydration is important, but at 1kg per litre, the weight of water is an issue. Judge the water situation on the ridge and plan accordingly. Drink as much as you can on the walk-in, but don't fill up and carry water until the last burn. There will probably be snow in early spring and it will be melting. The Ridge doesn't have much water later in the summer, but there are two usually reliable springs. The first is at about NG 4512 2065 near the foot of the gully below the T-D Gap, the second is the burn in upper Fionn Choire, about 75m down from the Bealach nan Lice.

It's also worth considering a carbohydrate additive for water such as SIS Go Electrolyte or carbohydrate/hydration tablets such as SIS Go Hydro.

Cuillin Ridge – The Route

*O*ne of the great mountaineering routes of the world, the Cuillin Ridge offers a roller coaster ride over uncompromisingly rugged terrain. It may not be the highest, or the longest, or the most technical and committing, but it punches well above its weight and should not be underestimated

Am Bàsteir and the Basteir Tooth from the head of Fionn Choire

Cuillin Ridge

Terrain: *Unavoidable Difficult Grade Rock Climb (avoidable sections of Severe Grade Rock Climb)*
Distance: *25km, 15.5 miles*
Ascent & Descent: *2980m; 9775ft*
Time: *15 – 20 hrs*
Start: *Glen Brittle Campsite*
Finish: *Sligachan Hotel*

NOTE – Indicated timings include some allowance for stops required for navigation, food, drink or rest.

Approach

The most popular approach to the Ridge is **from Glen Brittle** Campsite. Ascend the Coire Làgan path to a junction at NG 4206 2035 and turn right onto a well-prepared path. Follow this south-east to the broad Allt Coire Làgan, crossed by boulder-hopping, and another junction at a small cairn (NG 4344 1960), where the Coire a' Ghrunnda path turns off left.

Continue on a rougher path crossing the Allt Coire a' Ghrunnda and Allt Coire nan Laogh, before branching off left and ascending the scree-covered south-western flank of Gars-bheinn (*see p163–5*). It's a tedious ascent (making the most of occasional grassy patches and careful footwork will help), which eventually gains the main Cuillin ridgeline just west of Gars-bheinn (*7km/4.25 miles; ascent 895m/2935ft; 3hrs*).

Some advocate approaching from **Coire a' Ghrunnda** by turning left at the small cairn, NG 4344 1960 mentioned above, following the path to Loch Coire a' Ghrunnda, and gaining the Ridge at Bealach a' Garbh-choire before Caisteal a' Garbh-choire (*see p154–5*). Sacks can be left here, while Sgùrr nan Eag, Sgùrr a' Choire Bhig and Gars-bheinn are climbed as an out and back route (*see p163–5*).

However, even in good visibility the rocky route into upper Coire a' Ghrunnda can be time-consuming for anyone unfamiliar with the terrain, and this is doubly so in poor visibility (*7.5km/4.5 miles; ascent 1100m/3610ft; descent 155m/510ft; 3hrs 30mins*).

It is also possible to access Gars-bheinn **from Coruisk**, reached on foot **from Sligachan** or **from Camasunary** via the Bad Step (*see p160, 190*). The most popular Coruisk approach is by boat **from Elgol**, but there are logistical constraints. The first boats usually depart around 8.30am, so a dawn start for a one-day traverse isn't possible and given good high season weather,

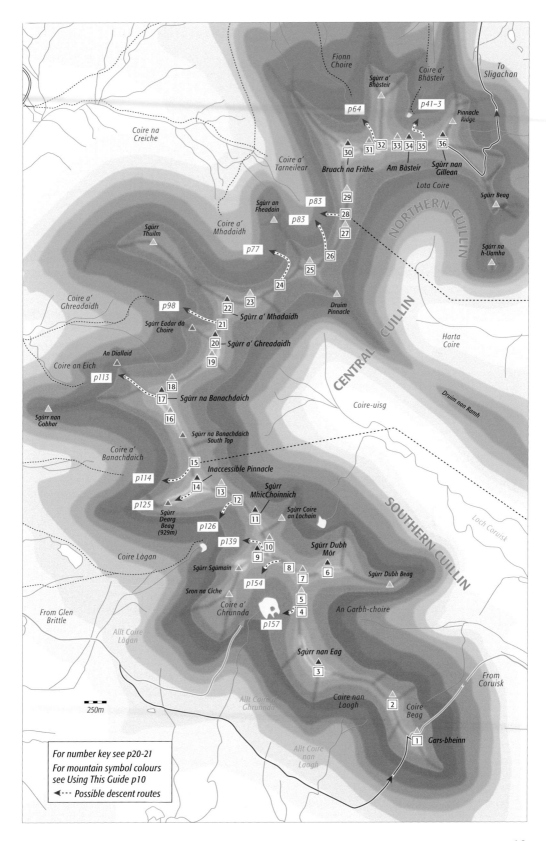

Fionn Choire

Coire a' Bhàsteir

To Sligachan

Coire na Creiche

Sgùrr a' Bhàsteir

p64

p41–3

Pinnacle Ridge

Coire a' Tarneilear

30 31 32   33 34 35   36

Bruach na Frithe   Am Bàsteir   Sgùrr nan Gillean

NORTHERN CUILLIN

Lota Coire

Sgùrr Beag

Sgùrr an Fheadain

p83

29

Sgùrr na h-Uamha

Coire a' Mhadaidh

p83   28

27

p77   26

25

Druim Pinnacle

Coire a' Ghreadaidh

24

CENTRAL CUILLIN

p98   23

22 Sgùrr a' Mhadaidh

Harta Coire

Sgùrr Eadar dà Choire

21

20 — Sgùrr a' Ghreadaidh

An Diallaid

19

Coire an Eich

p113   18

17 Sgùrr na Banachdaich

Coire-uisg

Druim nan Ramh

16

Sgùrr nan Gobhar

Sgùrr na Banachdaich South Top

Coire a' Banachdaich

15   Inaccessible Pinnacle

p114   14   13   Sgùrr MhicChoinnich

SOUTHERN CUILLIN

p125   12

Sgùrr Dearg Beag (929m)   11   Sgùrr Coire an Lochain

p126

Loch Coruisk

Coire Làgan

p139

Sgùrr Dubh Mòr

10

9   Sgùrr Sgùmain

8   7   6   Sgùrr Dubh Beag

Sron na Ciche   p154

From Glen Brittle

Coire a' Ghrunnda

5   An Garbh-choire

4

Allt Coire Làgan

p157

Sgùrr nan Eag

3

From Coruisk

Allt Coire a' Ghrunnda

Coire nan Laogh

2   Coire Beag

250m

1   Gars-bheinn

Allt Coire nan Laogh

For number key see p20-21
*For mountain symbol colours
see Using This Guide p10*
◄--- *Possible descent routes*

19

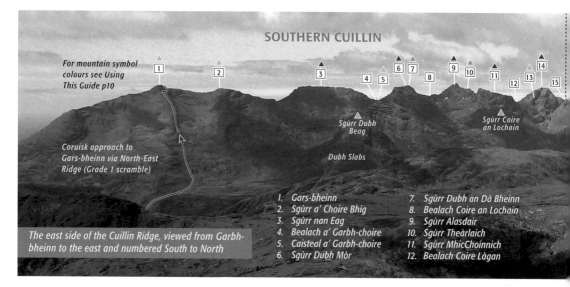

SOUTHERN CUILLIN

For mountain symbol colours see Using This Guide p10

[1] [2] [3] [4] [5] [6] [7] [8] [9] [10] [11] [12] [13] [14] [15]

Sgùrr Dubh Beag

Sgùrr Coire an Lochain

Coruisk approach to Gars-bheinn via North-East Ridge (Grade 1 scramble)

Dubh Slabs

1. Gars-bheinn
2. Sgùrr a' Choire Bhig
3. Sgùrr nan Eag
4. Bealach a' Garbh-choire
5. Caisteal a' Garbh-choire
6. Sgùrr Dubh Mòr

7. Sgùrr Dubh an Dà Bheinn
8. Bealach Coire an Lochain
9. Sgùrr Alasdair
10. Sgùrr Theàrlaich
11. Sgùrr MhicChoinnich
12. Bealach Coire Làgan

The east side of the Cuillin Ridge, viewed from Garbh-bheinn to the east and numbered South to North

you'll need to book in advance and compete with guided parties for a place. You'll also need to sort transport to Elgol and possible car collection later. From Coruisk, the main Cuillin ridgeline is gained via **Gars-bheinn**'s North-East Ridge, or via the scree gully at the head of **Coire Beag**, an hour's less effort than approaching from Glen Brittle (*diagram above*). Approaching from Elgol and Coruisk is a good option if you plan to take two days with a bivvi and can arrange transport to Elgol *www.mistyisleboattrips.co.uk*, or *www.bellajane.co.uk*, *(3km/1.75 mile; ascent 895m/2935ft; 2hrs 30mins)*.

The Route
SOUTHERN CUILLIN – From the summit of **Gars-bheinn**, follow the well-defined ridge over **Sgùrr a' Choire Bhig** and ascend rocky ground to the summit of **Sgùrr nan Eag**. There are reasonable bivvi sites just south and 20m below the Sgùrr a' Choire Bhig and Sgùrr nan Eag col (*see p163–5*). Cross the boulder summit of Sgùrr nan Eag and descend the North Ridge to **Bealach a' Garbh-choire** before **Caisteal a' Garbh-choire**. Climb over this or go round it on the right (*diagram* [1] & *p155–6*).

There are now **two options: (1)** To take in the Munro **Sgùrr Dubh Mòr**, go north-east across the top of An Garbh-choire and gain access to a rubble gully via a slabby wall. Ascend the gully, then broken ground up and right to the South Face. Climb this to the summit (*diagram* [1] & *p157*). Descend the South Face, then climb the East Ridge of Sgùrr Dubh an Dà Bheinn to the summit. **(2)** Alternatively, climb the blocky South Ridge of **Sgùrr Dubh an Dà Bheinn**, going left on ledges near the top, then back right to the summit.

Descend the North-West Ridge of **Sgùrr Dubh an Dà Bheinn** to **Bealach Coire an Lochain** and follow

Sgùrr Dubh an Dà Bheinn

South Ridge

East Ridge

col on pinnacled ridge

Sgùrr Dubh Mòr

option 2

option 1

rubble gully

slabby wall

Caisteal a' Garbh-choire

yellow scar

An Garbh-choire

Bealach a' Garbh-choire

[1] – Caisteal a' Garbh-choire to Sgùrr Dubh Mòr

the transverse ridge beyond for about 130m, passing over a rocky knoll to a small col at NG 4519 2064, before the ridge merges with the vertical cliffs of **Sgùrr Theàrlaich** (*diagram* [2]).

There are now **two options: (1)** Ascending straight ahead leads to the gap between Sgùrr Dubh an Dà Bheinn and Sgùrr Theàrlaich, the (Theàrlaich–Dubh) **T-D Gap**. Continue up the ridge and climb an exposed wall on the left to easier ground and the top of the pinnacle overlooking the **T-D Gap** (*diagram* [2] & *p141*). Abseil into the gap (10m) and climb the

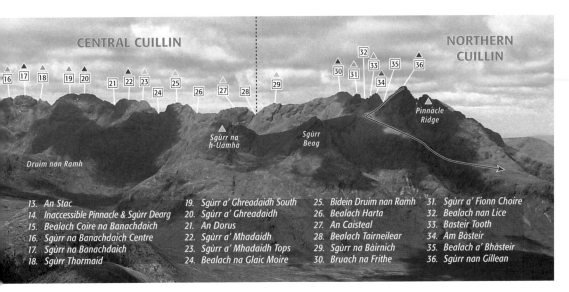

CENTRAL CUILLIN

NORTHERN CUILLIN

Pinnacle Ridge

Sgùrr na h-Uamha

Sgùrr Beag

Druim nan Ramh

13. An Stac
14. Inaccessible Pinnacle & Sgùrr Dearg
15. Bealach Coire na Banachdaich
16. Sgùrr na Banachdaich Centre
17. Sgùrr na Banachdaich
18. Sgùrr Thormaid

19. Sgùrr a' Ghreadaidh South
20. Sgùrr a' Ghreadaidh
21. An Dorus
22. Sgùrr a' Mhadaidh
23. Sgùrr a' Mhadaidh Tops
24. Bealach na Glaic Moire

25. Bidein Druim nan Ramh
26. Bealach Harta
27. An Caisteal
28. Bealach Tairneilear
29. Sgùrr na Bàirnich
30. Bruach na Frithe

31. Sgùrr a' Fionn Choire
32. Bealach nan Lice
33. Basteir Tooth
34. Am Bàsteir
35. Bealach a' Bhàsteir
36. Sgùrr nan Gillean

[2] – T-D Gap and South-West Flank of Sgùrr Alasdair

the cliffs (water possible and bivvi sites). Traverse the base of the cliffs west to below the pinnacled **Bealach Sgùmain**, then cut back right to a chimney (NG 4496 2072) on **Sgùrr Alasdair**'s South-West Flank (*diagrams* **[2] [3]** & *p157*). Climb the chimney and the face above to the summit. Descend the South-East Ridge to the col before Sgùrr Theàrlaich, then down right (Coire a' Ghrunnda) side, on scree for about 35m.

Both options now climb onto the steep South Ridge of **Sgùrr Theàrlaich** (Grade 3) and ascend it to the summit (*diagram* **[2]** & *p139–41, photo p146*). Go down the North Ridge to a rocky platform at

polished 25m chimney (Severe) on the opposite side. Continue up easier ground to about 35m short of the col (the top of the Great Stone Shoot), dividing **Sgùrr Alasdair** on the left and **Sgùrr Theàrlaich**. Sgùrr Alasdair is just a short ascent by its South-East Ridge from this col. (2) Alternatively, the **T-D Gap** can be avoided by traversing left below the cliffs and ascending **Sgùrr Alasdair**. Scramble down left (west) from the rocky knoll before the small col at NG 4519 2064, and descend into the shallow hanging corrie directly below

[3] – Chimney on the South-West Flank of Sgùrr Alasdair

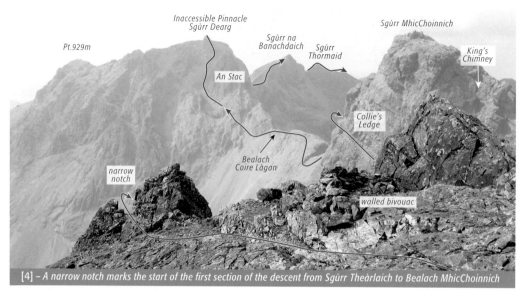

[4] – *A narrow notch marks the start of the first section of the descent from Sgùrr Theàrlaich to Bealach MhicChoinnich*

NG 4505 2093, with a walled bivouac and what looks like a sheer drop beyond to **Bealach MhicChoinnich**. Descend on the left (Coire Làgan) side to a prominent notch (*diagram* **[4]**), go through it and climb down until moves lead right (looking down) to a slab. Cross the top of the slab behind large boulders to the top of another impasse (*diagram* **[5]**). Descend the loose gully on the left (Coire Làgan) side to the top of a blocky black pillar. Go over this rightwards (looking

down) and descend friable rock to easier ground (Moderate), then up to **Bealach MhicChoinnich** (*diagrams* **[6] [7]**).

Traverse out right and climb a steep corner crack to the start of **Collie's Ledge** (named Hart's Ledge in some guidebooks). The big corner near the start is **King's Chimney** (Very Difficult). Traverse Collie's Ledge round **Sgùrr MhicChoinnich**'s West Face to join the North-West Ridge below a chimney. Climb the

[5] – *First section of the descent from Sgùrr Theàrlaich to Bealach MhicChoinnich*

[6] – *First and second sections of the descent from Sgùrr Theàrlaich to Bealach MhicChoinnich*

[7] – *The loose gully to the black pillar on the second section of the descent to Bealach MhicChoinnich*

chimney and exposed ridge beyond to the summit (*diagrams* [7] [8] & *p151*).

Return back down the North-West Ridge to near its end. Scramble down on the Coire Làgan side with some awkward moves (Grade 2) round large boulders, to the foot of the ridge (*see p136*). Traverse the top of Upper Coire Làgan to the pinnacles of **Bealach Coire Làgan** above the **An Stac Screes** (*see p126*).

Although it can be climbed direct (*see p150*), the tower of **An Stac** is usually skirted on its left (Coire Làgan) side, on a path that descends initially, then ascends scree and stone-covered ramplines up and right to the base of the **Inaccessible Pinnacle**. Climb the East Ridge (Moderate) and abseil 20m down the West Ridge (*see p129*). Descend the scree slopes of **Sgùrr Dearg**'s North-West Ridge to the **Bealach Coire na Banachdaich**.

CENTRAL CUILLIN – Gain the South Ridge of **Sgùrr na Banachdaich** and ascend via easy scrambling to the impressive tower of the **Centre Top**, before the summit. Traverse over this (Grade 2), or avoid it easily on the left, to reach the top of **Sgùrr na Banachdaich** (*see p114–5*). From the summit, follow the crest of the corrie north-west for about 50m. Don't be tempted to follow a path east down an open scree gully, but work a way north and then east, down boulders and loose rock to **Bealach Thormaid** (not named on maps), where the ridge turns sharply right (east).

Go round pinnacles and follow the worn crest to the summit of **Sgùrr Thormaid**. Cross over the summit and down to the **Three Teeth**. They are easily traversed by a worn path and some mild scrambling, or can be avoided most easily on the right, to reach the grassy col of **Bealach a' Coire Ghreadaidh** (not named on maps) and some good walled bivvi sites (*see p118*).

The long South-West Ridge of **Sgùrr a' Ghreadaidh** follows, climbed on the crest (Grade 3) or much more easily via ledges on the left, to gain the peak's **South Top**. Descend the short arete of the Top's North Ridge and continue to a steep nose on the crest beyond,

[8] – *Sgùrr Theàrlaich to Bealach MhicChoinnich and the North-West Ridge of Sgùrr MhicChoinnich*

[9] – *Descent to the stubby tower and the Three Tops, from the summit of Sgùrr a' Mhadaidh*

before the main summit. Climb this and traverse a rock fin to gain the summit (*p102–3*). Descend ledges on the left, passing left of **The Wart**, the squat rocky tower on the ridge. Descend slabby rocks with a few tricky moves (Grade 2) close to the crest (*photo p96*), to reach the slot of **Eag Dubh**. Cross over and

continue down the ridge, first on its crest then to its left, to above the col of **An Dorus** (*see p101–3*).

Looking down into **An Dorus** from above, paths go right and left. Descend the crack and corner on the left (Grade 3) to gain **An Dorus**. Move right, scramble up ramps to a worn path and follow this, or go more directly up the rock on the right, to the summit of

[10] – *The stepped corner on the Third Top*

[11] – *Corner and flake on the Second Top*

24

Sgùrr a' Mhadaidh (*see p99*).

Descend the summit crest north and drop down slabby ground on the right (Coruisk) side to a stubby tower, where the ridge turns sharply east to the **Three Tops of Sgùrr a' Mhadaidh**. Turn the stubby tower on its north (Coire a' Mhadaidh) side via a rocky break and descend the fine airy rib to the foot of the **Third Top**. Ascend easy ground to a corner-line just right of the nose of the Third Top and climb it to easier ground (Moderate). Pass over the summit to the foot of the **Second Top**. Traverse left from the boulder choke to a shallow right-slanting corner which leads to a flake. Climb the flake to its top and the short wall above to the summit (Difficult), (*diagrams* **[9] [10] [11]** *& p90–1*). Descend to the **First Top**, climb easily over this and down slabby ground to the **Bealach na Glaic Moire**.

Cross the broad bealach and swing up and left to a parallel-sided basalt staircase (*diagram* **[12]** *& p80–1*). Follow the ridge above to an upper basalt staircase on the West Ridge of the **West Peak** of **Bidein Druim nan Ramh**. Ascend this and down a slab on the other side. Some tricky downclimbing in a right-to-left spiral (Moderate) gains **Bridge Rock**, a massive boulder spanning the gullies separating West and Central Peak (*diagram* **[13]** *& p80*).

Ascend directly from **Bridge Rock**, or traverse right then up on the wall to the right, to the foot of a parallel-sided chimney and climb it to the crest and

[12] – *Bealach na Glaic Moire to Bidein Druim nan Ramh*

the summit of the **Central Peak** of **Bidein Druim nan Ramh** on the right (*diagram* **[14]**). The North-East Ridge leads down to the **North Peak** beyond. This ridge can be downclimbed (Very Difficult – Severe)

[13] – *Tricky descent to Bridge Rock from the West Peak*

[14] – *Ascent to Central Peak from Bridge Rock*

[15] – *Abseils on the Central Peak, viewed from North Peak*

but the route is very exposed and the climbing tricky and most descend it by making two abseils.

Follow the crest north to abseil slings and abseil north down a slabby wall to a cleft formed by a subsidiary summit. Scramble round this on the left (Coire a' Tairneilear) side then make a second abseil to the gap before the **North Peak** (*diagram* [15] *& p92–3*). North Peak can be climbed by traversing out left and up in an exposed position (Moderate), or avoided entirely by descending a short distance right to pick up a path which traverses round onto its East Ridge (*diagram* [16]). Zigzag down the slabby East Ridge to **Bealach Harta** (*see p83*).

It is also possible to avoid the abseils on the North-East Ridge, but still climb all three peaks, by utilising North Gap and South Gap Gully between them, but this will be time-consuming (*see p80–3*).

Continue over the long ridge beyond, crossing three clefts to reach **An Caisteal** (*diagram* [16]). The first two clefts can be crossed via ledges on the left (Coire a' Tairneilear) side, but the third requires a bold step or jump. Just short of the summit of An Caisteal descend on the left (Coire a' Tairneilear) side to gain the top of a large orange slab on the ridge beyond (*diagram* [17]) and descend it towards Bealach Tairneilear, first right, then back left to regain the crest.

[16] – *The first abseil on Bidein Druim nan Ramh Central Peak and the continuation routes on North Peak*

Bruach na Frithe   Sgùrr na Bàirnich   Sgùrr a' Fionn Choire   Am Bàsteir

orange col

An Caisteal

no!

[17] – *The route to the orange col at the top of An Caisteal's North Ridge. It is important to keep on the left (Coire a' Tairneilear) side of the summit as the right (Harta Corrie) side leads to the top of the vertical cliff shown in the photo below*

A steep final wall bars access to the bealach. Descend this first on the left (looking down) to ledges, then back right (looking down), then straight down on small positive holds (Moderate) to **Bealach Tairneilear** (*diagram* [18] *& p93–5*).

NORTHERN CUILLIN – From the bealach, ascend loose ground left of the crest then better rock, to reach the pleasant summit of **Sgùrr na Bàirnich** and a fine view of the final objectives. Sgùrr na Bàirnich can also be avoided by a traverse below the peak to reach the South Ridge of **Bruach na Frithe** (*diagram* [16] *& p95*).

Ascend the crest of the rather broken and loose South Ridge, avoiding some pinnacles on the right (Lota Corrie side) near the top. There are good bivvi spots near the summit. From **Bruach na Frithe**, descend scree on the east side to the pyramidal lump of **Sgùrr a' Fionn Choire**, which is most easily climbed up and down by its Central Gully (*see p65*).

Cross the **Bealach nan Lice** to the **Basteir Tooth** with **Am Bàsteir** behind. Most will elect to climb **Naismith's Route** (Severe) on the South Face of the **Basteir Tooth** (*diagram* [19]). If this appears too daunting, the route is wet, or there is a queue, then the only alternative on the Tooth is to descend into Lota Corrie and climb **Collie's Route** (Moderate), (*diagram* [19] *& p55–7*). From the Tooth's summit, descend to the **Basteir Nick**, the cleft between the Tooth and Am Bàsteir (*photo p54*), ascend a short

An Caisteal

orange col

no!

slabs

North Ridge

abseil

crux wall

Bealach Tairneilear

[18] – *The crux wall to Bealach Tairneilear from An Caisteal*

[19] – *Collie's Route and Naismith's Route on the Basteir Tooth, and the Basteir Tooth – Am Bàsteir Link*

slot on the right to gain grassy ledges on **Am Bàsteir** and follow them round to below a short parallel-sided chimney (at the top of Collie's Route), (*diagram* [19] [20]). Above is the Basteir Tooth – Am Bàsteir Link (*see p55–7*). Climb the chimney to an overhanging corner and chockstone (Severe) and continue to easier ground and the summit of **Am Bàsteir**, (*photo opposite*).

Descend towards the 'bad step' the short wall before the East Summit. Although this gives Difficult rock climbing in descent, it is less awkward in ascent (*see p51–3*). Scramble down the crest of the East Ridge to **Bealach a' Bhàsteir** and up the rocky arete towards **Sgùrr nan Gillean**'s **West Ridge** (*photos p52, 58*).

Go left round a detached pinnacle forming the base of the ridge on a good path overlooking Coire a' Bhàsteir, to reach a recess with two boulders on a large ledge, below a series of chimneys separated by ribs (*diagram* [21]). The long, wide chimney forming the left side of the recess has a chockstone near the bottom and is **Tooth Chimney** (Difficult). To the right are two prominent cracks forming an inverted-V, then a broad rib. Right of the broad rib is a shorter, stepped groove leading to the rocky arete. This is **Tooth**

[20] – *From the Basteir Nick below the Basteir Tooth, a slot on the Am Bàsteir side gains grassy ledges which lead to below the square-cut chimney of the Basteir Tooth – Am Bàsteir Link*

Groove & The Arete (Moderate) and the easiest line, although it necessitates traversing the exposed and rocky arete beyond. **The Arete** is polished and tricky in places with some suspect rock, but finally leads to a

28

[21] – *Tooth Groove & The Arete, the principal start to the West Ridge of Sgùrr nan Gillean*

ledge above **Tooth Chimney** (*see p43–5, photo p40*).

From the ledge, zigzag up the **West Ridge** mostly on the right, past the topknot pinnacle and towards the finger pinnacle looming above. The steep rib below the finger pinnacle can be avoided on the right. Traverse round the left side of the pinnacle, go though the key-hole window and climb the final narrow arete directly to the summit of **Sgùrr nan Gillean** (*photo p30–1*); from **Gars-bheinn** (*12km/7.5 miles; ascent 2065m/ 6775ft; descent 2015m/6610ft; 10-15hrs*).

Descent
It isn't over yet! Cross Gillean's narrow summit to the top of the **South-East Ridge**. Descend the slabby rock fin of the frontal face directly (Grade 3) (*option 1 & 2 p39*). Alternatively, near the start of the slabby rock fin, drop down right (Harta Corrie side) and descend a short distance, then traverse left (looking down), step down to broken ledges (*option 3 p39, photo 61*) and descend them to the foot of the fin.

Follow bouldery ground leftwards, then back right to a parallel-sided chimney which leads to the easier lower ridge. From this point the best route down into **Coire Riabhach** can be hard to find and requires special concentration when tired or in poor visibility.

To get the best line through the boulder-strewn corrie below, it is essential to follow the ridge right down to a small col (NG 4742 2498) with a large square boulder in it and a finger-like rock above (*see p38*).

From there, follow a scree path north-east for about

Roped climbers on the Basteir Tooth – Am Basteir Link. The lower section involves a strenuous overhang

250m, then north through boulders for about 35m to a cairn marking the top of a stony gully-rampline and go down this to the lower corrie. Descend beside the burn, then north on a good path through **Coire Riab-hach** to the plank bridge over the **Allt Dearg Beag**. Turn right and the path leads to a footbridge over the **Allt Dearg Mòr** and **Sligachan**; (*6km/3.75 miles; ascent 20m/65ft; descent 965m/3166ft; 2hrs*).

NORTHERN CUILLIN

Descending the West Ridge of Sgùrr nan Gillean to Bealach a' Bhàsteir.
Am Bàsteir, Sgùrr a' Fionn Choire and Bruach na Frithe behind and
Sgùrr a' Bhàsteir on the right

Sgùrr na h-Uamha from Sgùrr nan Gillean, showing the crux wall above the col separating the North and South Buttresses (see p34). The twin summited peak in the background is Sgùrr na Stri.

Sgùrr Beag & Sgùrr na h-Uamha

Two very different peaks lie at the north end of the main Cuillin ridgeline. While Sgùrr Beag is little more than a pleasant ridge walk, Sgùrr na h-Uamha is in a totally different league; a serious and committing route in both ascent and descent

Sgùrr Beag and Sgùrr na h-Uamha from the col on Gillean's South-East ridge – Blàbheinn left and Gars-bheinn right

West Ridge & North Ridge

Summits: *Sgùrr Beag* ▲ *; Sgùrr na h-Uamha* ▲
Terrain: *Hillwalk (Sgùrr Beag); Moderate Grade Rock Climb (Sgùrr na h-Uamha)*
Distance: *13km; 8 miles*
Ascent & Descent: *1060m; 3475ft*
Time: *5–6hrs*
Start & Finish: *Sligachan Hotel (NG 4853 2989)*

Some guidebooks suggest Sgùrr na h-Uamha (736m) as a potential 'consolation prize' for anyone failing on Sgùrr nan Gillean's South-East Ridge. Be warned – anyone expecting an 'easier day out' will get a very nasty shock. Careful route-finding is needed, the hardest section is steep, committing and very exposed and the same moves have to be reversed on the descent. An ascent is not recommended in anything but settled, dry conditions with good visibility and many will require the security of a rope.

Sgùrr Beag (764m), however, is a pleasant rocky walk with a spectacular view north to Gillean. Both peaks offer unhindered views over Glen Sligachan to the Western Red Hills and Blàbheinn.

Approach
Approach as for Sgùrr nan Gillean's South-East Ridge, to the small col above upper Coire Riabhach (NG 4742 2498), *(see p37)*.

Ascent
Ascend slightly, then descend the broad continuation ridge south-east round the rocky rim of the corrie to below Sgùrr Beag, then ascend to its summit with little difficulty. Return to the ridge, then descend south over steeper grass and scree to reach Bealach a' Ghlas-choire, below the North Ridge of Sgùrr na h-Uamha.

An initial scramble (Grade 2) leads to easier ground along a broad rocky ridge, then the top of the North Buttress. A small col separates this from the steep tower of the South Buttress and the main difficulties of the route; a traverse on grassy stone-covered ledges on the West Face, followed by a steep and committing wall overlooking the col between the buttresses.

Descend to the col between the buttresses from where a faint path goes up and right, following a rampline of shattered basalt and grassy ledges *(see p34)*. Follow this round the corner onto the West Face overlooking Lota Corrie and continue traversing on

Sgùrr Beag and the steep West Face of Sgùrr na h-Uamha from Druim nan Ramh. Marsco in the background

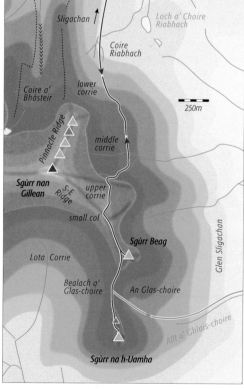

Sgùrr na h-Uamha's North Ridge

facing corner. There are good if slightly rattly, blocky holds and it is steep, off-balance, and very exposed.

Once above the wall, look down and mentally mark the location for the return, as the wall is hidden from above. Scramble up to the summit ridge, turn round and mentally mark the location of the wall again. The wall is not in the direct line of descent from the summit ridge, but slightly off to the left. Continue along the summit ridge to the highest point, which is a large boulder with a smaller boulder on top.

Descent

Return down the ridge to above the cracked wall and descend the steep, awkward, and very committing moves to regain the grassy ledges. Reverse the route back to Bealach a' Ghlas-choire, make a long trudge up to the col on Gillean's South-East Ridge and reverse the approach route to Sligachan. It is also possible to descend east from the bealach into An Glas-choire, then cross the River Sligachan to gain the path in Glen Sligachan. The terrain can be very wet.

Alternatives

There are slightly easier scrambling routes on Sgùrr na h-Uamha, but all are long and unless they are also used for descent, the only way off is via the steep crux of the North Ridge, but without any prior knowledge of the intricacies of its descent, gained by ascending it first.

The cracked wall on Sgùrr na h-Uamha's North Ridge

grassy ledges for about 20m, to where the ledges fade.

Ascend a short rock slab to gain higher grassy ledges and follow them back left for almost the same distance, to the exposed crest overlooking the col between the two buttresses (Grade 2). Now climb straight up a steep cracked wall (Moderate) below a small left-

The South Face of Sgùrr na h-Uamha, left, and Sgùrr Beag from Sgùrr na Stri to the south

Sgùrr nan Gillean, left, and Coire a' Bhàsteir from the Allt Dearg Mòr. The South-East Ridge follows the left-hand skyline

Sgùrr nan Gillean

*G*illean *has inspired climbers in the Cuillin since its ascent by Skye-men Duncan MacIntyre and James Forbes in 1836, the first recorded ascent of a principal Cuillin summit. The so called 'Tourist Route' up the South-East Ridge is the easiest way to the top, but it still requires a final steep and exposed scramble to gain the spectacular summit*

Sgùrr nan Gillean's South-East Ridge from the small col above upper Coire Riabhach. The right-hand ridge is Pinnacle Ridge

South-East Ridge

Summits: *Sgùrr nan Gillean*▲
Terrain: *Grade 2–3 Scramble*
Distance: *12km; 7.5 miles*
Ascent & Descent: *970m; 3180ft*
Time: *5–6hrs*
Start & Finish: *Parking near Sligachan Hotel (NG 4853 2989)*

The rugged profile of Sgùrr nan Gillean (965m) and its proximity to the main road, make it a prime target for 'have-a-go' tourists. This is unfortunate as it's one of the harder summits in the Cuillin and one of the most exposed. Care also needs to be taken with the approach route from middle Coire Riabhach to the upper corrie and the start of the South-East Ridge. The best line isn't immediately obvious (there are either too many paths or none!) and the scree and boulderfields are very disorientating in poor visibility.

Approach

Walk 150m west up the 'old road' parallel to the A863 Dunvegan road, passing the Mountain Rescue

Post building. Go diagonally over the road to a path on the left (NG 4839 2974), follow it to a footbridge and cross the Allt Dearg Mòr. Ascend south over the moor to reach a plank bridge on the Allt Dearg Beag (NG 4764 2793).

Continuing straight ahead without crossing here leads up the right side of the Bhasteir Gorge into Coire a' Bhàsteir (see p41–3, Approach option 1).

Cross over and ascend to gain the spur projecting north from the base of Sgùrr nan Gillean's Pinnacle Ridge and a large cairn overlooking lower Coire Riabhach and Loch a' Choire Riabhach.

The path that branches off right (west) from the cairn, leads up the spur towards Pinnacle Ridge, then round the left side of the Bhasteir Gorge into Coire a' Bhàsteir (see p41–3, Approach option 2).

From the large cairn, remain on the main path and descend south into lower Coire Riabhach and past the loch, with fine views east to Marsco and Blàbheinn. A steep and stony zigzag path ascends out of the corrie to reach middle Coire Riabhach and a burn draining from the mass of rock slabs and walls below Gillean's East Face and Pinnacle Ridge.

Although there are cairns on the grassy spur on the far (south) side of the burn, do not cross over, but

The route from middle Coire Riabhach to the rampline leading to upper Coire Riabhach

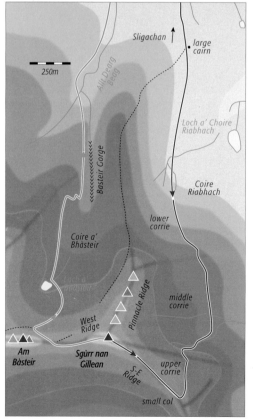

ascend the burn's right (north) side up a wide boulder and scree-filled gully. Initially the path is ill-defined then a lot clearer, hemmed in on both sides by rock walls.

About half-way up, where the scree gully swings right, there is a large arrow-shaped black overhang in the cliff above, at which point a steep stony gully-

The route from upper Coire Riabhach to the small col

Descending the lower section of the South-East Ridge with Pinnacle Ridge behind

rampline leads out left through the rock walls.

Ascend this ramp to gain the lip of the shallow boulder-strewn basin of upper Coire Riabhach. From there, head up and left over initially boulder-strewn ground to gain a scree path leading to a small col (NG 4742 2498) on the South-East Ridge. The col has a large square boulder in it and a finger-like rock above and to the left.

Ascent

From the small col, scramble up the South-West Ridge to reach a parallel-sided chimney on the left. Climb this (Grade 2), then ascend broken ground and rock-steps on the right, before moving back left to the base of the upper section of the ridge, at the point where it narrows and becomes a steep fin of homogenous rock.

There are now **three options: (1)** Climb the frontal face of the fin direct and ascend via a narrow and exposed slab (Grade 3); **(2)** Follow broken ledges up and left, then move right via a ledge to gain the narrow slab (Grade 3); **(3)** Follow broken ledges further up and left, from where a high step on the right leads to an ascending traverse (Grade 2), left then right.

All three options gain the final section of the summit ridge, from where a narrow gap has to be negotiated to gain the spectacular summit (*photo p43*).

Descent

The easiest descent is to reverse the line of ascent

(*photo p61*). A rope may be of assistance, especially in descent. The West Ridge (*see p43–5*) can also be descended. This is mostly Grade 2 scrambling until Tooth Groove & The Arete (Moderate) at the end. It is also possible to abseil down Tooth Chimney (Difficult), but this will require a rope, harness and abseil device. There are usually abseil slings in place.

The summit tower at the top of the South-East Ridge

Crossing The Arete on the exposed crux section at the start of the West Ridge of Sgùrr nan Gillean. The peaks behind are, from right, Am Bàsteir, Bruach na Frìthe and Sgùrr a' Fionn Choire

Looking up the West Ridge of Sgùrr nan Gillean to the prominent finger pinnacle and people on the summit

West Ridge

Summits: *Sgùrr nan Gillean* ▲
Terrain: *Moderate Grade Rock Climb*
Distance: *12km; 7.5 miles*
Ascent & Descent: *970m; 3180ft*
Time: *5–6hrs*
Start & Finish: *Parking near Sligachan Hotel
(NG 4853 2989)*

Gillean's West Ridge is harder and more exposed than the South-East Ridge, although much of the route is straightforward. The crux section is at the start, where a choice of short rock climbs give access to a rocky arete. This used to be topped by a tooth-like pinnacle called The Gendarme, which fell down in 1987. The rock on The Arete is polished and a little unstable in places. Beyond The Arete, the ridge is a Grade 2 scramble by the easiest line.

Approach
Walk 150m west up the 'old road' parallel to the A863 Dunvegan road, passing the Mountain Rescue Post building. Go diagonally over the road to a path on the left (NG 4839 2974), follow it to a footbridge and cross the Allt Dearg Mòr. Ascend south over the moor to reach a plank bridge on the Allt Dearg Beag (NG 4764 2793).

There are now **two Approach options** for Coire a' Bhàsteir and Bealach a' Bhàsteir. **(1)**: The route on

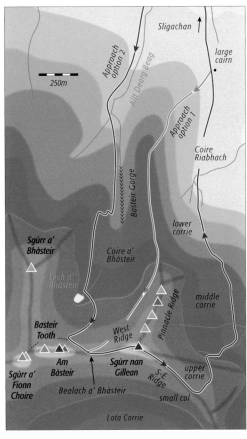

Approach option 2 – *The initial zigzags at the toe of Sgùrr a' Bhàsteir on the route into Coire a' Bhàsteir. Circles indicate people. Approach option 1 traverses the east side of Coire a' Bhàsteir, below Pinnacle Ridge in the background*

Approach option 2 – *The slabby upper section of the route into Coire a' Bhàsteir*

Approach option 2 – Above the slabs, the route traverses below Sgùrr a' Bhàsteir's North-East Ridge to reach Coire a' Bhàsteir. The viewpoint is on Approach option 1 below Pinnacle Ridge on the east side of Coire a' Bhàsteir

the left (east) side of the Allt Dearg Beag crosses the bridge, continues to the large cairn (NG 4763 2700) overlooking lower Coire Riabhach, as for the South-East Ridge, ascends the north spur towards Pinnacle Ridge (*see p46–7*), then traverses round the east side of the corrie to the Bealach a' Bhàsteir. This path is intermittent in places, passes over scree and through boulders and often retains snow into the spring.

(2): The route on the right (west) side of the Allt Dearg Beag is more direct, but requires some easy scrambling and route-finding where it crosses the North-East Ridge of Sgùrr a' Bhàsteir. The final scree slope to the Bealach a' Bhàsteir is direct but tedious. This route offers a useful and quick way off the main Cuillin ridgeline and is the more frequented route in ascent and descent. It is described in more detail as follows.

Don't cross the plank bridge but continue ascending towards the triangular frontal buttress of Sgùrr a' Bhàsteir, until progress is blocked by the deep cleft of the Bhasteir Gorge and the rock slabs forming the toe of Sgùrr a' Bhàsteir's North-East Ridge.

A path, slightly hidden from below, zigzags up scree to the right of the lower rocks, then moves out left onto the lower slabs. Ascend these following crampon scratches here and there and the line of least resistance, via long zigzags, **[A]** & **[B]** on the diagrams, until more level rocky ground is reached.

The path now heads up and left over more slabby rock and grass, to reach rounded rock slabs on the crest of the ridge **[C]**. From here the path continues traversing horizontally past a wide cave in a large crag **[D]** to reach Coire a' Bhàsteir and its lochan.

Go left round the lochan to gain a path which swings round the corrie to the final scree slopes,

which are climbed to Bealach a' Bhàsteir left of Am Bàsteir (NG 4683 2526).

Ascent

From Bealach a' Bhàsteir, scramble left (east) up the rocky arete towards Gillean's West Ridge (*photo p58*), to reach the detached pinnacle forming the base of the ridge. Go left round this on a good path overlooking Coire a' Bhàsteir, to reach a recess with two boulders on a large ledge, below a series of chimneys separated by ribs (*see p45*).

The long wide chimney forming the left side of the recess has a chockstone near the bottom and is Tooth Chimney (Difficult). To the right are two prominent cracks forming an inverted V, then a broad rib. Right of the broad rib is a shorter stepped groove, leading to a rocky arete. This is Tooth Groove (Moderate). It is the

Starting Gillean's spectacular summit ridge

43

A final narrow arete beyond the finger pinnacle and window on the West Ridge gains the summit; Sgùrr a' Bhàsteir behind

The start of Tooth Groove & The Arete

easiest of the lines, in ascent and descent, although it does necessitate traversing the exposed and rocky Arete beyond. The Arete (Moderate), is polished and tricky in places with some suspect rock, but finally leads to a ledge above Tooth Chimney (*photo p40*).

The rest of the route is Grade 2 scrambling via the easiest line (*photo p30–1*). From the ledge, zigzag up ledges on the right past the topknot pinnacle and towards the finger pinnacle looming above. The steep rib below the finger pinnacle can be avoided on the right. Traverse round the left side of the pinnacle, go though the keyhole window and climb the final narrow arete directly to the summit.

Descent

The only alternatives are to return down the West Ridge to Coire a' Bhàsteir, or down the South-East Ridge (*see p37–9, photo p61*) to Coire Riabhach. The descent of Coire a' Bhàsteir is slightly quicker, especially if the route through the slabs at the toe of Sgùrr a' Bhàsteir is already known from the ascent. Both descents are tricky in poor visibility.

Tooth Groove & The Arete may feel harder in descent than it was in ascent. Abseiling down Tooth Chimney is an alternative option, but this will require a rope, harness and abseil device. There are usually abseil slings in place.

Tooth Chimney and Tooth Groove & The Arete, the principal starts to the West Ridge

The line of the West Ridge in its upper section

The four pinnacles of Pinnacle Ridge and the summit of Sgùrr nan Gillean from the Allt Dearg Beag before the Bhasteir Gorge

Pinnacle Ridge

Summits: *Sgùrr nan Gillean* ▲ *; Knight's Peak* ▲
Terrain: *Difficult Grade Rock Climb (optional abseil)*
Distance: *11km; 6.75 miles*
Ascent: *1050m; 3445ft*
Time: *6–8hrs*
Start & Finish: *Parking near Sligachan Hotel*
(NG 4853 2989)

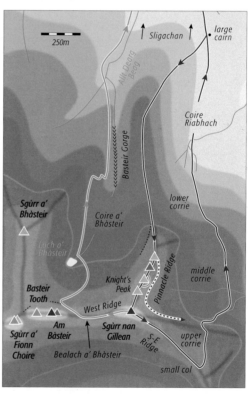

Pinnacle Ridge is the longest of Sgùrr nan Gillean's three ridges and while it is nominally the hardest, the difficulties can be reduced if the easiest line is taken.

However, this isn't always obvious and 'alpine-style' route-finding skills are useful. The hardest section is the short steep wall above the col separating the Fourth Pinnacle, known as Knight's Peak, from the main summit of Sgùrr nan Gillean. This requires a committing and exposed sequence on small holds, although an easier alternative exists to the right.

Compared with Gillean's other ridges, the rock quality is quite poor in places and there is much unstable terrain, with detached blocks and loose stones lying on the ledges. Helmets are recommended, especially if climbers ahead are 'pitching' with ropes, as the resulting ropework can cause significant stonefall.

Although the route includes a lot of walking, many parties carry full rock climbing equipment (60m rope, harness, belay/abseil device, slings, some protection wires) and 'pitch' the steeper sections (see p11, 17). This also facilitates the 25–30m abseil down the steep south face of the Third Pinnacle. However, this

abseil is easily avoided by traversing below the pinnacle on its left (middle Coire Riabhach) side, allowing a confident party with minimal climbing equipment and a quiet day, to ascend all the pinnacles without having to abseil or climb down the exposed Difficult rock climb from the Third Pinnacle.

Knight's Peak became a Munro Top (see p10) in 1997 and was recorded on Ordnance Survey maps at 915m (3002ft), making it a target for anyone climbing all 508 Munros and Munro Tops. However, a survey in 2013 found the height to be just 914.24m, or 2999ft. No longer a Munro Top and with insufficient 'drop' between it and Sgùrr nan Gillean to make it a Corbett, Knight's Peak was demoted. It is recorded here as an Other Fine Summit.

Approach

Walk 150m west up the 'old road' parallel to the A863 Dunvegan road, passing the Mountain Rescue Post building. Go diagonally over the road to a path on the left (NG 4839 2974), follow it to a footbridge and cross the Allt Dearg Mòr. Ascend south over the moor to a plank bridge on the Allt Dearg Beag (NG 4764 2793). Cross over and continue to the large cairn overlooking lower Coire Riabhach, turn right (west) and ascend the broad spur to the toe of the First Pinnacle (*Approach option 1, see p41–3*),

Ascent

One of the easiest lines is described here, but many variations are possible. Above the broken lower rocks of the **First Pinnacle**, traverse left to the end of a grassy ledge and climb a grassy groove. Where it steepens, go left to a second groove and climb that to where the rock steepens again (Grade 2). Traverse horizontally right on an initially grassy ledge, cross over the top of the continuation of the first groove and reach the base of a blocky rampline. Continue for about 6m up and right on a long rising traverse over mixed ground, until the face opens out and it is possible to ascend to a shallow square-cut cleft capped by a small overlap. Climb the cleft and overlap to a grassy terrace, above which the cleft continues. Bypass this continuation by ascending a ramp up and right, then a horizontal terrace back left and go slightly round the corner to an orange wall (Grade 2).

Ascend the steep wall on good holds (Grade 2–3) to rougher black rock and zigzag up in the vicinity of a dyke, to easier ground and a small grassy col on the crest. Climb the tower directly ahead via a groove on its right side (Grade 2) and follow the easy crest of a fine rocky arete in a great position, to easier ground and a grassy col.

Ahead is a buttress with a wide scree gully on its left and broken rocks on the right. Ascend the broken rocks on a rough bouldery path, until it is possible to traverse back left before the final steepening, to gain an easy-angled rocky slope leading to the cairned top of the First Pinnacle. From here it is possible to escape from the ridge by traversing south-west over the rocky eastern slopes below all the pinnacles, then south-

The intricate route on the First Pinnacle

east into middle Coire Riabhach and the path to Gillean's South-East Ridge and Sligachan.

Cross the wide gully to the **Second Pinnacle** and ascend easy scree and boulders to the summit. Go round another big gully and ascend scree paths to the base of the **Third Pinnacle** (*diagram p48*).

There are now **three options: (1)** The hardest requires either abseiling from the Third Pinnacle, or downclimbing a Difficult grade rock climb. The foot of the Third Pinnacle is separated from a small tower on the right by a short white gully of eroded scree and broken rock. Climb part-way up this, then move out left and zigzag up rocky shelves to a bay capped by a small bulging overlap. Above, unpleasant gravelly grooves lead to a rocky platform a little below the final tower. Ascend a worn crack and corner on the right (Grade 2–3) to gain the summit blocks and the abseil slings.

A 30m abseil gains a ledge in the gully separating the Third Pinnacle and Knight's Peak (Fourth Pinnacle) on the Coire a' Bhàsteir side. A 25m abseil leads to a higher ledge, from where a flake chimney (Grade 2–3) must be descended to the ledge in the gully. Alternatively, climb down the steep and exposed corner-line below the abseil, approached from either arete (Difficult).

(2) This involves exposed Grade 3 scrambling over grass and rock, with some tricky route-finding. Good visibility and dry conditions are essential. Ascend to the rocky platform below the final tower of the Third Pinnacle as above and leave your rucksack here. Climb

47

Near the summit of Knight's Peak, Sgùrr a' Bhàsteir behind and MacLeod's Tables in the distance (photo Rab Anderson)

Third Pinnacle

option 1 abseil

Knight's Peak

option 2

white gully

small tower

option 3

escape

East - middle Coire Riabhach - face

The three options for tackling the Third Pinnacle

Pinnacle. Ascend to the summit as above, then return to the foot of the small tower. Traverse left down grass and boulders to pass below the Third Pinnacle and ascend scree to the gully separating the Third Pinnacle and Knight's Peak. Scramble up the left side of this (Grade 1) to its top, then make a short descent on the Corrie a' Bhàsteir side to a ledge. This gully would also offer an escape from the ridge into middle Coire Riabhach and the path to Sligachan and

to the summit, then back down to the rocky platform.

From there, traverse down and left onto the East Face of the pinnacle overlooking middle Coire Riabhach and cross a slabby shelf of grass and rock to where it ends at a patch of orange rock. Beyond this, traverse a narrow footledge round bulging gabbro (Grade 3) to grassy ledges and the gully separating the Third Pinnacle from Knight's Peak. Enter the gully and climb it, then descend to a ledge on the Coire a' Bhàsteir side.

(3) This is the easiest option. Leave your rucksack below the small tower at the base of the Third

Abseiling from the Third Pinnacle in poor conditions

Sgùrr nan Gillean's South-East Ridge. All the options finish at the ledge between the Third Pinnacle and Knight's Peak on the Corrie a' Bhàsteir side.

The lower part of **Knight's Peak (Fourth Pinnacle)** is cut by a right-slanting rubble-covered rampline. Follow the ramp via a couple of airy steps and continue round the corner to a broken line leading diagonally back left. Follow this over worn ground to reach much steeper corners. Avoid these via an orange right-slanting rampline, which leads to just below the ridge crest. From here, follow a short groove back left to easier ground and a boulder-filled col between two summits (Grade 1–2). Both are easily climbed from the col, the North (left facing Gillean) is slightly higher.

A ridge with two small towers links Knight's Peak to Sgùrr nan Gillean. From the summit col, gain a columnar ledge, then traverse left (looking down) and descend a slabby wall (Grade 2) to a notch before the first small tower on the ridge. Descend the notch and continue down, heading slightly right on a path and worn rocks to a grassy ledge. From here the route cuts back left on a rocky ledge to a notch on the ridge at the second small tower. Skirt this to gain a rocky crest linking the ridge with Sgùrr nan Gillean.

The crux wall onto **Sgùrr nan Gillean** follows. Climb the exposed slabby wall up and right on small holds (Difficult), to where the angle eases and continue up and right to less steep ground. An easier alternative

The crux wall and routes to the summit of Sgùrr nan Gillean

Descent from Knight's Peak to Sgùrr nan Gillean

(Grade 3) steps horizontally right from the base of the crux wall on a footledge and goes round the corner to a grassy ledge. Follow it to its end, from where a loose crack and groove cuts back up left. If neither of these appeal, then descending some 12m down the gully on the right (Coire a' Bhàsteir side) to where it narrows, opens other potential lines onto Sgùrr nan Gillean.

Easier ground leads to a large terrace, which can be followed rightwards without difficulty to join the West Ridge. However, to keep climbing, go round to the left and shuffle up a shallow, square-cut chimney to a terrace (Grade 2). Climb the continuation chimney above with a grunt over a small chockstone (Grade 2) to easier scrambling. Broken ground leads up and right to meet the West Ridge just before the window in the finger pinnacle. Go through the hole and ascend the ridge to the summit of Sgùrr nan Gillean (*photo p44*).

Descent

Most will go down the South-East Ridge (*see p37–9, photo p61*), but if you have abseiled on the Third Pinnacle then the rope, harness and abseil device increase the descent options on the West Ridge (*see p43–5*). This is mostly a Grade 2 scramble until Tooth Groove & The Arete (Moderate) have to be down-climbed at the end. Alternatively, the rope can be used to abseil down Tooth Chimney (Difficult). There are usually abseil slings in place.

Roping down the 'bad step' beyond the East Summit on the East Ridge of Am Bàsteir, Sgùrr nan Gillean behind

Am Bàsteir & Basteir Tooth

*A*long with the Inaccessible Pinnacle, the jutting silhouette of the Basteir Tooth is an unmistakeable feature of the Cuillin skyline. Like many Cuillin peaks, Am Bàsteir presents a glacially sculptured Matterhorn-style profile when viewed end-on. Not surprisingly perhaps, the easiest way up both peaks involves some climbing

West from below Bealach a' Bhàsteir to climbers descending from the main summit of Am Bàsteir towards the East Summit

Am Bàsteir – East Ridge

Summits: Am Basteir ▲; East Summit ▲
Terrain: Difficult Grade Rock Climb or Grade 2 Scramble
Distance: 12km; 7.5 miles (excluding Tooth)
Ascent & Descent: 920m; 3020ft
Time: 5–6hrs
Start & Finish: Parking near Sligachan Hotel (NG 4853 2989)

The East Ridge of Am Bàsteir (935m) offers the only line of ascent without significant technical rock climbing, the main summit being separated from the easily attained East Summit by a short wall. It's only a few moves but the rock is undercut and awkward to downclimb and the position very exposed. Many will find a rope reassuring on this 'bad step', especially in descent. It is possible to avoid the 'bad step' by traversing the South (Lota Corrie) Face at a lower level than the East Ridge. However,

this exposed route includes grass and stone-covered ledges and requires route-finding skill and very great care. Good visibility and dry conditions are essential.

Am Bàsteir and the Basteir Tooth (917m) are described via Coire a' Bhàsteir in ascent and descent, but the North-East Ridge of Sgùrr a' Bhàsteir offers a pleasant scrambling approach, as for the Round of Coire a' Bhàsteir (see p59). Approaching via this route it is probably best to climb the Tooth first, then descend back into Coire a' Bhàsteir after Am Bàsteir.

Approach

Walk 150m west up the 'old road' parallel to the A863 Dunvegan road, passing the Mountain Rescue Post building. Go diagonally over the road to a path on the left (NG 4839 2974), follow it to a footbridge and cross the Allt Dearg Mòr. Ascend south over the moor to a plank bridge on the Allt Dearg Beag (NG 4764 2793). Don't cross over, but follow the right (west) side of the Allt Dearg Beag to enter Coire a' Bhàsteir. Ascend the scree to Bealach a' Bhàsteir, left of Am Bàsteir (NG 4683 2526), (Approach option 2, see p41–3).

51

Sgùrr a'
Fionn Choire

Am Bàsteir
summit

Basteir
Tooth

East Summit

'bad
step'

Bealach
nan Lice

East Ridge

rampline
between
summits

descent to
Collie's Route

orange
slab

Coire a'
Bhàsteir

alternative
avoiding
'bad step'

Bealach a'
Bhàsteir

Collie's
Route

Lota Corrie

Am Bàsteir's South, Lota Corrie, Face showing the principal East Ridge route, the alternative avoiding the 'bad step' and
Collie's Route on the Basteir Tooth

Am Bàsteir
summit

'bad
step'

East Summit

East Ridge

rampline separating
Am Bàsteir east &
main summits

orange
slab

alternative
avoiding
'bad step'

Bealach a'
Bhàsteir

Am Bàsteir's South, Lota Corrie, Face showing the principal East Ridge route and the alternative avoiding the 'bad step'

Ascent

Principal Route: From Bealach a' Bhàsteir, follow the ridge to the first rocks which are crossed to the left, then cut back right on a well-worn route and ascend diagonally on the curving crest of the ridge via short rocky steps (Grade 2).

Higher up, a slabby section leads to a stubby pinnacle which is turned on the left, followed by the East Summit. Continue beyond this to above the 'bad step' on the very edge of the buttress. There is a ledge a short distance down which offers a good belay for anyone roping down the step (*photo p50*).

Climb down the wall of the 'bad step' which is tricky and undercut at its base (Difficult), or make a short abseil. Cross over the ramp dividing the summits and ascend easily to the main summit of Am Bàsteir.

Alternative Route Avoiding 'Bad Step': From Bealach a' Bhàsteir, cross the first rocks as above, but continue traversing down and left over broken ground to reach a narrow orange slab. Climb this for about 6m, then traverse out left onto stony ramps on the South (Lota Corrie) Face and follow them round via some rock steps, to gain the rampline separating the east and main summits. This section is exposed Grade 2 scrambling, the route isn't obvious and the unstable terrain requires **very great** care. Scramble easily up the rampline past the 'bad step' to gain the summit.

Descent

Return to Bealach a' Bhàsteir by the line of ascent, or by reversing the Principal Route described above. The 'bad step' is still tricky, but feels easier in ascent.

If the only objective is Am Bàsteir, then descend the scree path from Bealach a' Bhàsteir back into Coire a' Bhàsteir. To include the Basteir Tooth, descend to below Am Bàsteir, then ascend beyond the Tooth to Bealach nan Lice, where the South Ridge of Sgùrr a' Bhàsteir abuts the main Cuillin ridgeline below Sgùrr a' Fionn Choire. The bealach gives access to Collie's Route – the easiest way up the Tooth (*see p54–7*).

orange
slab

The start of the alternative route avoiding the 'bad step'

Am Bàsteir and the Basteir Tooth, divided by the prominent slot of the Basteir Nick. Sgùrr nan Gillean in shadow to the left

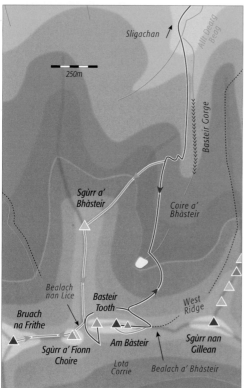

Basteir Tooth – Collie's Route

Summits: *Basteir Tooth* ▲
Terrain: *Moderate Grade Rock Climb*
Distance: *1km; 1,090yds*
Ascent & Descent: *330m; 1080ft*
Time: *1–2hrs*
Start & Finish: *Bealach nan Lice (NG 4643 2526)*

Norman Collie and the famous Skye guide John Mackenzie made the first ascent of the Basteir Tooth (917m) from Lota Corrie in 1888 and their route is the easiest way to climb this Munro Top. It is mostly an enclosed and straightforward scramble with a couple of short, steeper chimneys. For ropeless scramblers, the route must be descended as well as ascended, because the Basteir Tooth – Am Bàsteir Link involves steep and exposed rock climbing which is only recommended with ropes.

Naismith's Route is the only 'reasonable grade' alternative to Collie's Route and is usually climbed as part of a traverse of the Cuillin Ridge. It is a Severe rock climb and only recommended with ropes.

Approach
Walk 150m west up the 'old road' parallel to the A863 Dunvegan road, passing the Mountain Rescue

Post building. Go diagonally over the road to a path on the left (NG 4839 2974), follow it to a footbridge and cross the Allt Dearg Mòr. Ascend south over the moor to a plank bridge on the Allt Dearg Beag (NG 4764 2793).

Don't cross over, but follow the right (west) side of the Allt Dearg Beag to enter Coire a' Bhàsteir. Ascend the scree to Bealach nan Lice to the right of Am Bàsteir (*Approach option 2, see p41–3*).

Alternatively, the North-East Ridge of Sgùrr a' Bhàsteir offers a pleasant scrambling approach to Bealach nan Lice, as for the Round of Coire a' Bhàsteir (*see p59*). From the bealach it would be possible to include Sgùrr a' Fionn Choire and Bruach na Frithe in the round (add approx 1hr), (*see p63–5*).

From Bealach nan Lice, descend the scree slope below the South (Lota Corrie) Face of Am Bàsteir. Just round from the lowest point is the open mouth of a narrow initially scree-filled gully on the left edge of the buttress. The gully has a prominent rock finger on its left side, just above the start (*see p56*).

Ascent

Climb the scree cone into the gully which soon narrows to form a parallel-sided fault. Go over a couple of small chockstones, then a larger one with a jammed sling (Grade 2). Continue in the same line until the going steepens at a fin of rock which is climbed on its left-hand side (Moderate). Above this a short parallel-sided chimney (Moderate) leads to small walls, easier slabby ground and grassy ledges. The top of the Basteir Tooth can now be seen over to the left, sticking up above the end of the ledges (*see p57*). Traverse left on the grassy ledges to pass round the corner and descend a slot-like chimney (Grade 2) into the Basteir Nick, the cleft between Am Bàsteir and the Basteir Tooth. Climb a rib, then the final slabby wall to the top of the Tooth.

The steep rock and square-cut chimney forming the continuation of the gully-line above the grassy ledges, leads to an overhanging wall below Am Bàsteir's summit. This is the Basteir Tooth – Am Bàsteir Link. It is steep and exposed (Severe) and best only attempted with ropes (*see p28–9, 56–7*).

Descent

Reverse the route and ascend back to the Bealach nan Lice. From here descend back into Coire a' Bhàsteir.

The Basteir Tooth, topped by the summit of Am Bàsteir with climbers, from Bealach nan Lice

Collie's Route and Naismith's Route on the Basteir Tooth and the Basteir Tooth – Am Bàsteir Link (see p28–9)

The scree-filled gully marking the start of Collie's Route

The central section of Collie's Route

From the Basteir Nick, easy climbing gains the summit

Below the square-cut chimney, traverse the slabby, grassy ledges left to gain the Basteir Tooth at the Basteir Nick

Looking towards the West Ridge, centre, and summit of Sgùrr nan Gillean from Bealach a' Bhàsteir

Round of Coire a' Bhàsteir
Sgùrr a' Bhàsteir, Basteir Tooth, Am Bàsteir, Sgùrr nan Gillean

*T*he round of this corrie takes in the iconic peaks of the Northern Cuillin. While there is a lot of easy scrambling, there are also some sections of steep and exposed rock climbing and only confident scramblers will forgo the reassurance of a rope at some point

Sgùrr a' Bhàsteir, right, Sgùrr a' Fionn Choire, Basteir Tooth and Am Bàsteir from the Allt Dearg Mòr

Round of Coire a' Bhàsteir

Summits: *Sgùrr a' Bhàsteir ▲; Basteir Tooth ▲; Am Basteir ▲; East Summit ▲; Sgùrr nan Gillean ▲*
Terrain: *Difficult Grade Rock Climb or Grade 2 Scramble (Am Bàsteir); Moderate Grade Rock Climb (Basteir Tooth); Moderate Grade Rock Climb (West Ridge Sgùrr nan Gillean)*
Distance: *15km; 9.25 miles*
Ascent & Descent: *1460m; 4790ft*
Time: *6hrs 30mins–7hrs 30mins*
Start & Finish: *Parking near Sligachan Hotel (NG 4853 2989)*

Tooth Groove & The Arete at the start of Sgùrr nan Gillean's West Ridge is easier in ascent than descent, so this round is best tackled in an anti-clockwise direction. This is excellent training for a South-North

traverse of the Cuillin Ridge and makes an ascent of Sgùrr a' Bhàsteir's North-West Ridge a pleasant warm-up to the day. From the summit of Sgùrr a' Bhàsteir (898m), the South Ridge is followed to where it joins the main Cuillin ridgeline at Bealach nan Lice.

The Munro Top Sgùrr a' Fionn Choire (936m) and the Munro Bruach na Frithe (958m) are easily reached from that point and could be included in the round (add approx 1hr), either before or after the Basteir Tooth (see p63–5).

Approach

Walk 150m west up the 'old road' parallel to the A863 Dunvegan road, passing the Mountain Rescue Post building. Go diagonally over the road to a path on the left (NG 4839 2974), follow it to a footbridge and cross the Allt Dearg Mòr. Ascend south over the moor to a plank bridge on the Allt Dearg Beag.

Don't cross over, but follow the right (west) side of the Allt Dearg Beag towards the triangular frontal

Looking down to the Allt Dearg Beag from the North-East Ridge of Sgùrr a' Bhàsteir

buttress of Sgùrr a' Bhàsteir and climb over the rock slabs forming the toe of Sgùrr a' Bhàsteir's North-East Ridge. Follow the path into Coire a' Bhàsteir to about NG 4698 2606, where it starts to traverse the hillside (*Approach option 2, see p41–3*).

Ascent

Leave the main path and zigzag up to gain the crest of Sgùrr a' Bhàsteir's North-East Ridge (*see p43*). Slabs ribs and walls linked by scree and grassy terraces offer interesting scrambling (Grade 1–2) in a fine position. The ridge is rocky but not intimidating, steep or particularly exposed and any difficulties can be avoided.

Beyond a couple of deep clefts marking the tops of gullies, the crest becomes rockier and better defined and leads past a small notch to a final rocky arete and the summit. There is a fair amount of shattered rock, so care is needed in places.

Apart from a small cairn and a change in direction, Sgùrr a' Bhàsteir's 898m summit isn't particularly well-defined, but offers fine views north to Am Bàsteir and the Basteir Tooth. Drop down onto the rocky

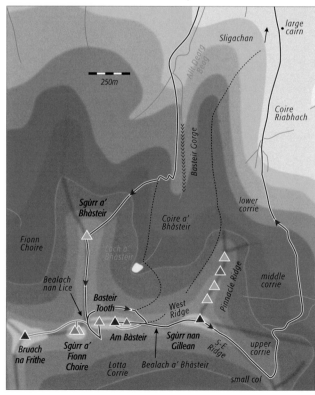

but easy South Ridge and follow it in a fine position to its very end, where it joins the main Cuillin ridgeline at Bealach nan Lice (NG 4643 2526), beyond the Basteir Tooth and below Sgùrr a' Fionn Choire. Bruach na Frithe and Sgùrr a' Fionn Choire (*see p63–5*) are easily reached from here (add approx 1hr).

The easiest route to the summit of the Basteir Tooth is Collie's Route (Moderate), (*see p54–7*). This is easier than Naismith's Route (Severe), but means ascending and descending the route, with a return back up the scree to Bealach nan Lice; the Basteir Tooth – Am Bàsteir Link (Severe) is only recommended with ropes (*see p28–9, 54–7*).

Once back at Bealach nan Lice having ascended and descended Collie's Route, skirt the scree below Am Bàsteir's North Face, then ascend to the Bealach a' Bhàsteir making the best use of the more stable rock on route. From the bealach, climb the East Ridge of Am Bàsteir (Difficult on the 'bad step') or via the Alternative Route (Grade 2), (*see p52–3*). Return to the bealach from the summit.

Scramble east along the main Cuillin ridgeline towards Sgùrr nan Gillean, then cut round left to the recess below the West Ridge. Ascend the ridge to the summit via Tooth Groove & The Arete (Moderate), (*see p43–5*).

The South Ridge of Sgùrr a' Bhàsteir

Decent

From the summit of Sgùrr nan Gillean, descend the South-East Ridge (*see p37–9*) into Coire Riabhach and back to the start at Sligachan. It would also be possible to include Sgùrr Beag and Sgùrr na h-Uamha in the route (*see p33–5*) with a return via Coire Rabiah, or via the Bealach a' Ghlas-choire and Glen Sligachan, adding perhaps 1–2hrs to the day.

Descending Sgùrr nan Gillean's South-East Ridge, high above Lota and Harta Corries. The slabby rock fin of the frontal face on the left can be downclimbed direct, or a more circuitous route on the right can be taken, as shown here

Bruach na Frithe, centre right, and the castle-like Sgùrr a' Fionn Choire, left, from upper Fionn Choire

Bruach na Frithe
& Sgùrr a' Fionn Choire

*G*aining the summit of Bruach na Frithe via Fionn Choire is a straightforward hillwalk and a pleasant respite from the steep and craggy peaks to the east. Although its upper slopes are rock and scree, the corrie has a lot of grass in its lower reaches. Alternatively, the rocky North-West Ridge offers an easy scrambling ascent or descent for anyone feeling deprived. Sgùrr a' Fionn Choire is a fine viewpoint and easily climbed via its rocky central gully

Spring snow at the head of Fionn Choire on the ascent to Bruach na Frithe

Bruach na Frithe – Fionn Choire
& East Ridge

Summits: Bruach na Frithe ▲
Terrain: Hillwalk
Distance: 14km; 8.5 miles
Ascent & Descent: 945m; 3104ft
Time: 5–6hrs
Start & Finish: Layby on A863 to Dunvegan, 700m west of the Sligachan Hotel (NG 4796 2979)

Bruach na Frithe (958m) and adjacent Sgùrr a' Fionn Choire (936m) can be climbed from Sligachan or from Glen Brittle. The former is possibly a little longer, but saves a sometimes tedious drive over to Glen Brittle, followed by a fight to get parked among the hundreds of tourists visiting the Fairy Pools at the foot of the

western approach path to Bealach a' Mhàim.

Fionn Choire is a large open bowl, grassy in its lower reaches and rockier higher up. It has few obvious features and this can be disorientating in poor visibility. There is a good path into the rockier upper corrie, but it then fades. The route stays left (east) of the Allt an Fhionn-choire (the left-hand burn draining the upper corrie), then climbs to Bealach na Lice, left of the castle-like Sgùrr a' Fionn Choire.

The South Ridge via Bealach Tairneilear and Sgùrr na Bàirnich offers the most scrambling, but the approach from Coire a' Tairneilear to the bealach is over unpleasantly steep boulders and scree and not specifically described here, (see p83, 95).

Approach
Start up the access track to Alt Dearg house, just south of the layby. The track can also be accessed

Looking down the North-West Ridge of Bruach na Frithe to the Bealach a' Mhàim and Fionn Choire

more directly from Sligachan by following the Sgùrr nan Gillean path (*see p37*) to the footbridge over the

Allt Dearg Mòr. Don't cross over, but follow the right (north) side of the burn (boggy) to reach the track.

Follow the track to just before Alt Dearg where a signposted path goes off right and skirts the house. Ascend beside the Allt Dearg Mòr into Coire na Circe past gorges pools and waterfalls, to where the path splits at a small cairn (NG 4542 2765).

Cross the Allt Dearg Mòr here and ascend towards Fionn Choire on a path to the right (west) of the Allt an Fhionn-choire draining from the corrie. Cross the burn before a large cairn (NG 4577 2630) and follow the increasingly rocky path on the left (east) side of the burn draining the upper corrie, to final scree slopes leading to Bealach nan Lice (NG 4643 2526), right of the Basteir Tooth and below Sgùrr a' Fionn Choire.

Ascent

Traverse right below Sgùrr a' Fionn Choire (for the easiest route up this Munro Top see opposite) and follow the easy East Ridge to the cylindrical trig point on the summit of Bruach na Frithe. The short rocky crest right of the path offers some pleasant scrambling (Grade 1–2) to gain the summit.

Descent

Descend by the same route, or down the rocky North-West Ridge (*see map & opposite*). Where the ridge splits lower down, swing right and go over Pt.585m to join the ascent path beside the Allt an Fhionn-choire.

Bruach na Frithe – North-West Ridge

Summits: *Bruach na Frithe▲*
Terrain: *Hillwalk or Grade 1–2 Scramble*
Distance: *10km; 6.25 miles*
Ascent & Descent: *860m; 2815ft*
Time: *4hrs 30mins–5hrs 30mins*
Start & Finish: *Fairy Pools (pay) car park (NG 4237 2588) or Forestry car park (NG 4227 2640)*

The rocky North-West Ridge is an easy scramble.

Approach
From Glen Brittle: Start on the Fairy Pools path, but branch off left after about 50m onto a grassy path. Cross the burn and ascend beside forestry towards the Bealach a' Mhàim at the foot of Bruach na Frithe's North-West Ridge. At the bealach there is a small lochan with a largish single cain before it (NG 4478 2689). Turn right and cross the outflow from the lochan to reach the grassy end of the North-West Ridge.

Ascent
Follow the broad North-West Ridge, keeping right of the scree and deeply incut gullies of the Allt Mòr an Fhionn Choire, to where the terrain steepens and becomes rockier. Scramble up the ridge to the summit of Bruach na Frithe. Difficulties can be avoided on the right (Coire a' Tairneilear) side, although this involves scree and loose rock which can make for a tedious ascent. In many respects, sticking to the crest may prove less tiresome.

Descent
Descend by the same route, or down the East Ridge and Fionn Choire (*see map & opposite*). Leave the path near the large cairn (NG 4577 2630) and traverse due west keeping above the scree and rocky gullies of the Allt Mòr an Fhionn Choire, to reach the ascent route on the North-West Ridge.

Sgùrr a' Fionn Choire – Central Gully

Summits: *Sgùrr a' Fionn Choire ▲ ; East Summit ▲*
Terrain: *Grade 1 Scramble*
Distance: *40m; 130ft*
Ascent & Descent: *40m; 130ft*
Time: *15–20mins*
Start & Finish: *Bealach nan Lice (NG 4643 2526)*

This squat Munro Top lies on the ridge between the Basteir Tooth and Bruach na Frithe and is easily climbed from Bealach nan Lice via its central gully-line. It offers good views of the Basteir Tooth.

Approach
Ascend Fionn Choire to Bealach nan Lice (NG 4643 2526) as for Bruach na Frithe (*see opposite*).

Ascent
Both summits are accessible from the central gully.

Descent
Via the ascent route.

Sgùrr a' Fionn Choire's central gully offers the easiest line of ascent

Bruach na Frithe from the head of Fionn Choire near Sgùrr a' Fionn Choire. The North-West Ridge is on the right

Round of Fionn Choire
Meall Odhar, Sgùrr a' Bhàsteir, Sgùrr a' Fionn Choire, Bruach na Frithe

*T*he easiest corrie round in the Cuillin offers a good introduction to the terrain
found on the main ridge. Once above the grass of lower Fionn Choire, the
ground is generally rough and rocky with scree and some shattered rock requiring
care when scrambling. Any difficulties can be avoided and the views are spectacular

Looking east to Sgùrr nan Gillean and the Western Red Hills from the summit of Bruach na Frithe

From Sligachan

Summits: *Meall Odhar* ▲ ; *Sgùrr a' Bhàsteir* ▲ ;
Sgùrr a' Fionn Choire ▲ ; *East Summit* ▲ ;
Bruach na Frithe ▲
Terrain: *Hillwalk (but sections of up to Grade 2
Scrambling on Sgùrr a' Bhàsteir & Bruach na
Frithe if desired)*
Distance: *13km; 8 miles*
Ascent & Descent: *995m; 3265ft*
Time: *5–6hrs*
Start & Finish: *Parking near Sligachan Hotel
(NG 4853 2989)*

From Glen Brittle

Summits: *As above*
Terrain: *Hillwalk (but sections of up to Grade 2
Scrambling on Sgùrr a' Bhàsteir & Bruach na
Frithe if desired)*
Distance: *12km; 7.5 miles*
Ascent & Descent: *910m; 2985ft*
Time: *4hrs 40mins–5hrs 40mins*
Start & Finish: *Fairy Pools (pay) car park (NG
4237 2588) or Forestry car park (NG 4227 2640)*

The shallow bowl of Fionn Choire is flanked on its
east side by the North-West and South Ridges of
Sgùrr a' Bhàsteir's shapely pyramid and on the west
by the North-West Ridge of Bruach na Frithe.

The round can be started from Sligachan or from
the Fairy Pools pay car park in Glen Brittle and offers
an interesting high-level circuit of Bruach na Frithe on
elevated ridges, with fine views of the impressive
peaks that make up the Northern Cuillin.

Approach
From Sligachan: Walk 150m west up the 'old road'
parallel to the A863 Dunvegan road, passing the
Mountain Rescue Post building. Go diagonally over
the road to a path on the left (NG 4839 2974),
follow it to a footbridge and cross the Allt Dearg Mòr.
Ascend south over the moor to a plank bridge on the
Allt Dearg Beag.

Don't cross over, but follow the right (west) side of
the Allt Dearg Beag towards the North Face of Sgùrr a'
Bhàsteir (*Approach option 2, p41–3*). Leave the path
at about NG 4696 2680 and ascend right (west) to
the northern tip of Meall Odhar (*photo p69*). Ascend
scree and grass to the summit, a spectacular viewpoint, then descend south to the col below the North-
West Ridge of Sgùrr a' Bhàsteir.

From Glen Brittle: Start on the Fairy Pools path, but branch off left after about 50m onto a grassy path. Cross the burn and ascend beside forestry towards Bealach a' Mhàim at the foot of Bruach na Frithe's North-West Ridge. At the bealach there is a small lochan with a largish single cairn before it (NG 4478 2689). Turn right, cross the outflow from the lochan to reach the grassy end of Bruach na Frithe's North-West Ridge and ascend it, keeping right of the scree and deeply incut gullies of the Allt Mòr an Fhionn Choire.

At about 500m altitude leave the ridge and traverse south-east to pass south of the grassy hump of Pt.585m (marked on OS 1:25k map) to enter Fionn Choire. Continue traversing round the corrie and ascend to the col between Sgùrr a' Bhàsteir and Meall Odhar. Climb Meall Odhar for its view, then return south to the col.

Pinnacle Ridge of Sgùrr nan Gillean, the long North-East Ridge and shorter North-West Ridge of Sgùrr a' Bhàsteir and, in the right foreground, the grass and rock dome of Meall Odhar; viewed from the Allt Dearg Mòr to the north

Ascent

The North-West Ridge of Sgùrr a' Bhàsteir looks steep from below, but is a lot easier in reality. From the col, a clear zigzag path leads up through the scree to a rocky path left of the lower buttress, which is ascended back and forth to the better defined upper section. The crest of the buttress to the right offers some scrambling up short steps, although the rock quality is poor.

Higher up the ridge becomes better defined and the scrambling more interesting and airy, although any difficulties are easily avoided on the left. From the small cairn on Sgùrr a' Bhàsteir's 898m summit, descend the rocky South Ridge to its very end where it joins the main Cuillin ridgeline at Bealach nan Lice, right of the Basteir Tooth and below Sgùrr a' Fionn Choire.

Traverse right below Sgùrr a' Fionn Choire (*for the easiest route up this Munro Top see p65*) to gain

Bruach na Frithe's easy East Ridge and follow it to the cylindrical trig point. The rocky crest right of the path offers a short scramble (Grade 1–2) to the summit.

Descent

The rocky North-West Ridge starts directly from the trig point and gives an easy scramble descent (Grade 1–2) which is largely avoidable on its left side. Follow this to where the ridge divides and a spur swings right to Pt.585.

To Sligachan: Turn right towards the grassy hump of Pt.585m and descend before it to gain Fionn Choire. Cross the Allt an Fhionn-choire, contour round Fionn Choire and below the scree-covered nose of Meall Odhar and descend to gain the approach path from Sligachan below the Basteir Gorge.

To Glen Brittle: Continue down the North-West Ridge to the approach route and Bealach a' Mhàim.

CENTRAL CUILLIN

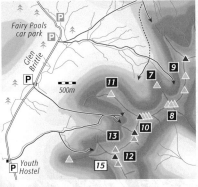

Descending the South Ridge of Sgùrr a' Ghreadaidh towards Sgùrr na Banachdaich on the Round of Coire a' Ghreadaidh

Sgùrr an Fheadain from the Fairy Pools path. The Spur ascends the central ridge, gained from the broad shoulder on the left

Sgùrr an Fheadain

*W*ith the internationally famous Fairy Pools at its foot and a classic mountain profile, split from top to bottom by the impressive cleft of Waterpipe Gully, Sgùrr an Fheadain must be the most photographed single summit in the Cuillin. The North-West Ridge is the line of The Spur; a superb and steady scramble in a magnificent position

Looking down into Coire na Crèche from high on The Spur, Sgùrr an Fheadain

Sgùrr an Fheadain – The Spur

& North-West Ridge of Bidein Druim nan Ramh

Summits: *Sgùrr an Fheadain* ▲
Terrain: *Grade 2 Scramble*
Distance: *10km; 6.25 miles*
Ascent & Descent: *830m; 2725ft*
Time: *4hrs 30mins–5hrs 30mins*
Start & Finish: *Fairy Pools (pay) car park (NG 4237 2588) or Forestry car park (NG 4227 2640)*

Sgùrr an Fheadain (688m) is the most rugged and mountain-like of all the westerly spurs that project from the main Cuillin ridgeline. Its arresting frontal face gives it great presence and the airy upper ridge below the summit is spectacular. The hardest moves are on the initial lower slabs, but these are short-lived.

The rest of the route is straightforward if the line of least resistance is followed. As with many scrambles, sticking to the rock can be less tiring than apparently easier lines on adjacent scree and grassy ledges.

Continuing up the North-West Ridge of Bidein Druim nan Ramh (869m) extends the day, but both descents, east into Coire a' Tairneilear and west into Coire a' Mhadaidh, involve a lot of scree and require careful route-finding in poor visibility. Of the two, that into Coire a' Mhadaidh from Bealach na Glaic Moire is probably the longest, but involves less boulder scree.

Approach
From Glen Brittle: Follow the Fairy Pools path past the pools themselves and continue into Coire na Creiche. As the path rises towards Coire a' Tairneilear it is squeezed into a small rocky narrows between the toe of The Spur and the base of Bruach na Frithe's North-West Ridge.

Sgùrr an Fheadain summit

The Spur

upper bowl

small rowan tree

steeper section

(2) easy approach

(1) scramble approach

The line of The Spur from the base of the route, showing the optional starts

Leave the path about 200m before this point, cross the Allt Coire a' Tairneilear and gain a path which traverses right (south-west) below the main face. After a short distance, ascend grass and scree to below the initial slabs.

From Sligachan: As for Bruach na Frithe and Fionn

Choire, but continue on the path to reach the lochans at Bealach a' Mhàim, with views to Glen Brittle and south to the triple peaks of Bidein Druim nan Ramh (*see maps p64, 68*).

Cross the outfall of the large lochan, cairn, gain a path and follow it round the base of Bruach na Frithe's

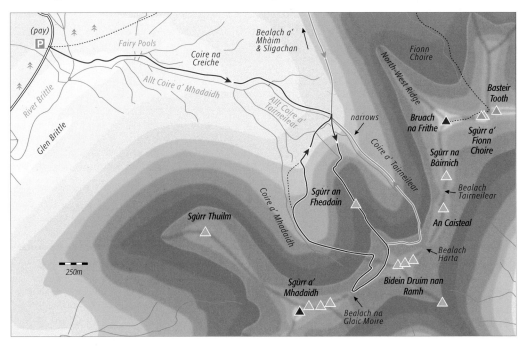

The summit of Sgùrr an Fheadain from the North-West Ridge of Bidein Druim nan Ramh

North-West Ridge into Coire na Creiche to meet the Fairy Pools path (*photo p76*). Cross straight over the Allt Coire a' Tairneilear and ascend to the initial slabs.

Ascent

Two starts are possible and both lead to a steeper section which is difficult to avoid. **(1)** Scramble up (Grade 2) and slightly right on the lower slab. **(2)** Start further left, immediately right of the overhangs and slabs at the toe of the ridge overlooking the burn, where a grassy ledge cuts up right above the lower slab.

Above the lower slab, a slightly steeper section (Grade 2) forces a zigzag left then right to reach an area of steep but straightforward slabs. These soon lead to easier grassy ground and the upper scree bowl, below the ridge taken by The Spur.

Follow a path rightwards across the scree towards a single small rowan tree growing from the rocks low on the ridge. Scramble up behind the tree to gain the ridge crest and climb it over grassy and mostly straight-

forward rocky sections, following a well-travelled line.

Higher up the crest starts to narrow and leads to a final rocky section (Grade 2) with a view into the upper reaches of Waterpipe Gully. A level area is soon reached with the summit straight ahead and beyond it the continuation North-West Ridge, leading to the triple summit of Bidein Druim nan Ramh.

Gain the summit of Sgùrr an Fheadain, then return to the level area and drop down right on an obvious path below the summit, to a small col (*diagram p77*). With care it is possible to descend left (east) from here down scree into Coire a' Tairneilear, but this makes for a short day and avoids the interesting continuation up Bidein Druim nan Ramh's North-West Ridge to the main Cuillin ridgeline and views of Loch Coruisk.

The rocky rib at the start of the North-West Ridge continuation is a little more shattered than the rock on The Spur, although the scrambling is of no great difficulty and it is possible to weave back and forth to find the easiest line.

Looking down to Sgùrr an Fheadain and the North-West Ridge of Bidein Druim nan Ramh above Coire a' Mhadaidh

A grassy ridge then leads to shattered pinnacles which are skirted on the right, followed by easy going along a grassy and stony crest to reach a grassy col directly below Bidein Druim nan Ramh. Ascend steeper terrain up and right to gain a short rocky ridge which leads to the lower section of the West Ridge of Bidein Druim nan Ramh.

It is also possible to escape horizontally left from the grassy col, over very rough and rocky terrain under Bidein Druim nan Ramh to below Bealach Harta, then down into Coire a' Tairneilear (*see opposite page*).

Descent

Go down Bidein Druim nan Ramh's West Ridge, keeping right before it ends at a steep crag to find a stone-scattered parallel-sided basalt staircase. Descend this, then traverse left on a path towards Bealach na Glaic Moire (*diagram* **[6]** *p82, 86*). Before the bealach, descend bouldery scree on the right (Coire a' Mhadaidh side) to gain a lower grassy platform. Follow this then scree north-east, keeping high and resisting the temptation to start descending, to reach the top of the scree gully formed between the North-West Ridge of Bidein Druim nan Ramh and the three

The path linking Bealach a' Mhàim and Coire na Creiche. Bidein Druim nan Ramh and Coire a' Tairneilear, left, Sgùrr an Fheadain, centre, Sgùrr a' Mhadaidh and Coire a' Mhadaidh, right

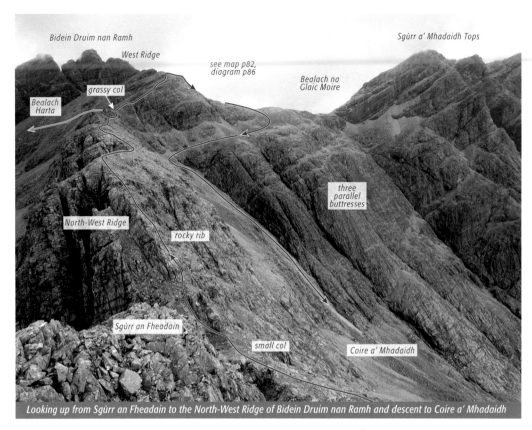

Bidein Druim nan Ramh

West Ridge

see map p82, diagram p86

Sgùrr a' Mhadaidh Tops

Bealach na Glaic Moire

grassy col

Bealach Harta

three parallel buttresses

North-West Ridge

rocky rib

Sgùrr an Fheadain

small col

Coire a' Mhadaidh

Looking up from Sgùrr an Fheadain to the North-West Ridge of Bidein Druim nan Ramh and descent to Coire a' Mhadaidh

large parallel buttresses below the bealach.

Descend the gully into Coire a' Mhadaidh, taking the line of least resistance on steep scree then grass and rock, to reach the burn in the corrie floor. Follow the right (east) side of the burn through a small ravine towards a gorge at the lip of the corrie. Veer right before the gorge and descend grassy slopes immediately left of Sgùrr an Fheadain to reach a path.

This leads rightwards below the prominent Waterpipe Gully to the Fairy Pools path and the path back to Bealach a' Mhàim and Sligachan. Note that the Bealach a' Mhàim path is ill-defined at first. The best start is from an area of eroded scree almost directly across from the traversing path, not at the cairned path lower down.

If descending via Coire a' Tairneilear from the grassy col, traverse hard left across very rough boulder scree to below Bealach Harta, beyond Bidein Druim nan Ramh's North Peak. Descend scree slopes in a northerly direction to where the two burns draining the upper corrie pass through gorges (*diagram* [8] *p83*).

Follow a path in the right-hand (northern) gorge to gain a path on the right (north) side of the Allt Coire a' Tairneilear. Descend to the small rocky narrows below Sgùrr an Fheadain and pass through to join the approach paths.

Bealach Tairneilear

An Caisteal

Bealach Harta

from Bidein Druim nan Ramh North- West Ridge

Coire a' Tairneilear diagram p83

Bidein Druim nan Ramh North-West Ridge

The descent into Coire a' Tairneilear from Bealach Harta

Bidein Druim nan Ramh's West Peak from the top of Central Peak. The climbers are on Bridge Rock below the tricky descent from West Peak, with South Gap Gully on the right. Sgùrr Thuilm is in the background and Bealach na Glaic Moire to the left

Bidein Druim nan Ramh & Druim nan Ramh

*C*limbed direct, the traverse of Bidein Druim nan Ramh's three peaks usually requires two abseils. However, these abseils can be avoided with individual ascents of each peak. The other route described here is an ascent of Druim nan Ramh from Glen Sligachan. This magnificent ridge gives a long day and should not be underestimated. The crux is at the very top and all descents involve long scree slopes

The peaks of Bidein Druim nan Ramh, centre right, with Bealach na Glaic Moire to their right. From left are Sgùrr na Bàirnich, Bealach Tairneilear, An Caisteal and Sgùrr an Fheadain split by Waterpipe Gully. The descent from Bealach na Glaic Moire into Coire a' Mhadaidh takes the scree gully immediately below Bidein Druim nan Ramh and left of three parallel buttresses

Bidein Druim nan Ramh

Summits: *Bidein Druim nan Ramh West Peak* ▲ ; *Central Peak* ▲ ; *North Peak* ▲
Terrain: *Moderate Grade Rock Climb (no abseils)*
Distance: *9.5km; 6 miles (via Sgùrr an Fheadain & North-West Ridge)*
Ascent & Descent: *845m; 2770ft*
Time: *5hrs 30mins–6hrs 30mins*
Start & Finish: *Fairy Pools (pay) car park (NG 4237 2588) or Forestry car park (NG 4227 2640)*

The abseils down the North-East Ridge of Bidein Druim nan Ramh's Central Peak (869m) can be avoided in two ways. The first is to ascend the West (c840m) and Central Peaks by their West Ridges to gain the highest point, then reverse both routes back to below the upper basalt staircase. Descend scree below all of the peaks on their western side and ascend to the Bealach Harta, from where the East Ridge of North

Peak (c850m) can be ascended and descended.

Alternatively, South Gap Gully between West and Central Peak and North Gap Gully between Central and North Peak can be utilised to avoid much of the backtracking. The gullies are short Grade 2–3 scrambles with some scree and loose rock, so the usual care is needed. They are also exposed to stonefall from parties above, so this must be considered when making a decision to descend or ascend them.

Approach

The best and most enjoyable is probably via an ascent of The Spur on Sgùrr an Fheadain and the continuation North-West Ridge of Bidein Druim nan Ramh (*see previous route*). This brings you out onto the main Cuillin ridgeline below the West Ridge of the West Peak and some way above the Bealach na Glaic Moire.

Other approaches involve tedious scree ascents; via Coire a' Mhadaidh and Bealach na Glaic Moire (*diagram p77*), or via Coire a' Tairneilear and Bealach Harta (*diagram* **[8]** *p83*).

[1] – *The West Face of Bidein Druim nan Ramh. North Peak, Central Peak and West Peak from the North-West Ridge*

Ascent

Go over Sgùrr an Fheadain and up the North-West Ridge of Bidein Druim nan Ramh, to where it merges into the main Cuillin ridgeline at the West Ridge (*diagram* [1]).

Ascend towards the **West Peak** to where the West Ridge steepens at the prominent dyke of the upper basalt staircase (*diagram* [2]). Scramble up its smooth rock with care (Grade 1–2) to gain a sloping platform below the shattered summit pinnacle.

The Central Peak is straight ahead, separated from West Peak by Bridge Rock and South Gap Gully on the left. With care, descend the slabby East Ridge right of West Peak's summit, then make some steep and tricky moves (Moderate) to gain Bridge Rock in the gap between the West and Central Peaks (*diagram* [3]). A spiral descent is the best way to tackle this, starting on the right looking down, to gain a ramp which cuts back left to a steep move onto Bridge Rock.

From Bridge Rock step onto the **Central Peak**, ascend a little bit, and traverse out right on narrow ledges (Grade 2–3) then up and left (*diagram* [4]). The steep corner can also be climbed directly at a similar grade. Cross over grass and climb a distinctive parallel-sided chimney (Grade 3) formed by an eroded basalt dyke, which leads via ledges to the crest of the Central Peak. Traverse right to the summit block.

Unless abseiling or downclimbing the North-East Ridge (*see p92–3*), the only way from here is to reverse back down Central Peak to Bridge Rock. Here, South

Gap Gully (Grade 3) can be descended north to the screes below the West Face. There is some loose rock in the gully but it is short. The gully is also exposed to stonefall from other parties traversing West and Central Peaks. Alternatively, traverse back over the West Peak,

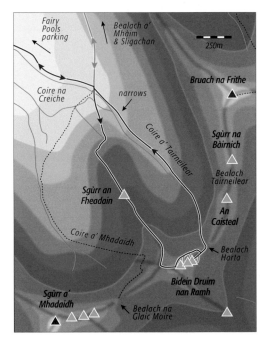

North Peak

West Peak summit

Central Peak

upper basalt staircase

Druim nan Ramh see p84–7

[2] – *The basalt staircase on the upper section of the West Ridge of Bidein Druim nan Ramh, West Peak*

West Peak

South Gap Gully

Bridge Rock

[3] – *Descent to Bridge Rock from the West Peak*

Central Peak

parallel sided basalt chimney

Bridge Rock

South Gap Gully

West Peak

[4] – *Ascent to Central Peak from Bridge Rock*

81

[5] – *Traverse of Bidein Druim nan Ramh's North Peak viewed from Central Peak*

then drop down on the north (Coire a' Tairneilear) side and traverse scree below the West Face, sticking close to the base of the buttresses (*diagrams* [1], [6], [8]).

The next option allows the **North Peak** to be traversed by ascending North Gap Gully. This is the gully immediately right (west) of North Peak, not the next gully

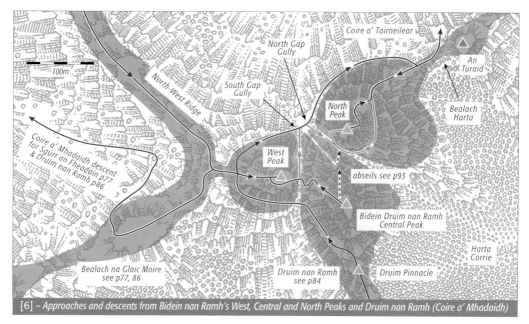

[6] – *Approaches and descents from Bidein nan Ramh's West, Central and North Peaks and Druim nan Ramh (Coire a' Mhadaidh)*

east from South Gap Gully, which separates Central Peak and a small subsidiary summit (*diagram* **[1]** & **[A]** *on diagrams p92–3*). Initial scree leads to short walls (Grade 3) which are climbed to a plinth in the gap between Central Peak and North Peak. Care is needed as this gully is also exposed to stonefall from parties above traversing Central Peak and North Peak (*diagrams* **[1]**, **[6]**, **[8]**).

From the plinth in the gap, follow a basalt terrace out left (Coire a' Tairneilear side) to the edge of the West Ridge of North Peak, then ascend a rib, a basalt staircase and a short wall to gain the summit. This section (Moderate) is very exposed (*diagram* **[5]**). If this is too intimidating, return to the gap and descend about 50m on the south (Harta Corrie side) to pick-up a worn ledge which traverses round to join the East Ridge some distance below the North Peak's summit.

Downclimb the East Ridge (Grade 2), initially via some slabs on the right which can be quite wet, then by cutting back left to gain a rockier ridge which can be descended to Bealach Harta (*diagrams* **[5]**, **[7]**).

If the North Gap Gully option isn't taken, then continue on the scree below the buttresses and ascend to Bealach Harta. Ascend and descend the North Peak via its East Ridge (*diagrams* **[1]**, **[6]**, **[8]**).

Decent

From Bealach Harta, descend scree slopes in a northerly direction into Coire a' Tairneilear where two burns draining the upper corrie pass through gorges. Follow a path in the right-hand (northern) gorge to gain a path on the right (north) side of the main burn (*diagram* **[8]**). Descend to the narrows below Sgùrr an Fheadain and pass through to join the approach paths.

[7] – *East Ridge of North Peak from Bealach Harta*

[8] – *Descent to Coire a' Tairneilear from Bidein Druim nan Ramh and Bealach Harta*

83

The impressive Druim Pinnacle near the top of the Druim nan Ramh, with Blàbheinn on the left in the distance

Druim nan Ramh from Sligachan

Summits: *Pt.500m* ▲ *; Pt.648m* ▲ *;*
Optional – Druim Pinnacle ▲
Terrain: *Grade 2 Scramble (one short section)*
Distance: *26km; 16 miles*
Ascent & Descent: *1250m; 4100ft*
Time: *8hrs 30mins–9hrs 30mins*
Start & Finish: *Glen Sligachan car park (NG 4877 2990)*

The Druim nan Ramh divides Coire-uisg and Loch Coruisk from Harta Corrie and offers a fine route with a panoramic view of the Cuillin Ridge and tremendous views of Coruisk. The route is mostly a high-level hillwalk, albeit one with an unexpected amount of rock and some rough terrain. The crux is at the top; a very short scramble to avoid a 'bad step', followed by some intricate route-finding round the southern flanks of Bidein Druim nan Ramh's Central Peak.

Approach

Druim nan Ramh is easily ascended from Coruisk, with a return via Bealach na Glaic Moire. But this will mean either an overnight stay, or coming in (and possibly out) by boat and an ascent 'against the clock'.

Ascending the ridge in a circuit from Sligachan

makes for a very long route, but given good weather, an early start and a long summer's day, it's a perfectly feasible expedition.

From Sligachan, the shortest route (by about 4km) is to ascend Pt.500m from Harta Corrie, skirt Bidein Druim nan Ramh to the east and descend the scree below Bealach Harta south-east, back into Harta Corrie. However, this doesn't take you to a satisfactory end point, misses the first section of the ridge and involves retracing your steps back along Glen Sligachan (more than two-thirds of the distance travelled).

The longer Sligachan route crosses over the main Cuillin ridgeline into Coire a' Mhadaidh and offers a more complete and satisfying circuit. From the car park, follow the old road and turn left onto the footpath before the old bridge. Keep immediately left past a circle of boulders with little cairns and go past a junction on the left with a gate.

Follow the path down Glen Sligachan for about 7km, fording the Allt na Measarroch at the foot of Marsco and continuing beyond on a slightly rougher path to reach the watershed at the twin pools of Lochan Dubha in the base of the glen. The path descends for about 350m to a junction with a cairn (NG 5018 2402). Turn right off the main path onto a clear path across the head of Srath na Crèitheach.

Ascend past a lochan to the col on the rocky shoulder of Druim Hain and a junction of paths, north

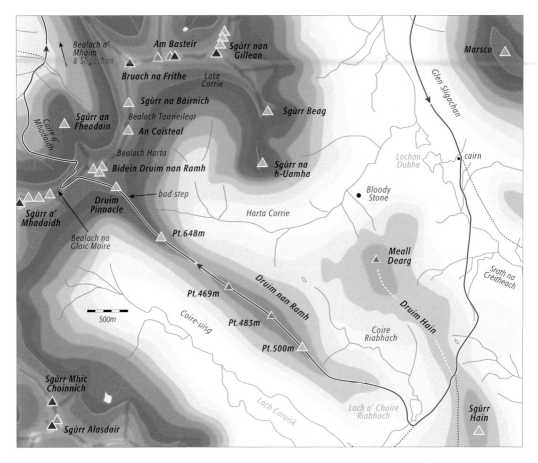

Bidein Druim nan Ramh, centre left, Harta and Lota Corries, from the central section of Druim nan Ramh

The 'bad step' and intricate traverse round Bidein Druim nan Ramh's South Face to the main Cuillin ridgeline

of Sgùrr Hain. The left-hand path contours below Sgùrr Hain to Sgùrr na Stri (see p190). Turn right towards Loch Coruisk, descend to the outflow of Loch a' Choire Riabhach and cross over to gain the ridge.

Approaching the 'bad step' beyond Pt.648m

Ascent

A long but gentle ascent, with lots of opportunities for easy scrambling gains the top of Pt.500m. Beyond this, undulating rockier ground scattered with lochans, leads to a steeper section of easy scrambling and the summit of Pt.648m. The ridge now narrows and leads towards the Druim Pinnacle. Before this, near the 720m contour, a gully cuts across the ridge creating a 'bad step' impasse (NG 4584 2363). It is possible to descend this (Difficult) via an awkward, sloping terrace about 6m below the crest (see *diagrams*).

However, a much easier alternative exists on the next terrace about 15m below. Gain this by reversing the crest a short way then scrambling down (Grade 2) and round on the Coruisk side, to a narrow grassy ramp of orange rock leading into the gully. Descend the ramp with care (Grade 2), some unstable rock, cross the enclosed gully and make a few moves up steep grassy rock, to a faint path leading out left.

Follow this round to below the Druim Pinnacle (easily climbed up and down by its East Ridge) and continue up the ridge to an area of slabs. Climb these to reach the top of the ridge where it abuts the steep nose of the Central Peak (see *above & opposite*).

Go left here to a cairn, then down a short scree-filled ramp-chimney. Make a short exposed descent to a lower terrace of grass and scree, then make a gently ascending horizontal traverse below the Central Peak to reach scree-covered orange slabs. Ascend these carefully to gain the main Cuillin ridgeline above a beaked rock and below the upper basalt staircase on the West Ridge of the West Peak (*see opposite & diagram* [2] *p81*).

Descent

Via Bealach na Glaic Moire and Coire a' Mhadaidh. Turn left (west) down the ridge, keeping right before it ends at a steep crag, to reach the stone-scattered parallel-sided lower basalt staircase. Descend this, then traverse left on a path towards Bealach na Glaic Moire. Before the bealach, descend coarse scree on the right (Coire a' Mhadaidh side) to gain a grassy platform.

Follow this then scree hard right (north-east), keeping high and resisting the temptation to start descending, to reach the top of the scree gully formed between the North-West Ridge of Bidein Druim nan Ramh and the three large parallel buttresses below the bealach (*diagram p77 & diagram* [6] *p82*). Descend the gully into Coire a' Mhadaidh over steep scree then grass and rock, to reach the burn in the corrie floor. Follow the left (east) side of the burn through a small ravine towards a gorge at the lip of the corrie. Swing right before this gorge, go over a shoulder and descend grassy and rocky slopes immediately left of Sgùrr an Fheadain to reach a path.

This leads right below the prominent Waterpipe Gully to the Fairy Pools path and the path back to Bealach a' Mhàim and Sligachan. Note that the Bealach a' Mhàim path is ill-defined at first. The best start is from an area of eroded scree almost directly across from the path below Waterpipe Gully (NG 4502 2519), not at the cairned path 150m lower down. Ascend to the Bealach a' Mhàim, turn right and follow the path beside the Allt Dearg Mòr back to Sligachan.

Looking back to the 'bad step' from the Druim Pinnacle

Meall Dearg 364m

Lying north of Druim Hain, near the pronounced division between granite and gabbro, this small hill's main claim to fame is geomorphological. Its bare granite summit is scattered with large gabbro boulders (erratics) deposited by glaciation.

The start of the traverse where the Druim nan Ramh abuts the steep nose of the Central Peak of Bidein Druim nan Ramh

Stepping off the flake on the crux Second Top of Sgùrr a' Mhadaidh; Difficult grade rock climbing

Round of Coire na Creiche
Sgùrr a' Mhadaidh, Bidein Druim nan Ramh, An Caisteal, Sgùrr na Bàirnich, Bruach na Frithe

*T*his spectacular round tackles two of the most technical sections of the Cuillin Ridge; the traverse of Sgùrr a' Mhadaidh's three tops and Bidein Druim nan Ramh's three peaks, which can involve two abseils. With a start up Sgùrr a' Mhadaidh's classic North-West Ridge and an intricate and awkward descent from An Caisteal to the Bealach Tairneilear near the finish, there's never a dull moment

Looking south from Sgùrr na Bàirnich to the orange col on An Caisteal, Bidein Druim nan Ramh and Sgùrr a' Mhadaidh

Round of Coire na Creiche

Summits: Sgùrr a' Mhadaidh ▲ ; Third Top ▲ ; Second Top ▲ ; First Top ▲ ; Bidein Druim nan Ramh West Peak ▲ ; Central Peak ▲ ; North Peak ▲ ; An Caisteal ▲ ; Bruach na Frithe ▲ ; Optional – Sgùrr na Bàirnich ▲

Terrain: Difficult Grade Rock Climb (Sgùrr a' Mhadaidh); Difficult Grade Rock Climb or optional 2 abseils (Bidein Druim nan Ramh); Moderate Grade Rock Climb (An Caisteal); Grade 2 Scramble (Bruach na Frithe)

Distance: 13km; 8 miles

Ascent & Descent: 1400m; 4595ft

Time: 6–7hrs

Start & Finish: Parking at the bridge over the River Brittle (NG 4175 2459)

Starting from the bridge over the River Brittle reduces the road walking and offers a straightforward if pathless ascent into Coire an Dorus. Most parties will carry a rope, harness and abseil device and use them on the traverse of Bidein Druim nan Ramh. These three peaks can be traversed without abseiling (see p80–3), but this removes some of the mountaineering challenge from a superb round.

Approach

Cross the bridge over the River Brittle and ascend the hillside directly making the most of the burn's grassy flanks, to where the ridge levels out. Cross the western spur of Sgùrr Thuilm at a col right of some rocks and a little below Pt.327m marked on the OS 1:25k map. From the col, contour above Coire a' Ghreadaidh and below the scree of the South-West Buttress. Either descend a little to meet the main path beside the Allt a' Choire Ghreadaidh, or make a

Approach from the North-West Ridge and descent to the stubby tower and the Third Top, from the summit of Sgùrr a' Mhadaidh

steady diagonal ascent over grass and occasional scree to meet the main path, then ascend left of a rocky gorge to the boulder-strewn grass, rocky slabs and scree of upper Coire an Dorus (*see p98*).

Keep left and ascend grass and scree left of the large boulderfield directly below the left-hand side of the West Face of Sgùrr a' Mhadaidh, to where two grassy rakes cut diagonally left across a short wall to the col between Sgùrr Thuilm and Sgùrr a' Mhadaidh's North-West Ridge (*diagrams p98–9, 107*). Gain the col by the higher rake.

Ascent

The steep North-West Ridge (Moderate) of Sgùrr a' Mhadaidh is exposed and quite awkward in places, although the holds are positive and the rock generally good (*photo p116*).

Rocky pinnacles lead to steeper ground made-up of two ribs, divided by a vertical cleft. Start up the right-hand rib, but soon cross over below the cleft to gain the broader left-hand rib and follow the line of least resistance, which is mostly just right of the edge. This leads to a slab forming the left wall of the cleft. Traverse left to the edge of the rib and ascend a steep chimney-recess.

Easier ground leads to a rocky arete, defined in its upper reaches by another cleft on the left (Deep

Gash Gully). The shattered ridge above is ascended to below the north end of Sgùrr a' Mhadaidh's summit ridge. Follow ledges rightwards, zigzaging up to gain the summit ridge, cross a cracked block on the crest and make a final short scramble to the summit.

Return to the north end of the summit ridge, where the main Cuillin ridgeline turns sharply south-east above a stubby tower. Descend slabs to the tower and climb it out left on a break. Go round the tower on its north (Coire a' Mhadaidh) side (Grade 2) and descend to a fine, airy rib leading to the Third Top.

Alternatively, descend the brown slab below the tower and make delicate, technical and exposed

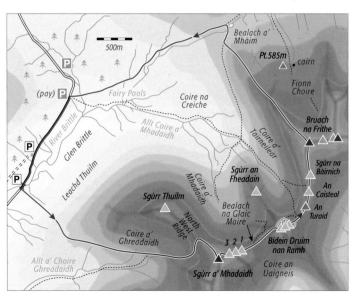

The descent from Sgùrr a' Mhadaidh to the Third Top

moves across the slab on small incuts (Grade 3) to a narrow gully, then exit this to gain the rib.

Sgùrr a' Mhadaidh's **Third Top** is best tackled directly via a stepped corner right of the prow. The climbing is steep but short, the holds are good and the line is obvious. Scramble up to the base, climb the first corner direct (Moderate), avoid the second by traversing out right and ascend to easier ground, which leads diagonally right to the top. If using a rope, the moves can be protected and a belay could be arranged at the end.

An alternative route zigzags up ledges and grassy grooves further right (Moderate), but the line isn't obvious and getting off-route could be serious. For this, descend the path below the stepped corner and go round a small jutting prow of black rock (about 50 paces, *see diagram p90*). A scree path continues beyond but leads nowhere – nowhere safe anyway!Zigzag up grass and slabs to a grassy ledge. Traverse this up and right to a rocky faultline with grass at its base, which cuts up left. (The grass ledge continues beyond, but the path soon fades). Ascend the faultline left then right, traversing out right to easier ground near the top.

Go over the summit and descend the ridge to the foot of the **Second Top**. Climb onto the boulder choke and traverse out left to a shallow, right-slanting corner. Follow this up and round right to a cracked flake. Ascend the steep crack on good holds to stand

The stepped corner on the South Face of the Third Top of Sgùrr a' Mhadaidh

Crux South Face of the Second Top of Sgùrr a' Mhadaidh

The First Top of Sgùrr a' Mhadaidh

on the flake (*photo p88*) and climb the blocky crack above to the summit (Difficult). This is the crux of the route. If using a rope, the climbing is easily protected and there is a good spike at the top on which to belay.

Descend to a narrow cleft which cuts over the ridge below the **First Top**. Cross this right, then left to a small gully and climb a steep wall, from where easier scrambling gains the summit. Descend the East Ridge

with a small step to reach Bealach na Glaic Moire. Cross the bealach and zigzag up left to the stone-scattered lower basalt staircase (*see p86*).

Ascend it and the easy ridge above to the steeper, upper basalt staircase on the West Ridge of Bidein Druim nan Ramh (*diagram* **[2]** *p81*). Climb over the **West Peak** and descend with difficulty to Bridge Rock below the Central Peak (Moderate), (*diagram* **[3]** *p81*). Cross the gap to the **Central Peak** and ascend a wall and parallel-sided chimney (Grade 3) to the summit above the North-East Ridge (*diagram* **[4]** *p81*).

There are now **three options**. (1) Climb down the North-East Ridge. The initial section is an open and exposed slab (Moderate) leading to a gap before the subsidiary summit, **[A]** on diagram below and right. Pass round the left side of this (looking down) then swing right on slabs to above an overhanging wall. Descend this via some horrible, steep and exposed climbing (Very Difficult – Severe).

(2) Alternatively, the North-East Ridge can be descended in two abseils (*diagram opposite*). The first leads to a cleft between the Central Peak and the small subsidiary summit. From here, scramble round and down left to a second shorter abseil into the gap between the Central and North Peaks. Care is needed here as the ropes run over sharp rock at the start of

The first abseil on Central Peak and the continuation routes on North Peak, Bidein Druim nan Ramh

Abseils on the Central Peak of Bidein Druim nan Ramh, viewed from North Peak

the abseil (*diagram above*).

(3) It is also possible to reverse the routes on the three peaks and utilise South Gap and North Gap Gully (Grade 3), which split the West Face on the Coire a' Tairneilear side (*see diagrams* **[1]**, **[6]**, **[8]** *p80–3*). Abseiling is probably quicker, depending on

ropework proficiency.

All of the options lead to a plinth in the gap between the Central Peak and the **North Peak**. Follow a basalt terrace out left (Coire a' Tairneilear side) to reach the edge of the West Ridge (*diagram p92*), then ascend a very exposed rib, a basalt staircase and a short wall to gain the summit (Moderate). If this is too intimidating, return to the gap and descend about 50m on the south (Harta Corrie) side to pick-up a worn ledge which traverses round to join the North Peak's East Ridge some distance below the summit.

Downclimb the East Ridge (Grade 2), initially via some slabs on the right which can be quite wet, then by cutting back left to gain a rockier ridge which can be descended to Bealach Harta (*diagram* **[7]** *p83*).

From Bealach Harta, the rocky lump of An Turaid blocks the continuation of the main Cuillin ridgeline to the north-east. Climb this direct or go round it on the right and continue along the initially rocky and grassy ridge towards An Caisteal (830m), the serrated peak facing Sgùrr na Bàirnich across the Bealach Tairneilear. Note that neither An Turaid (*see also p82-3*), An Caisteal, nor Bealach Tairneilear are named on OS maps.

Three eroded dykes create significant clefts and give An Caisteal its serrated appearance. The first two can be crossed via ledges on the left (Coire a' Tairneilear side), but the third needs a bold step across (Grade 2). All are deep and awkward and care is needed. An Caisteal's summit lies above a vertical cliff, which must be avoided via a descending traverse on the left (Coire a' Tairneilear side) to reach a prominent orange col at the top of a large orange slab (*see following pages*).

Scramble down the slab via a basalt trough. From the bottom of this, make a leftwards descending

The three clefts of An Caisteal and orange col at the top of the North Ridge descent to Bealach Tairneilear

The route to the orange col at the top of An Caisteal's North Ridge. It is important to keep on the left (Coire a' Tairneilear) side of the summit as the right (Harta Corrie) side leads to the vertical cliff shown in the photo on the right

The start of the North Ridge descent to Bealach Tairneilear from the orange col on An Caisteal

The crux wall at the end of the North Ridge descent

traverse below the crest of the ridge, with a short wall (Grade 2) en route, to reach the top of the final undercut crux wall above the Bealach Tairneilear. This can be abseiled or downclimbed (Moderate) via a spiral line. Descend to the left (looking down) to reach ledges, then traverse back right (looking down) towards the bealach, then straight down. The final handholds are small but positive.

Head straight up from the bealach, not as intimidating as it looks from below, keeping to the crest via the line of least resistance (Grade 1–2). Cross over a squat pinnacle to a gap created by an eroded orange dyke and avoid the steep wall ahead on the right. Easier ground leads to the summit of Sgùrr an Bàirnich (860m). From the top, a short scramble on good rock gains the South Ridge of Bruach na Frithe. Sgùrr an Bàirnich is a pleasant summit and a good viewpoint, but it can be avoided by traversing left on lower ledges (*see below*). Near the top of Bruach na Frithe's South Ridge, avoid some pinnacles on their right (Lota Corrie side), then regain the crest and continue to the summit (Grade 2). The rock on this section of ridge is quite broken and loose in places.

Descent

From Bruach na Frithe, descend via the North-West Ridge or Fionn Choire to the Bealach a' Mhàim (*see p63–5*) and down to the Fairy Pools car park. Follow the road back to the starting point.

The route over Sgùrr na Bàirnich to Bruach na Frithe. The summit of Sgùrr na Bàirnich can be avoided by a lower traverse

Below The Wart on Sgùrr a' Ghreadaidh, descending slabby ground towards An Dorus. The summit of Sgùrr a' Mhadaidh is on the left with the Third, Second and First Tops to its right. Bruach na Frithe, Am Bàsteir and Sgùrr nan Gillean in the distance

Sgùrr a' Mhadaidh
& Sgùrr a' Ghreadaidh

Sgùrr a' Mhadaidh is the lower and easier of the two peaks, although it has a lot of scree and shattered rock. An Dorus, the notch separating Sgùrr a' Mhadaidh and Sgùrr a' Ghreadaidh, is one of the best known features on the Cuillin Ridge and the steep corner on its south side needs to be ascended and descended when climbing Sgùrr a' Ghreadaidh, making it the crux of that route

Approaching the summit of Sgùrr a' Mhadaidh at the top of the North-West Ridge

Sgùrr a' Mhadaidh – An Dorus

Summits: *Sgùrr a' Mhadaidh* ▲
Terrain: *Grade 2 Scramble or Hillwalk*
Distance: *8km; 5 miles*
Ascent & Descent: *905m; 2965ft*
Time: *4–5hrs*
Start & Finish: *Parking near Glen Brittle Youth Hostel (NG 4092 2250)*

Sgùrr a' Mhadaidh and Sgùrr a' Ghreadaidh are often climbed together. An ascent via An Dorus gives a route of 9.5km/6 miles, 1035m/3400ft of ascent & descent, 5–6hrs

The West Face of Sgùrr a' Mhadaidh (918m) overlooks Coire a' Ghreadaidh and offers a relatively sunny and short approach to this impressive

mountain and its next door neighbour, Sgùrr a' Ghreadaidh (973m). Both are most commonly climbed from the notch of An Dorus and while the white grooves forming the Sgùrr a' Mhadaidh side feel a little easier than the steep corner on the Sgùrr a' Ghreadaidh side, they are still tricky in places.

An approach via An Dorus isn't the only option and there are two alternative routes on the West Face.

Regardless of approach, all of the popular routes on Sgùrr a' Mhadaidh involve copious amounts of scree and shattered rock and care is required, not least to make sure nothing is knocked down onto other parties.

Approach
From the Youth Hostel, follow the firm path on the right (south) side of the Allt a' Choire Ghreadaidh and ascend past pools and deep ravines. After about 1.7km the path to Sgùrr na Banachdaich breaks off

Looking up Coire An Dorus to An Dorus and the West Faces Sgùrr a' Mhadaidh and Sgùrr a' Ghreadaidh

right at a stone water drain (NG 4236 2320).

Continue on the main path which steepens and the quality deteriorates, the going becoming a lot rougher and stonier. The path then levels out and arrives at a point where the burn forms a waterslide over slabby rocks. While it is possible to keep to the right (south) side of the burn, the best route crosses to the left (north) side.

Cross over and ascend the rock for a short distance to regain the path, which leads over a gravel dome to gain the floor of upper Coire a' Ghreadaidh. Continue over a section of grassy moorland with the prominent pointed peak of Sgùrr Eadar dà Choire straight ahead, to meet the burn draining upper Coire an Dorus, which is hidden from the approach in a right to left gully.

Alternative approach to Sgùrr a' Mhadaidh avoiding scramble from An Dorus

West Face of Sgùrr a' Mhadaidh from the North Ridge of Sgùrr a' Ghreadaidh

A prominent path beside the burn leads to a leveling out, then a final rise left of a rocky gorge to the boulder-strewn grass, rocky slabs and scree of upper Coire an Dorus. Sgùrr a' Mhadaidh lies straight ahead, defined on its left by the steep North-West Ridge which separates it from Sgùrr Thuilm and on its right by the prominent notch of An Dorus. To the right of this is the greater bulk of the significantly higher Sgùrr a' Ghreadaidh, whose summit ridge is split by the prominent gash of Eag Dubh.

Ascent

The classic route ascends from Coire an Dorus to the notch of An Dorus. From upper Coire an Dorus, cross over the burn and ascend over grass into the scree trough directly below An Dorus. Follow the long and rather tedious scree slope in the trough to An Dorus, with some scrambling at the top. In poor visibility it is important to keep left, as the paths leading straight up lead to Eag Dubh.

From the far side of the An Dorus notch, scramble up smooth grooves of white rock, in the wall on the left (north) side (Grade 2). These are short but can be tricky in the damp. Zigzag up Mhadaidh's South Ridge via paths and small bits of scrambling to the summit. There is a fair amount of rubble on the ledges hereabouts so care is needed.

An Dorus Alternative: This avoids the white grooves via scree and is little more than a walk. Follow the route up the scree trough as for An Dorus, but some 10m before the notch, follow a worn scree path horizontally out left. Pass round a rock buttress to reach the right edge of the upper scree slope. Ascend directly past some walled bivouac sites to reach the main path from An Dorus and follow this to the summit. Mark the point where you joined the main path if you wish to return by the same route and visibility is poor.

Descent

Any combination of routes on Sgùrr a' Mhadaidh can be used for ascent and descent. If Sgùrr a' Ghreadaidh is to be added, then any descent needs to return to An Dorus so that its steep crack and corner can be climbed, or a traverse made to Eag Dubh (*see p101–3*).

99

Sgùrr a' Mhadaidh – West Face

Summits: *Sgùrr a' Mhadaidh* ▲
Terrain: *Grade 1–2 Scramble*
Distance: *9km; 5.5 miles*
Ascent & Descent: *905m; 2965ft*
Time: *4–5hrs*
Start & Finish: *Parking near Glen Brittle Youth Hostel (NG 4092 2250)*

This route involves reasonable scree paths lower down, but scrambling on less stable ground near the top of the North-West Ridge. It is mostly straightforward but requires careful route-finding.

Approach
Follow the description to upper Coire an Dorus as for Sgùrr a' Mhadaidh (*see p97–9*).

Ascent
From upper Coire an Dorus, keep left and ascend grass and scree left of the large boulderfield directly below the left-hand side of the West Face, to gain grassy ledges below the cliffs (*diagram p98*).

Follow the ledges rightwards to gain the large lower scree slope and ascended diagonally leftwards heading for a notch at its top left edge. Go through the notch on stony ledges, then continue diagonally up and right to gain the North-West Ridge above its difficulties, where the angle eases.

When the ridge reaches the steep north end of the summit ridge, follow ledges rightwards, zigzaging up to gain the summit ridge. Cross a cracked block on the crest (probably the hardest moves) and make a final short scramble to the summit.

Looking down across the West Face to Sgùrr Thuilm

Descent
Any combination of routes on Sgùrr a' Mhadaidh can be used for ascent and descent. However, the upper section of the West Face is on complex and in places unstable terrain and could be confusing and dangerous if descending in poor visibility, having ascended by a different route. If Sgùrr a' Ghreadaidh is to be added, then any descent needs to return to An Dorus so that the steep and crack and corner can be climbed, or a traverse made to Eag Dubh (*see p101–3*).

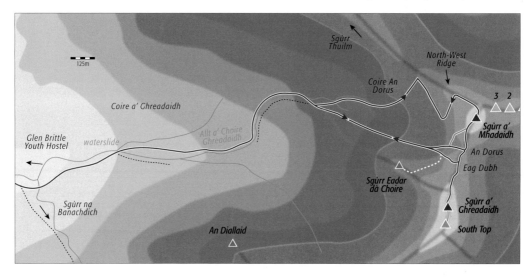

Sgùrr a' Ghreadaidh – An Dorus

Summits: *Sgùrr a' Ghreadaidh* ▲ ;
Optional – South Top ▲
Terrain: *Grade 3 Scramble*
Distance: *9km; 5.5 miles*
Ascent & Descent: *960m; 3145ft*
Time: *4hrs 30mins–5hrs 30mins*
Start & Finish: *Parking near Glen Brittle Youth
Hostel (NG 4092 2250)*

*Sgùrr a' Mhadaidh and Sgùrr a' Ghreadaidh are
often climbed together. An ascent via An Dorus
gives a route of 9.5km/6 miles, 1035m/3400ft
of ascent & descent, 5–6hrs*

*The higher of the two peaks by 55m, Sgùrr a'
Ghreadaidh (973m) offers more continuous
scrambling on better rock. The usual ascent is via An
Dorus and involves climbing out of the notch on its
right (south) side via a steep crack and corner.*

Approach
Follow the description to upper Coire an Dorus as for
Sgùrr a' Mhadaidh (*see p97–9*).

The steep crack and corner at An Dorus

The North Ridge of Sgùrr a' Ghreadaidh showing the route from An Dorus

Ascent

From upper Coire an Dorus, cross over the burn, ascend rightwards over grass to the scree directly below An Dorus and ascend to the notch. In poor visibility it is important to keep left, as the paths leading straight up lead to Eag Dubh (*see p98*). Climb the right (south) side of the notch by a crack and corner with a few steep moves on positive holds (Grade 3).

Gain the worn crest of the ridge and follow it past the deep cleft of Eag Dubh on the right. Scramble up to an orange break in a small overlap and climb this on good holds (Grade 2, trickier in descent). Go right from there, then left to slabby ground leading to the prominent tower of The Wart (*photo p117*). Pass this to its right to reach the summit, marked by a small cairn.

Beyond is the South Top (970m), a Munro Top, which is just a few metres lower. To reach this continue along a narrow rock fin to a steep nose. Descend the nose in a left to right spiral, go round the next section of ridge on the right and ascend a steep arete (Grade 3) to the South Top. The nose can be avoided by a ledge system below, gained by scrambling down to the right (Coire a' Ghreadaidh side) from the main summit (Grade 2).

Descent

Retrace your steps. Looking down into An Dorus from above, paths go right and left. The crack and corner is on the left. The corner may feel more intimidating in descent and many use a rope here. The downclimbing is very short and there is a good belay at the top. Descend the scree to Coire an Dorus.

The crack and corner at An Dorus. The climbing is just a few moves, but feels harder in descent

Descending the crack and corner to An Dorus feels significantly more awkward and exposed

Looking towards the South Top. From the summit of Sgùrr a' Ghreadaidh a rock fin leads towards the South Top, which is lower by just three metres.The fin ends in a steep nose. The fin and the nose can be avoided by descending from the summit to the rocky ledges below, shown here, which can be traversed to the South Top

Sgùrr a' Ghreadaidh – Eag Dubh

Summits: *Sgùrr a' Ghreadaidh* ▲ *;*
Optional – South Top ▲
Terrain: *Grade 2 Scramble (Grade 3 to the South Top)*
Distance: *9km; 5.5 miles*
Ascent & Descent: *960m; 3145ft*
Time: *4hrs 30mins–5hrs 30mins*
Start & Finish: *Parking near Glen Brittle Youth Hostel (NG 4092 2250)*

The steep corner out of An Dorus can be avoided via the slot of Eag Dubh on the West Face of Sgùrr a' Ghreadaidh, south of An Dorus. However, it is possibly better used for descent than ascent. The enclosed nature of the slot means it is often wet and slimy and it can retain snow into early summer.

Approach
Follow the description to upper Coire an Dorus as for Sgùrr a' Mhadaidh (see p97–9).

Ascent
From upper Coire an Dorus, cross over the burn and ascend rightwards over grass into the scree trough directly below An Dorus. Where the path swings left towards An Dorus, continue straight up and right to below the slot chimney of Eag Dubh and climb it to emerge on the ridge below The Wart. Continue to the summit as for the route from An Dorus opposite.

Descent
Possibly a better route in descent than ascent. Descend the cleft with care, there is loose rock and stonefall is particularly dangerous in enclosed spaces, to gain the scree and Coire an Dorus.

> ### Sgùrr Eadar dà Choire 809m
> *This western outlier of Sgùrr a' Ghreadaidh (see map p100) is easily gained by a simple traverse south-west across the boulderfield below Eag Dubh. The summit lies right of an obvious gendarme and offers good views over Coire a' Ghreadaidh (25mins return from the An Dorus path)*

Starting the fine South-East Ridge of Sgùrr Thuilm. An elevated rocky arete with panoramic views of the surrounding peaks

Sgùrr Thuilm

*D*espite its 881m height, Sgùrr Thuilm falls just 20m short of the 152m drop required for Corbett status. Nevertheless, it's a classically proportioned mountain in a tremendous position, with a magnificent South-East Ridge. A peak for the mountain connoisseur

Looking west over Coire a' Mhadaidh from Bidein Druim nan Ramh, to Sgùrr Thuilm's South-East Ridge

South-East Ridge

Summits: *Sgùrr Thuilm* ▲
Terrain: *Hillwalk (optional Grade 2 Scramble)*
Distance: *9km; 5.5 miles*
Ascent & Descent: *865m; 2845ft*
Time: *4–5hrs*
Start & Finish: *Parking near Glen Brittle Youth Hostel (NG 4092 2250)*

Sgùrr Thuilm (881m) makes an excellent objective in its own right for a shortish day, although it is often included prior to ascending Sgùrr a' Mhadaidh's North-West Ridge on either the Round of Coire na Creiche (see p89) or the Round of Coire a' Ghreadaidh (see p117). The mountain's West Ridge soon merges into extensive scree and boulder slopes and that side of the mountain is best left for descent.

Approach

From the Youth Hostel, follow the firm path on the right (south) side of the Allt a' Choire Ghreadaidh and ascend past pools and deep ravines. After about 1.7km the path to Sgùrr na Banachdaich breaks off right at a stone water drain (NG 4236 2320).

Continue on the main path which steepens and the quality deteriorates, the going becoming a lot rougher and stonier. The path then levels out to reach a point where the burn forms a waterslide over slabby rocks. While it is possible to keep to the right (south) side of the burn, the best route crosses to the left (north) side.

Cross over and ascend the rock for a short distance to regain the path which leads over a gravel dome to gain the floor of Coire a' Ghreadaidh. Continue over a section of grassy moorland with the prominent pointed peak of Sgùrr Eader dà Choire straight ahead, to meet the burn draining upper Coire an Dorus, which is hidden from the approach in a right to left gully.

A prominent path on the burn's left bank leads to a leveling out, then a final rise left of a rocky gorge to the boulder-strewn grass, rocky slabs and scree of upper Coire an Dorus. From here, Sgùrr Thuilm lies to the left, its long South-East Ridge leading down to the col separating it from Sgùrr a' Mhadaidh.

From upper Coire an Dorus, keep left and ascend

High on Sgùrr Thuilm's South-East Ridge. A superb if easy rocky ridge

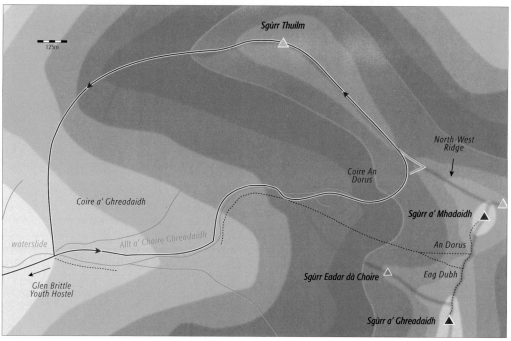

grass and scree left of the large boulderfield directly below the left-hand side of the West Face of Sgùrr a' Mhadaidh, to where two grassy rakes cut diagonally left across a short wall to the col between Sgùrr Thuilm's South-East Ridge and Sgùrr a' Mhadaidh's North-West Ridge (*see also p98–9*).

Ascent

Follow the higher of the two rakes diagonally left to gain the col and the start of the South-East Ridge. Follow the sharp rocky ridge to the summit.

For anyone wanting some Grade 2 scrambling at the start, an alternative takes in the small towers on the lower section of Sgùrr a' Mhadaidh's North-West Ridge. To gain these, continue past the grassy rakes, to the foot of Sgùrr a' Mhadaidh's West Face. From here, follow a rocky chimney-slot diagonally left to gain the North-West Ridge. Descend the lower section of the ridge towards Sgùrr Thuilm, passing over some short pinnacles with a couple of tricky moves, to gain the col and the South-East Ridge.

Descent

Descend the West Ridge to where it merges with the srcee and continue down that to clear the crags on the southern tip. When clear, turn south and contour south-east to meet the Allt a' Choire Ghreadaidh at the waterslide on the approach route. Cross to the far (south) side of the burn and follow the path back to the Youth Hostel.

See also diagrams p98–9

North-West Ridge

Sgùrr a' Mhadaidh

Sgùrr Thuilm South-East Ridge

upper grassy rake

Sgùrr a' Mhadaidh West Face

Coire an Dorus

Approaches to Sgùrr Thuilm's South-East Ridge from upper Coire An Dorus

The South Ridge of Sgùrr na Banachdaich, left, from Sgùrr Dearg. Right of Banachdaich is Sgùrr Thormaid and the Three Teeth, then the South Ridge of Sgùrr a' Ghreadaidh. The lower pointed summit right of Ghreadaidh is Sgùrr a' Mhadaidh, with its Three Tops beyond. Sgùrr Thuilm is central in the middle distance and The Storr on the right in the far distance

Coire na Banachdaich from the Allt Coire na Banachdaich. From left, Sgùrr nan Gobhar, Sgùrr na Banachdaich and Sgùrr Dearg

Sgùrr na Banachdaich

*T*he standard route up Banachdaich via Coire an Eich and An Diallaid involves a steep scree ascent out of the corrie, but the rest of the route up the broad and rubble strewn West Face is at an easier angle and straightforward. In poor visibility the face can be a confusing place, especially in descent

Looking towards the peaks of the Southern Cuillin from the summit of Sgùrr na Banachdaich

West Face via Coire an Eich

Summits: Sgùrr na Banachdaich ▲ ; South Top ▲ ;
Optional – Centre Top ▲ ; An Diallaid ▲ ;
Sgùrr nan Gobhar ▲
Terrain: Hillwalk
Distance: 8km; 5 miles
Ascent & Descent: 950m; 3120ft
Time: 4–5hrs
Start & Finish: Parking near Glen Brittle Youth Hostel (NG 4092 2250)

Sgùrr na Banachdaich (965m) is a bit of a scree lump when climbed via the West Face from Coire an Eich, but this makes it one of the easiest and most popular Munros in the Cuillin, with fine views north and south over the dramatic ridges connecting it to Sgùrr a' Ghreadaidh (see p118) and Sgùrr Dearg (see p115). The West Face offers the easiest route on the mountain in ascent and descent.

Sgùrr nan Gobhar (630m) and the West Ridge offer an alternative descent, albeit with a little more scrambling. The final section is over rock and scree, making Sgùrr nan Gobhar and the West Ridge a better proposition for descent than ascent.

It should be noted that on their maps, the Ordnance

Survey have updated the spelling of Banachdaich for the mountain, but failed to update the burn, coire, or bealach names, which remain Banachdich.

Approach

From the Youth Hostel, follow the firm path on the right (south) side of the Allt a' Choire Ghreadaidh and ascend past pools and deep ravines. After about 1.7km, at a stone water drain (NG 4236 2320), turn right off the main path onto an earth path.

Ascend this path south-east across the moorland to gain a grassy spur right (west) of the Allt Coire an Eich, and climb this into Coire an Eich. Continue up the stony corrie, then cross over the burn, heading for the far left-hand side of the corrie, from where the zigzag ascent to An Diallaid starts.

Ascent

As the path steepens the scree becomes harder going but the angle soon relents. Traverse into a trough with the burn in its base, then ascend to reach the broad West Face at the col between An Diallaid and Sgùrr na Banachdaich, with views over Coire an Dorus to Sgùrr Thuilm, Sgùrr a' Mhadaidh and Sgùrr a' Ghreadaidh (see following pages).

To the north, the small rocky top of An Diallaid is easily climbed and worth taking in, either on the

The upper reaches of Coire an Each below An Diallaid. The West Ridge and Sgùrr nan Gobhar are on the left

ascent or descent. From the col, follow the broad ridge initially keeping near to the corrie edge, then open boulder slopes and occasional easy scrambling to reach the rocky summit of Sgùrr na Banachdaich.

Descent

The easiest descent is to reverse the West Face via Coire an Eich. When descending the boulder slopes west of the summit, it is essential, especially when visibility is poor, to keep on the right-hand path closer to the edge of upper Coire a' Ghreadaidh, as the natural lie of the land takes you left to the West Ridge leading to Sgùrr nan Gobhar (*see photo opposite*).

The West Ridge via Sgùrr nan Gobhar also offers an enjoyable way down, but involves some scrambling and a steep section on scree at the end. For this route, follow the broad boulder slopes west from the summit, sticking to the left-hand path. Pass over Pt.776m and scramble down some short steps (Grade 2), from where a fine grassy and rocky crest

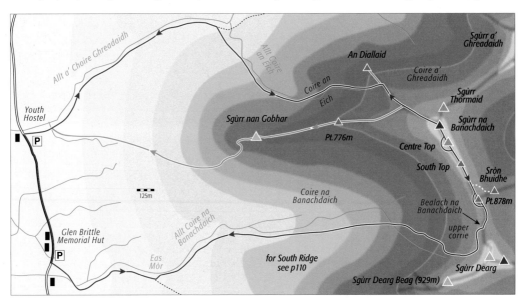

The broad scree plateau below the summit of Sgùrr na Banachdaich. If descending in poor visibility it is important to keep right towards An Diallaid and Coire an Eich, rather than be drawn left to the West Ridge and Sgùrr nan Gobhar

leads to the summit of Sgùrr nan Gobhar.

All of the descents from Sgùrr nan Gobhar involve some steep scree. The best is probably south-west into Coire na Banachdaich. From the summit, descend in a westerly direction then south-west zigzaging down between scree, grass and rocky steps, to where the angle eases to scree. Descend this in a more southerly direction to reach Coire na Banachdaich and cross the moor to join the outward path near the Youth Hostel.

It is also possible to descend the South Ridge to Bealach Coire na Banachdaich below Sgùrr Dearg and down into Coire na Banachdaich. This is largely a rocky and in places exposed hillwalk, with some easy scrambling if the Centre Top (Grade 2) is left out. The route from the bealach into Coire na Banachdaich also requires care, especially in poor visibility. This route is described in more detail on the following pages.

Approach and descent from Coire an Eich and the West Ridge, viewed from Sgùrr nan Gobhar

Approach and descent to the South Ridge of Sgùrr na Banachdaich from Coire na Banachdaich

South Ridge via Coire na Banachdaich

Summits: *Sgùrr na Banachdaich* ▲ *; South Top* ▲ *;*
Optional – Centre Top ▲ *; An Diallaid* ▲ *;*
Sgùrr nan Gobhar ▲
Terrain: *Grade 1 Scramble (Grade 2 if Centre Top is ascended).*
Distance: *9km; 5.5 miles*
Ascent & Descent: *960m; 3150ft*
Time: *4–5hrs*
Start & Finish: *Parking near the Glen Brittle Memorial Hut (NG 4117 2160)*

Sgùrr na Banachdaich's South Ridge via Coire na Banachdaich and Bealach Coire na Banachdaich offers a long and impressively rocky, but generally straightforward ridge with the option of a Grade 2 Scramble if the Centre Top (a Munro Top) is climbed.

The approach from Glen Brittle up Coire nan Banachdaich follows a clear path for much of the way, but the final section up the headwall below Sgùrr Dearg to gain the upper corrie, requires careful route-finding, especially when descending in poor visibility without 'prior knowledge', having ascended Sgùrr na Banachdaich by a different route.

Approach
Park in the vicinity of the Glen Brittle Memorial Hut,
just south of the Skye Mountain Rescue building in Glen Brittle (NG 4117 2160). Walk 55m south along the road to a path on the left before the sheep pens and follow it south-east to cross a footbridge over the Allt Coire na Banachdaich.

Continue on the right (south) side of the burn to a junction above the impressive Eas Mòr waterfall. Turn left (the right-hand path leads to Coire Làgan) and continue beside the burn up into Coire na Banachdaich. Steep, slabby buttresses form the corrie headwall below Sgùrr Dearg and Bealach Coire na Banachdaich, the lowest point on Sgùrr na Banachdaich's South Ridge.

Cross over the deeply incut burn draining the corrie below Sgùrr Dearg, then ascend the grassy slabs on the left to reach a shallow gully which cuts through the right side of the slabby headwall, to reach the scree slopes of the upper corrie.

Ascend these diagonally left below Sgùrr Dearg's North-West Face to reach a scree shoot and follow this up to gain the South Ridge at Bealach Coire na Banachdaich *(map p112)*.

Ascent
Traverse round or over Pt.878m (marked on Harvey map), then ascend steadily to gain the rocky ridge of the South Top and descend the other side to below the steeper and homogeneous Centre Top. Climbing this and descending the steeper side to the col below the summit buttress gives a Grade 2 scramble.

Approach and descent to upper Coire na Banachdaich and Bealach Coire na Banachdaich

Alternatively, skirt below the Centre Top on shattered ledges to reach a col and continue ascending over similar ground to the summit.

Descent
By the same route, the West Face via Coire an Eich or the West Ridge via Sgùrr nan Gobhar (*see p111–3*).

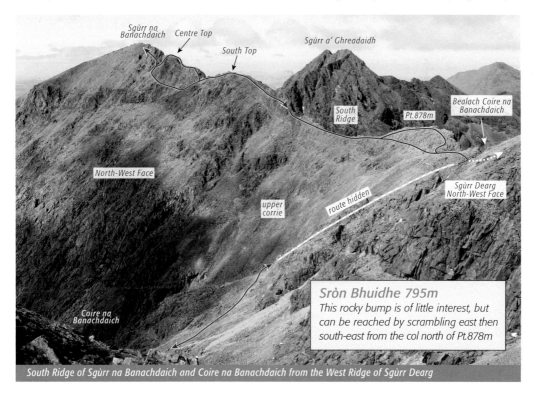

Sròn Bhuidhe 795m
This rocky bump is of little interest, but can be reached by scrambling east then south-east from the col north of Pt.878m

South Ridge of Sgùrr na Banachdaich and Coire na Banachdaich from the West Ridge of Sgùrr Dearg

The imposing North-West Ridge of Sgùrr a' Mhadaidh offers Grade 3 scrambling in big mountain surroundings

Round of Coire a' Ghreadaidh
Sgùrr Thuilm, Sgùrr a' Mhadaidh, Sgùrr a' Ghreadaidh, Sgùrr Thormaid, Sgùrr na Banachdaich & Sgùrr nan Gobhar

*T*his fine round offers a superb, sustained and committing outing. Once the intimidating North-West Ridge of Sgùrr a' Mhadaidh has been ascended the hardest section is the climb out of An Dorus. However, once beyond Sgùrr a' Ghreadaidh, there is no escape from the ridge until Sgùrr na Banachdaich

The Wart on the North Ridge of Sgùrr a' Ghreadaidh

Round of Coire a' Ghreadaidh

Summits: Sgùrr Thuilm ▲ ; Sgùrr a' Mhadaidh ▲ ; Sgùrr a' Ghreadaidh▲ ; South Top▲ ; Sgùrr Thormaid ▲ ; Sgùrr na Banachdaich▲ ; Sgùrr nan Gobhar▲

Terrain: *Moderate Rock Climb (Sgùrr a' Mhadaidh); Grade 3 Scramble (Sgùrr a' Ghreadaidh); Grade 2 Scramble (Sgùrr Thormaid); Grade 1 Scramble (Sgùrr na Banachdaich); Grade 2 Scramble (Sgùrr nan Gobhar)*

Distance: *11.5km; 7 miles*
Ascent & Descent: *1340m; 4375ft*
Time: *7–8hrs*
Start & Finish: *Parking near Glen Brittle Youth Hostel (NG 4092 2250)*

One of the top corrie rounds in the Cuillin, this route is best done in a clockwise direction. This may not give the best reconnaissance for a south-north traverse of the Cuillin Ridge, but an anti-clockwise route would mean descending Sgùrr a' Mhadaidh's steep North-West Ridge and even the most hardened scrambler might baulk at that suggestion on looking down it from above for the very first time.

Approach
As for Sgùrr Thuilm up Coire a' Ghreadaidh and Coire an Dorus to below the col between the South-East Ridge of Sgùrr Thuilm and the North-West Ridge of Sgùrr a' Mhadaidh (*diagrams p98, 107*).

Ascent
Gain the col by the lower grassy rake, then follow the South-East Ridge to the summit of Sgùrr Thuilm. Reverse the route back to the base of the North-West Ridge and climb it (Moderate) to the summit of Sgùrr a' Mhadaidh (*see p97–9, 107*). Descend the broken ledges of the broad South Ridge and scramble down into An Dorus. Climb the crack and corner on the right (south) side (Grade 3), and follow the North Ridge to

South Ridge of Sgùrr a' Ghreadaidh and the Three Teeth from Sgùrr na Banachdaich

the summit of Sgùrr a' Ghreadaidh (*see p101–2*). Continue to the South Top (Grade 3), then descend the long South Ridge to Bealach Coire a' Ghreadaidh (not named on maps) and the base of the Three Teeth, a small, three summited tower before the larger tower of Sgùrr Thormaid (926m), named after Normal Collie and a Munro Top. The ridge is Grade 3 via the crest but significantly easier via ledges on the right (Coire a' Ghreadaidh) side (*photo p70–1*).

A pleasant scramble leads over the Three Teeth (they can be avoided on either side or rock climbed more directly), followed by slabby rocks to the summit of Sgùrr Thormaid. From the summit, scramble down the ridge to the Bealach Thormaid (not named on maps) below Sgùrr na Banachdaich. The moves aren't hard but require care as the best line isn't obvious and the terrain is steep, slabby and very exposed (Grade 2). Ascend from the bealach passing small pinnacles on the right to the broad summit of Sgùrr na Banachdaich.

Descent

The West Face via Coire an Eich or the West Ridge via Sgùrr nan Gobhar (Grade 2) offer the most appropriate descents (*p111–3*). The South Ridge of Banachdaich to Bealach na Banachdaich and Coire na Banachdaich would be another option, (*p114–5*).

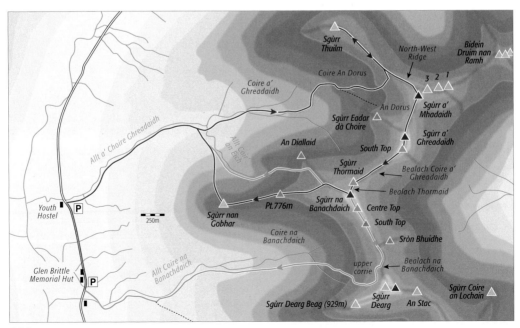

The descent from Sgùrr Thormaid to Bealach Thormaid is exposed and requires careful route-finding

SOUTHERN CUILLIN

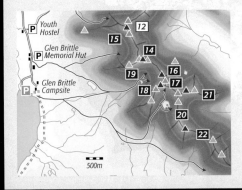

*The Inaccessible Pinnacle from the summit of An Stac
on the Round of Coire Làgan*

The 20m abseil down the steep West Ridge of the Inaccessible Pinnacle. The East Ridge follows the right edge

Sgùrr Dearg
& the Inaccessible Pinnacle

"The pinnacle had attracted much attention in the district, and had often been attacked by local climbers; but it deserved its name of Inaccessible till 1880, when my brother and I climbed it by its east edge. The following year a shepherd got up, after having taken off his shoes."

Charles Pilkington writing of the Inaccessible Pinnacle's first ascent

The Inaccessible Pinnacle is a prominent feature on the Cuillin skyline. Seen here from Beinn Dearg Mhòr, 14km to the east

Sgùrr Dearg – North-West Face

Summits: *Sgùrr Dearg* ▲ *; Sgùrr Dearg Beag* ▲
Terrain: *Hillwalk*
Distance: *7.5km, 4.5 miles*
Ascent & Descent: *970m; 3180ft*
Time: *4–5hrs*
Start & Finish: *Parking near Glen Brittle Memorial Hut (NG 4112 2163)*

Like Sgùrr na Banachdaich (965m), its close neighbour to the north, Sgùrr Dearg involves a lot of scree when climbed via its broad North-West or South-East Faces.

The Inaccessible Pinnacle (986m) is Sgùrr Dearg's highest point, but the lower summit (978m) is still an excellent destination in its own right, providing a platform to stretch out and watch the climbing and abseiling antics on the Pinnacle and admire the views south to Sgùrr MhicChoinnich (948m) and Sgùrr Alasdair (992m).

Approach

From the Glen Brittle Memorial Hut just south of the Skye Mountain Rescue building, walk 55m south along the road to a path on the left before the sheep pens and follow it over the Allt Coire na Banachdaich at a footbridge.

Continue on the right (south) side of the burn to a junction above the impressive Eas Mòr waterfall. Turn left (the right-hand path leads to Sgùrr Dearg's West Ridge and Coire Làgan) and continue beside the burn up into Coire na Banachdaich. Steep, slabby buttresses form the corrie headwall below Sgùrr Dearg and Bealach Coire na Banachdaich, the lowest point on Sgùrr na Banachdaich's South Ridge.

Cross over the deeply incut burn draining the corrie below Sgùrr Dearg, then up grassy slabs to the burn's left to a shallow gully and ascend through the right side of the slabby headwall to reach the scree slopes of the upper corrie. Ascend these diagonally left below Sgùrr Dearg's North-West Face to reach a scree shoot below Bealach Coire na Banachdaich and follow this to the main Cuillin ridgeline (see p114–5).

Scree and boulders on Sgùrr Dearg's North-West Face above Coire na Banachdaich. The West Ridge is behind

Ascent

Climb a rocky trough to gain Sgùrr Dearg's North-West Face and ascend to a ridge overlooking a gully cutting down left below the North Face. Follow the ridge round the top of the gully, beyond which the path merges into a slope of scree and boulders. Ascend this, making the best of any stable ground, to the rocky summit below the Inaccessible Pinnacle (*diagrams p114–5*).

Descent

Any of the routes on Sgùrr Dearg can be used. When descending, the section from Bealach na Banachdaich south below the North-West Face of Sgùrr Dearg to gain the route down into Coire na Banachdaich, requires care with route-finding, especially when descending in poor visibility without 'prior knowledge', having ascended Sgùrr Dearg by a different route.

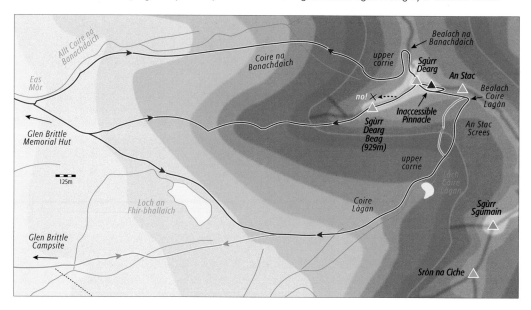

Sgùrr Dearg – West Ridge

Summits: *Sgùrr Dearg* ▲ *; Sgùrr Dearg Beag* ▲
Terrain: *Hillwalk – Grade 2 Scramble*
Distance: *7km, 4.25 miles*
Ascent & Descent: *980m; 3215ft*
Time: *4–5hrs*
Start & Finish: *Parking near Glen Brittle Memorial Hut (NG 4112 2163)*

The Inaccessible Pinnacle aside, the West Ridge is by far the most interesting route on the mountain in ascent and descent, with some pleasant scrambling on reasonable rock, although the lower section has its fair share of scree and boulders.

Approach
From the Glen Brittle Memorial Hut just south of the Skye Mountain Rescue building, walk 55m south along the road to a path on the left before the sheep pens and follow it over the Allt Coire na Banachdaich at a footbridge. Continue on the right (south) side of the burn to a junction above the impressive Eas Mòr waterfall. Keep right on the main path (the left turn leads to Coire na Banachdaich), for about 250m to another turn on the left and follow this to the start of the West Ridge.

Ascent
The path leads over grassy moorland, then zigzags up

scree to a prominent vertical yellow cleft on the left side of the rocky frontal face. Climb this, then continue ascending left of the crest to reach a grassier ridge where the angle eases.

Grass and scree lead up the broad ridge to the craggy face of Sgùrr Dearg Beag (point 929m on the OS 1:25k map). Scramble up onto this by the line of least resistance, go over the summit and descend to a col marked by large russet blocks of peridotite rock.

Beyond this, the ridge steepens significantly. Either scramble up the crest (Grade 2) or follow basalt ledges round on its right (Coire Làgan) side (Grade 1–2), until it is possible to ascend a shattered cleft to regain the crest. Follow the crest, initially on the right then on the left, to the lower summit of Sgùrr Dearg in front of the Inaccessible Pinnacle.

Descent
Any of the routes on Sgùrr Dearg can be used. In poor visibility the West Ridge requires care as both routes – scrambling down the crest, or traversing ledges on the left (Coire Làgan) side – weave around following the best line.

From the col, it is important to go over Sgùrr Dearg Beag (*see map opposite & p114–5, 128*). The prominent path on the right (north) side should be avoided as it leads into a hanging, rocky gully. An awkward and exposed exit can be made from the gully back onto the ridge just below Sgùrr Dearg Beag, but it is best avoided altogether.

The upper section of the West Ridge with the lower summit of Sgùrr Dearg topped by the Inaccessible Pinnacle beyond

Sgùrr Dearg – South-East Face

Summits: *Sgùrr Dearg* ▲ *; Sgùrr Dearg Beag* ▲
Terrain: *Grade 1–2 Scramble*
Distance: *9km, 5.5 miles*
Ascent & Descent: *970m; 3180ft*
Time: *4hr 30mins–5hr 30min*
Start & Finish: *Parking near Glen Brittle Memorial Hut (NG 4112 2163) or Glen Brittle Campsite (NG 4090 2065)*

An Stac Screes routes and An Stac approach to Sgùrr Dearg

Although a relatively straightforward route, the South-East Face has little to recommend it, being mostly scree and rubble-covered slabby ramplines linking the base of An Stac with the Inaccessible Pinnacle. In ascent, the worst of the An Stac Screes can largely be avoided to their left.

Approach

From the Glen Brittle Memorial Hut just south of the Skye Mountain Rescue building, walk 55m south along the road to a path on the left before the sheep pens and follow it over the Allt Coire na Banachdaich at a footbridge.

Continue on the right (south) side of the burn to a junction above the impressive Eas Mòr waterfall. Keep right here on the main path (the left turn leads to Coire na Banachdaich), and pass another turn on the left after about 250m (which leads to Sgùrr Dearg's West Ridge), to reach Loch an Fhir-bhallaich. Beyond this the path ascends, merges with the path from Glen

Brittle Campsite and the terrain becomes rougher.

If approaching from the campsite then go past the toilet block and ascend to a track. Follow this for a short distance, then turn left back onto the main path. Continue past Loch an Fhir-bhallaich to join the path from the Glen Brittle Memorial Hut.

Ascend through an area of heavily eroded slopes to gain a final steepening tackled by a stony zigzag path

Ascent routes up the An Stac Screes to Bealach Coire Làgan, viewed from Loch Coire Làgan

Climbers waiting their turn for the Inaccessible Pinnacle. The West Ridge is on the right

and rocky slabs and grooves, to gain the upper corrie and Loch Coire Làgan.

Straight ahead is the inclined table-top of Sgùrr MhicChoinnich with the An Stac Screes on the left and the Great Stone Shoot on the right (*photo p135*). Sgùrr Dearg, the Inaccessible Pinnacle and the smaller top of An Stac are the northernmost summits in the corrie, but they are largely obscured from below by the impressive rock face of Sgùrr Dearg's South Buttress, which overlooks the loch's north side.

Follow the path round the north side of the loch (it's more of a lochan, despite the name) towards the An Stac Screes and make the tedious and laborious ascent to gain the start of the route up the South-East Face below Bealach Coire Làgan.

Alternatively, follow the path round the loch, but leave it for the longest tongue of grass below South Buttress. Ascend the grass, then stable blocks of scree to gain a stony path which leads to the lowest rock walls of South Buttress.

Make an ascending traverse up and right, on a well-worn route towards Bealach Coire Làgan. It is possible to avoid much of the scree by simple scrambling on the lowest rocks, although the terrain requires care. When the angle eases, traverse horizontally right across scree and occasional rocks to join the route up the South-East Face, below the bealach. The last section is exposed to possible stonefall from parties on the South-East Face above.

Ascent
Follow the scree path leftwards, then a slabby orange

rampline below An Stac. Pass through a 'nick' on the right and scramble (Grade 1–2) to an upper rampline, which leads to the red slab, left of the Inaccessible Pinnacle and below the summit of Sgùrr Dearg.

Descent
Any of the routes on Sgùrr Dearg can be used. The South-East Face is rather tedious and great care is needed as there are many loose stones on the path and parties below are exposed to any stonefall. If descending in poor visibility without 'prior knowledge', having ascended Sgùrr Dearg by a different route, it is important to keep left through the 'nick' and stick close to the base of An Stac towards Bealach Coire Làgan. The speed you descend the An Stac Screes will depend on how much you care for your boots!

The alternative ascent route up the An Stac Screes

Descending the crest of the West Ridge towards Sgùrr Dearg Beag (point 929m on OS 1:25k map). To avoid the crest which is exposed in places, descend to and traverse the rock ledges which can be seen below and left of the figure. Pass over Sgùrr Dearg Beag – do not take the path on the right, below the summit, that can be seen in this picture

Setting up the abseil on the Inaccessible Pinnacle. Undoubtedly the most frequented abseil in the UK

Inaccessible Pinnacle – East Ridge

Summits: *Inaccessible Pinnacle* ▲
Terrain: *Moderate Grade Rock Climb (abseil)*
Distance: *65m, 215ft*
Ascent: *35m; 115ft* **Descent:** *20m; 65ft*

Sgùrr Dearg's main claim to fame is providing a plinth for the Inaccessible Pinnacle (986m), the 35 metre rock fin that tops the lower summit by just 8 metres, adding an 'In' to Sgùrr Dearg's otherwise very accessible summit. The Pinnacle is unavoidable for anyone 'ticking' The Munros and can be a bit of a bun fight on sunny summer days, with guides and their clients forming long queues on the East Ridge.

Approach
Any of the routes on Sgùrr Dearg can be used. From the lower summit descend the red slab right of the pinnacle, firstly right then back left, to the foot of the East Ridge. There is a lot of rubble on the red slab

and great care must be taken not to knock rocks down onto parties ascending the South-East Face from Coire Làgan directly below.

Ascent
The East Ridge faces the summit of An Stac and Sgùrr MhicChoinnich and offers the easiest line of ascent. The ridge is narrow with considerable drops on both sides and the rock is polished in places. It is exposed to the wind and requires extra care in the damp.

Start some 8m in from the lowest point of the ridge, ascend a chimney and flakeline to gain the crest and climb this (crux) to a belay at about 30m. Continue up the crest above to the top, 35m.

South Crack on the South Face is significantly harder (Hard Very Difficult), but shorter at 30m, more direct and better protected.

Descent
Make a 20m abseil down the 'short' West Ridge from fixed anchors below the summit. Any of the routes on Sgùrr Dearg can be used to descend to Glen Brittle.

129

Approaching the Central Top of Sgùrr na Banachdaich from the summit, with the North-West Face of Sgùrr Dearg behind. Sgùrr MhicChoinnich, Sgùrr Theàrlaich and Sgùrr Alasdair are to the left, with Sgùrr Dubh an Dà Bheinn in the distance

Round of Coire na Banachdaich
Sgùrr Dearg Beag, Sgùrr Dearg,
Sgùrr na Banachdaich, Sgùrr nan Gobhar

B *anachdaich's South Ridge provides the main excitement of this route. It has fine views and a high mountain ambiance, especially if the Central Top is taken en route, but the copious amounts of scree on Sgùrr Dearg and Sgùrr na Banachdaich can become wearisome*

The Central Top and summit of Sgùrr na Banachdaich just beyond, from the South Top on the South Ridge

Round of Coire na Banachdaich

Summits: *Sgùrr Dearg Beag* ▲ *; Sgùrr Dearg* ▲
Sgùrr na Banachdaich ▲ *; Centre Top* ▲ *;*
South Top ▲ *; Sgùrr nan Gobhar* ▲
Terrain: *Hillwalk or Grade 2 Scramble (Sgùrr Dearg); Grade 2 Scramble (Sgùrr na Banachdaich); Grade 2 Scramble (Sgùrr nan Gobhar)*
Distance: *9km, 5.5 miles*
Ascent & Descent: *1130m; 3705ft*
Time: *5–6hrs*
Start & Finish: *Parking near Glen Brittle Memorial Hut (NG 4112 2163)*

Any of the routes on Sgùrr Dearg (986m) can be used for the approach and any of the routes on Sgùrr na Banachdaich (965m) can be used in descent.

However, the West Ridges of both mountains offer the most interesting routes. Climbing the Inaccessible

Pinnacle will add interest to the day, but climbing equipment will add a lot more weight. Good practice for a full Cuillin Ridge traverse though!

Approach
From the Glen Brittle Memorial Hut just south of the Skye Mountain Rescue building, walk 55m south along the road to a path on the left before the sheep pens and follow it over the Allt Coire na Banachdaich at a footbridge.

Continue on the right (south) side of the burn to a junction above the impressive Eas Mòr waterfall. Keep right here on the main path (the left turn leads to Coire na Banachdaich), to another turn on the left after about 250m and follow this to the start of Sgùrr Dearg's West Ridge.

Ascent
The path leads over grassy moorland then zigzags up scree to a prominent vertical yellow cleft on the left side of the rocky frontal face. Climb this, then continue

The South Ridge of Sgùrr na Banachdaich. The small South Top and larger Centre Top are in the upper section of the ridge

ascending left of the crest to reach a grassier ridge where the angle eases. Grass and scree lead up the broad ridge to the craggy face of Sgùrr Dearg Beag (point 929m on the OS 1:25k map). Scramble up

onto this by the line of least resistance and descend to a col marked by large russet blocks of peridotite rock (*see photo opposite*).

Either climb the crest of the ridge ahead (Grade 2),

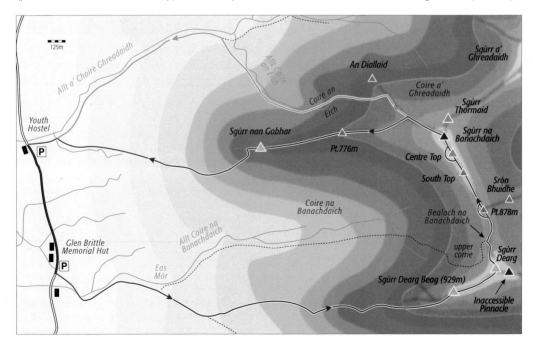

or follow basalt ledges on its right (Coire Làgan) side (Grade 1–2) until it is possible to ascend a shattered cleft to regain the crest and continue to the lower summit of Sgùrr Dearg, below the Inaccessible Pinnacle. From there, zigzag down the scree of the North-West Face and make a short scramble into Bealach Coire na Banachdaich.

Traverse round or over Pt.878m (marked on Harvey map), then ascend steadily to gain the rocky ridge of the South Top of Sgùrr na Banachdaich. Descend the other side to below the steeper and homogeneous Centre Top (*diagram p115*). Climbing this (Grade 2) and descending the steeper side to a col below the summit buttress gives the hardest scrambling on the route. Alternatively, skirt below the Centre Top on shattered ledges to reach the col and continue ascending over similar ground to the summit.

Descent

The West Ridge via Sgùrr nan Gobhar offers the most interesting descent, although descending the West Face via Coire an Eich (*see p111–3*) is also an option.

For the West Ridge via Sgùrr nan Gobhar, follow the broad boulder slopes west from the summit, sticking to the left-hand path. Pass over Pt.776m and scramble down some short steps (Grade 2), from where the route follows a fine grassy and rocky crest to the summit of Sgùrr nan Gobhar.

From the summit, descend in a westerly direction

The lower section of the West Ridge below Sgùrr Dearg Beag

then south-west, zigzaging down between scree, grass and rocky steps to where the angle eases to scree. Descend this in a more southerly direction to reach Coire na Banachdaich and cross the pathless moor to join the outward path near the Youth Hostel.

If descending the West Face via Coire an Eich it is essential, especially when visibility is poor, to keep to the right on paths closer to the edge of Coire a' Ghreadaidh, as the natural lie of the land takes you left towards the West Ridge and Sgùrr nan Gobhar (*photo p113*). Descend Coire an Eich on a path beside the Allt Coire an Eich to reach the path beside the Allt a' Choire Ghreadaidh.

Follow this back to the road at the Youth Hostel. A short walk along the road leads back to the start at the Glen Brittle Memorial Hut.

Looking east on Sgùrr Dearg's West Ridge, to the russet blocks of peridotite rock at the col before the ridge steepens. Beyond, the top of the Inaccessible Pinnacle sticks above the lower summit of Sgùrr Dearg

Looking across the top of Rotten Gully to climbers on the steep initial tower of Sgùrr MhicChoinnich's North-West Ridge

Sgùrr MhicChoinnich

*N*amed after the great Skye guide John Mackenzie of Sconsor who was in the first ascent party along with Charles Pilkington of Inaccessible Pinnacle fame, Sgùrr MhicChoinnich is a Cuillin gem. The 'easiest' route to the summit is via its long North-West Ridge which offers a lot of scrambling in some wonderfully exposed situations

Sgùrr MhicChoinnich and Loch Coire Làgan, with the An Stac Screes on the left and the Great Stone Shoot on the right

North-West Ridge

Summits: *Sgùrr MhicChoinnich* ▲
Terrain: *Grade 2 Scramble (sustained)*
Distance: *11km, 6.75 miles*
Ascent & Descent: *960m; 3145ft*
Time: *5–6hrs*
Start & Finish: *Parking before Glen Brittle Campsite (NG 4090 2065), or near Glen Brittle Memorial Hut (NG 4112 2163)*

One of the rockier Cuillin Munros, Sgùrr MhicChoinnich (948m) is a sustained route requiring a steady head for heights. The hardest section is the initial tower, tackled by a zigzag route on the Coire Làgan side. The exposure of the upper ridge can be mitigated by slabbier ground on the Coruisk side, but this still needs great care and some may find a rope reassuring. There are a number of variations en route, so it pays to seek out the line of least resistance.

Approach

The most direct approach is from the parking at the entrance to Glen Brittle Campsite. Walk through the campsite past the toilet block and ascend to a track. Follow this for a short distance, then turn left back onto the main path. Continue on this ignoring all turnings to the right and left, to pass Loch an Fhir-bhallaich and join the path from the Glen Brittle Memorial Hut.

If starting from the Glen Brittle Memorial Hut to the north, walk 55m south along the road to a path on the left before the sheep pens and follow it east to cross a footbridge over the Allt Coire na Banachdaich.

Continue on the right (south) side of the burn to a junction above the impressive Eas Mòr waterfall. Keep right here on the main path (the left turn leads to Coire na Banachdaich) and pass another turn on the left after about 250m (which leads to the West Ridge of Sgùrr Dearg), to reach Loch an Fhir-bhallaich. Beyond this, the path merges with the route from Glen Brittle Campsite and the terrain becomes rougher.

Ascend through an area of heavily eroded slopes to

A steep initial tower leads to the exposed crest of the North-West Ridge of Sgùrr MhicChoinnich. Climbers are circled

gain a final steepening tackled by a stony zigzag path and rocky slabs and grooves, to gain the upper corrie and Loch Coire Làgan.

Straight ahead is the inclined table-top of Sgùrr MhicChoinnich with the An Stac Screes on the left and the Great Stone Shoot on the right. Sgùrr Dearg, the Inaccessible Pinnacle and the smaller top of An Stac are the northernmost summits in the corrie, but are largely obscured from below by the impressive rock face of Sgùrr Dearg's South Buttress, which over-looks the loch's north side. The south side of the corrie is dominated by the north-west faces Sgùrr Alasdair and Sgùrr Sgùmain.

Follow the path round the north side of the loch (it's more of a lochan despite the name), towards the An Stac Screes and make the tedious and laborious ascent up them to the Bealach Coire Làgan.

Alternatively, follow the path round the loch, but leave it for the longest tongue of grass below South Buttress and ascend this, then stable blocks of scree, to gain a stony path which leads to the lowest rock walls of South Buttress (*diagram p126*). Make an ascending traverse up and right on a well-worn route towards Bealach Coire Làgan. It is possible to avoid much of the scree by simple scrambling on the lowest rocks, although the terrain requires care. When the

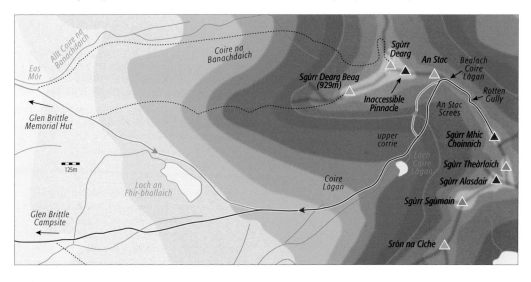

The easy if exposed crest below the prominent chimney at the start of Collie's Ledge. Sgùrr Alasdair on the right

angle eases, traverse horizontally right across scree and occasional rocks to the Bealach Coire Làgan. The last section is exposed to possible stonefall from parties on the South-East Face of Sgùrr Dearg above.

The final ridge leading to the summit

Ascent

From the spectacularly airy Bealach Coire Làgan, scramble east, in and out of the thin pinnacles to gain a wider grassier path. Descend this to cross the prominent deep cleft of Rotten Gully on the Coruisk side, then ascend to the steep initial tower.

Tackle this directly for a few moves to below a large and prominent section of pale rock. Follow a rightward traverse to easier ground and ascend directly via some awkward rock steps (Grade 2). Weave up and right over more broken ground following the line of least resistance to reach the ridge crest.

Traverse along the more level rocky ridge, easy but exposed, and across a notch to a grassier section. This leads to a rocky col above which the ridge steepens. A ledge leads rightwards to a left-slanting chimney formed by an eroded dyke (NG 4498 2113), which cuts through the small buttress. The ledge is Collie's Ledge (Hart's Ledge in some guidebooks), utilised on the Round of Coire Làgan (*see p149*). Climb the chimney (Grade 2) and traverse left on the Coruisk side over slabby boulders (Grade 2) to where the ridge narrows again. Scramble up this and ascend broken ledges on the Coire Làgan side to the summit.

Descent

Reverse the route of ascent., stopping at the foot of the An Stac Screes to empty your boots of stones.

The Great Stone Shoot from upper Coire Làgan. Sgùrr Alasdair centre, Sgùrr Theàrlaich left and Sgùrr Sgùmain right

Sgùrr Alasdair & Sgùrr Theàrlaich

Sgùrr Alasdair, Skye's highest peak, is named after local Cuillin explorer Sheriff Alexander Nicolson, who made the first recorded ascent in 1873. The easiest and most popular line is via the 365m Great Stone Shoot which separates it from Sgùrr Theàrlaich to the east. This gives a straightforward if rather laborious route, with a short final section of scrambling to gain the summit. Sgùrr Theàrlaich (named after Charles Pilkington and a Munro Top), can also be climbed from the shoot by a more technical scramble

Descending to the col at the head of the Great Stone Shoot and Sgùrr Theàrlaich's South Ridge

Via Great Stone Shoot

Summits: *Sgùrr Alasdair* ▲ *; Sgùrr Theàrlaich* ▲
Terrain: *Grade 2 Scramble (Sgùrr Alasdair South-East Ridge); Grade 3 Scramble (Sgùrr Theàrlaich South Ridge)*
Distance: *9.5km, 6 miles*
Ascent & Descent: *1045m; 3430ft*
Time: *5–6hrs*
Start & Finish: *Parking before Glen Brittle Campsite (NG 4090 2065), or near Glen Brittle Memorial Hut (NG 4112 2163)*

The Great Stone Shoot is easy in ascent and descent, but the abundance of scree and boulders, especially in the enclosed upper section, makes it a dangerous place. The recommended line is to keep as close as possible to the right side of the scree fan below the main gully, hugging the base of the rock for as long as possible. The only easy descent is back down the gully,

and it is then that great care must be taken not to send rocks down onto parties below. The route can be extended to include Sgùrr Theàrlaich (978m).

The use of 'Shoot' instead of 'Chute' is a Cuillin guidebook tradition. The Collins Dictionary defines Shoot: "to discharge down as if out of a chute". The Great Stone Shoot certainly discharges you... hopefully still on your feet.

Approach
The most direct approach is from the parking at the entrance to Glen Brittle Campsite. Walk through the campsite past the toilet block and ascend to a track. Follow this right for a short distance, then left back onto the main path. Continue on this ignoring all turnings to the right and left to pass Loch an Fhir-bhallaich and join the path from the Glen Brittle Memorial Hut.

If starting from the Glen Brittle Memorial Hut to the north, walk 55m south along the road to a path on the left before the sheep pens and follow it east to cross a footbridge over the Allt Coire na Banachdaich.

The east and south sides of upper Coire Làgan from Sgùrr Dearg to the north. From left, Sgùrr MhicChoinnich, Sgùrr Theàrlaich, the Great Stone Shoot, Sgùrr Alasdair, Sgùrr Sgùmain and Loch Coire Làgan

Continue on the right (south) side of the burn to a junction above the impressive Eas Mòr waterfall. Keep right here on the main path (the left turn leads to Coire na Banachdaich) and pass another turn on the left after about 250m (which leads to Sgùrr Dearg's West Ridge), to reach Loch an Fhir-bhallaich. Beyond this the path merges with the route from Glen Brittle Campsite and the terrain becomes rougher underfoot.

Ascend through an area of heavily eroded slopes to gain a final steepening tackled by a stony zigzag path and rocky slabs and grooves, to gain the upper corrie

and Loch Coire Làgan.

Straight ahead is the inclined table-top of Sgùrr MhicChoinnich flanked by the An Stac Screes to the left and the Great Stone Shoot to the right. The big north-west faces of Sgùrr Alasdair and Sgùrr Sgùmain form the south side of the corrie, with Sgùrr Dearg and the Inaccessible Pinnacle forming the north side. The enclosed nature of the corrie makes it difficult to identify the northern summits from below.

The Great Stone Shoot separates 992m Sgùrr Alasdair and 978m Sgùrr Theàrlaich (hidden from below by

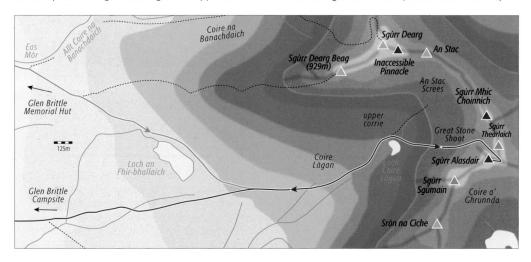

Alasdair) and is easily gained by a path leading from the east end of Loch Coire Làgan.

Ascent

Leave the main path at the far (eastern) end of Loch Coire Làgan and follow a path over grass towards the tip of the scree fan below Sgùrr Alasdair. Do not ascend the worn line in the centre, but keep to the right edge of the scree fan, sticking close to the rock for as far as possible to maximise upward progress on more stable ground and minimise exposure to any stonefall created by descending parties above.

When the enclosed upper gully is reached and the col separating Sgùrr Theàrlaich and Sgùrr Alasdair is visible, move over to the left side of the gully and ascend to the col. On the right, a 30m (Grade 2) scramble over slabs and steps on the South-East Ridge leads to the summit of Sgùrr Alasdair.

Once back at the col, Sgùrr Theàrlaich can also be climbed via its South Ridge. This is a more technical and exposed scramble with some dubious rock in places, which will need to be reversed back to the col, unless continuing by the harder route to Sgùrr MhicChoinnich as described in the Round of Coire Làgan (*see 148–51*).

For Sgùrr Theàrlaich, descend the scree on the opposite (Coire a' Ghrunnda) side from the Great Stone Shoot for about 35m until the South Ridge is easily gained (*photo below*) Climb it (Grade 3) in an exposed position to a slabby crest leading to Sgùrr Theàrlaich's summit (*photo p139, 146*). Reverse the route with care back to the col.

Descent

Descend the Great Stone Shoot back to Coire Làgan, taking care not to dislodge stones onto parties who may not be visible in the curved gully below.

The south (Coire a' Ghrunnda) side of Sgùrr Alasdair and Sgùrr Theàrlaich with climbers on the T-D Gap (see p20–1). The lower team is starting the approach, the centre team is nearing the top of the pinnacle and the 10m abseil into the Gap and the higher team is exiting the crux chimney and ascending towards the access point onto the South Ridge of Sgùrr Theàrlaich

141

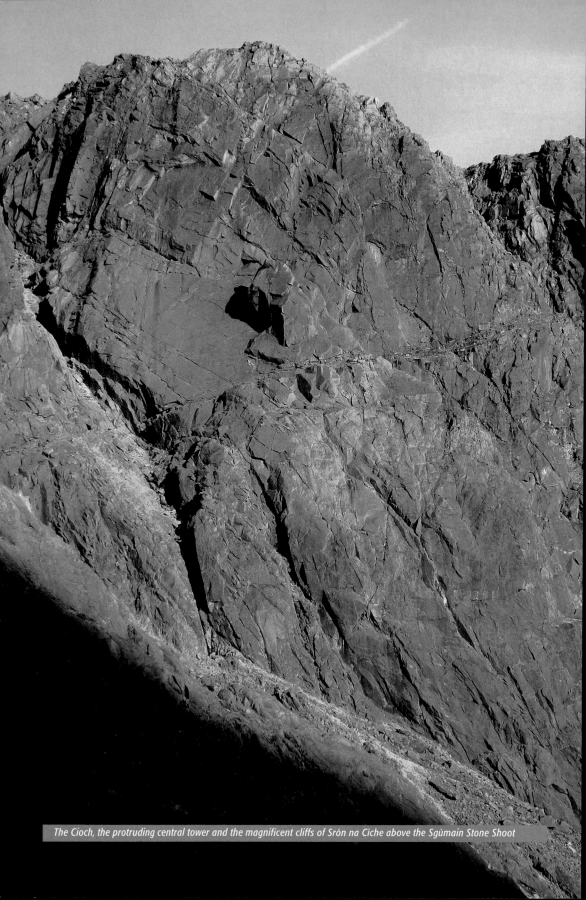

The Cioch, the protruding central tower and the magnificent cliffs of Sròn na Cìche above the Sgùmain Stone Shoot

Sròn na Cìche & Sgùrr Sgùmain

S gùmain is a fine mountain in it's own right and a Munro Top, but rather dwarfed by Sgùrr Alasdair to its east. The summit of Sròn na Cìche is little more than a highpoint on a broad ridge; but what a ridge. On the Coire Làgan side a sweep of gabbro cliffs 1000m long and more than 250m high, presents one of the most impressive mountain walls in Britain

The summit of Sròn na Cìche, lower left and the South Ridge of Sgùrr Sgùmain, viewed across Coire a' Ghrunnda

Sròn na Cìche & Sgùrr Sgùmain

Summits: Sròn na Cìche ▲ ; Sgùrr Sgùmain ▲
Terrain: Hillwalk
Distance: 9.5km, 6 miles
Ascent & Descent: 957m; 3140ft
Time: 4hrs 30mins–5hrs 30mins
Start & Finish: Parking before Glen Brittle Campsite (NG 4090 2065)

Sròn na Cìche (859m) and Sgùrr Sgùmain (947m), can be climbed from Coire Làgan via the Bealach Coire a' Ghrunnda which separates them, but this involves ascending and descending the scree-filled Sgùmain Stone Shoot. It's a rough place, full of scree, large boulders and loose rubble from recent rockfalls and tackling it once in the day is probably enough.

The alternative circuit described here, is to ascend the broad South-West Ridge of Sròn na Cìche, continue to Sgùrr Sgùmain, then descend the Sgùmain Stone Shoot back to Coire Làgan.

The South-West Ridge of Sròn na Cìche is a bit of a trudge, but there are fine views south over the Isle of Soay to Rùm and Eigg. Sgùrr Sgùmain's South Ridge is a pleasant route in a fine position.

Approach

Walk through Glen Brittle Campsite past the toilet block and ascend to a track. Follow this right for a short distance then turn left back onto the main path. Continue ascending for about 650m to where a path turns off to the right (NG 4206 2035). This is the path into Coire a' Ghrunnda.

Turn right here onto the well-prepared path and cross over the burn. Continue on the path to reach

The South-West Ridge of Sròn na Cìche above Loch Coire a' Ghrunnda. Bealach Coire a' Ghrunnda is at the far right

the wide Allt Coire Làgan which is crossed by boulder-hopping. This can be awkward if there is a lot of water running. About 380m beyond the burn, the path splits at a small cairn (NG 4344 1960).

Keep left here, remaining on the path into Coire a'

Ghrunnda (the right-hand path continues to below Gars-bheinn, *see p164*) and start ascending below the rocky spur of Sròn na Cìche's South-West Ridge, heading for a prominent perched boulder on the skyline. At the boulder, about 200m after the junction,

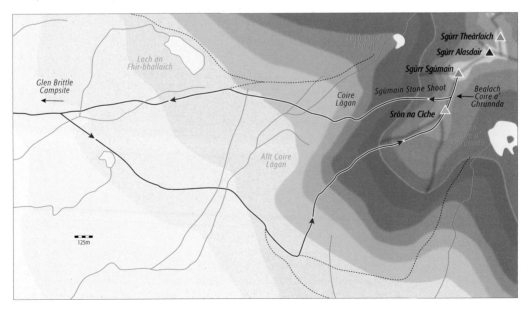

Looking up the Sgùmain Stone Shoot

keep to its left (western) edge overlooking Coire Làgan. A stony path is soon gained and leads to steep scree-covered slopes, beyond which the angle eases. Continue near the edge of the corrie, over rocky ground scattered with boulders and skirt round the incut top of Eastern Gully, to gabbro slabs and small steps leading to the summit cairn.

Avoid the cliff north-east of the summit by traversing right (east) away from the corrie edge, then return back towards the corrie edge and descend slabby ground to Bealach Coire a' Ghrunnda and a large cairn. From the bealach, ascend Sgùrr Sgùmain's straightforward South Ridge in a fine position to reach the summit.

Descent

Return to Bealach Coire a' Ghrunnda. From there, descend right (west) down the Sgùmain Stone Shoot into Coire Làgan, sticking beside the left-hand cliffs of Sròn na Cìche. Initially the going is straightforward, but as the boulders increase in size the terrain becomes trickier. Negotiate a boulder constriction with some route-finding, to a better defined path below the cliffs. If there are climbers on the cliffs, then be aware of potential stonefall from above when traversing below.

Follow the path down to beyond The Cìoch, then descend through boulder-covered grass and scree on a path that is indistinct in places, to the floor of Coire Làgan. Cross this in a north-westerly direction passing over the Allt Coire Làgan to meet the main path (NG 4339 2061). Turn left and descend to the campsite.

leave the path and head north over grassy ground towards the small crags that guard the foot of the broad South-West Ridge.

Ascent

Weave through the crags to gain the broad ridge and

Coire Làgan from the west. From left, Sgùrr MhicChoinnich, Sgùrr Sgùmain with the South Ridge on the right, Sgùmain Stone Shoot and Sròn na Cìche with the broad South-West Ridge on the right

The steep South Ridge of Sgùrr Theàrlaich. Sgùrr nan Eag, Sgùrr a' Choire Bhig and Gars-bheinn behind

Round of Coire Làgan
Sgùrr Sgùmain, Sgùrr Alasdair, Sgùrr Theàrlaich, Sgùrr MhicChoinnich, An Stac, Sgùrr Dearg

*T*his is a long, exposed and testing round on sometimes dubious rock, requiring a cool head and good route-finding skills. If you find it just a bit too easy, then you can include the Inaccessible Pinnacle at the end for good measure!

Descending the slabby but exposed upper section of the North-West Ridge of Sgùrr MhicChoinnich

Round of Coire Làgan

Summits: Sgùrr Sgùmain ▲; Sgùrr Alasdair ▲; Sgùrr Theàrlaich ▲; Sgùrr MhicChoinnich ▲; An Stac ▲; Sgùrr Dearg ▲; Sgùrr Dearg Beag ▲; Optional – Inaccessible Pinnacle ▲

Terrain: Grade 2–3 Scramble (Sgùrr Sgùmain); Grade 3 Scramble (Sgùrr Alasdair); Moderate Grade Rock Climb (Sgùrr Theàrlaich); Grade 2 Scramble (Sgùrr MhicChoinnich); Grade 3 Scramble (An Stac); Grade 2 Scramble (Sgùrr Dearg)

Distance: 11km, 6.75 miles

Ascent & Descent: 1273m; 4176ft

Time: 7hrs 30mins–8hrs 30mins

Start & Finish: Parking before Glen Brittle Campsite (NG 4090 2065)

This high level traverse is a magnificent Alpine-like adventure, climbing seven distinct 900m summits and crossing some complex terrain. There are a number of places where a rope may be required for extra reassurance and security.

Approach

Walk through Glen Brittle Campsite past the toilet block and ascend to a track. Follow this right for a short distance, then turn left back onto the main path. Continue on this for about 2km and pass a path turning off right over a burn (to Coire a' Ghrunnda), to reach a second path on the right (NG 4339 2061).

This path, indistinct in places, leads over the Allt Coire Làgan and up through boulder-covered grass and scree to the base of Sròn na Cìche's cliffs (*diagram p145*). If there are climbers on the cliffs, then be aware of potential stonefall from above when traversing below.

Follow the path below the cliffs over rough ground

[1] – *South-West Flank of Sgùrr Alasdair from Sgùrr Sgùmain*

Labels on image: Sgùrr Alasdair *see also p157*; South-East Ridge; South West Ridge; summit; chimney; pinnacles; Bealach Sgùmain; Sgùrr Sgùmain Coire Làgan side

into the Sgùmain Stone Shoot to reach a constriction of large boulders, which requires some route-finding and scrambling. Continue more easily above to reach Bealach Coire a' Ghrunnda.

Ascent

From Bealach Coire a' Ghrunnda, ascend the straightforward South Ridge of Sgùrr Sgùmain to the summit.

There are now **two options** for reaching Bealach Sgùmain between Sgùrr Sgùmain and Sgùrr Alasdair.

(1) Descend the North-East Ridge mostly on the right (Coire a' Ghrunnda side) with some awkward moves (Grade 3), to gain ledges leading round to the pinnacles at Bealach Sgùmain. (2) Descend the North-East Ridge to small col, then drop down on the left (Coire Làgan side) and make an exposed and tricky move across a stony slab (Grade 2) to a path leading round to the pinnacles at Bealach Sgùmain.

From the bealach, continue ahead descending slightly to gain a chimney on the South-West Flank of Sgùrr Alasdair, right of the well-defined South-West Ridge, which rises from the bealach (*see left & p157*). The chimney (Grade 3) is quite steep but the holds are positive and it feels relatively secure (*diagram* [1]).

The face above is technically easy, but open and exposed and the terrain broken. Follow the line of least resistance up and right, then back left to gain the better-defined South-West Ridge at about two-thirds height and climb it (Grade 2) to the summit.

Descend Alasdair's short South-East Ridge (Grade 2) to the col below Sgùrr Theàrlaich. The Great Stone Shoot is the wide gully on the left. Descend the scree on the opposite (Coire a' Ghrunnda) side from the Great Stone Shoot for about 35m (*photos p139, 141*), until Theàrlaich's South Ridge is easily gained and climb it (Grade 3) in an exposed position to the summit.

The slabby North Ridge now leads down towards Sgùrr MhicChoinnich. Cross over a notch, beyond which the ridge levels out, then a second notch, to reach a rocky platform with a walled bivouac, with what appears to be a sheer drop barring access to Bealach MhicChoinnich. On the left (Coire Làgan side), a devious route leads down to the bealach in two sections. Both

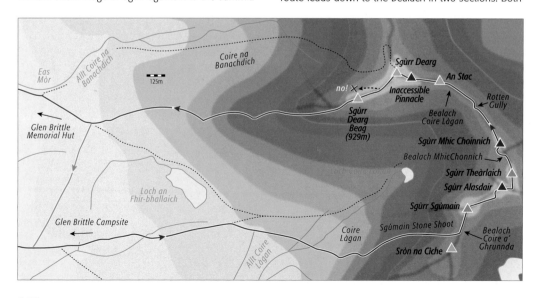

Map labels: Eas Mòr; Allt Coire na Banochdich; Coire na Banachdich; 125m; Sgùrr Dearg; An Stac; Inaccessible Pinnacle; no! ✕; Rotten Gully; Sgùrr Dearg Beag (929m); Bealach Coire Làgan; Glen Brittle Memorial Hut; Sgùrr Mhic Choinnich; Bealach MhicChonnich; Loch an Fhir-bhallaich; Sgùrr Theàrlaich; Sgùrr Alasdair; Glen Brittle Campsite; Sgùrr Sgùmain; Coire Làgan; Sgùmain Stone Shoot; Bealach Coire a' Ghrunnda; Allt Coire Làgan; Sròn na Cìche

[2] – *The route from Sgùrr Theàrlaich to Bealach MhicChoinnich and the North-West Ridge of Sgùrr MhicChoinnich*

could be abseiled. The first section starts at a distinctive narrow notch, with a small path leading to it, down and left of the walled bivouac (*diagram* [3]).

Go through the notch and descend a steep and very exposed dyke (Moderate) until moves lead round right (looking down) to the top of a slab. Keeping high, cross the top of the slab and pass behind two large boulders to reach the top of the second section, where another steep wall bars direct access to the bealach (*diagram* [4]).

Descend a rough and loose gully on the left (Coire Làgan side) – cairn at the start – to gain the top of a distinctive blocky pillar of black rock. Go over this rightwards (looking down) and descend on friable rock

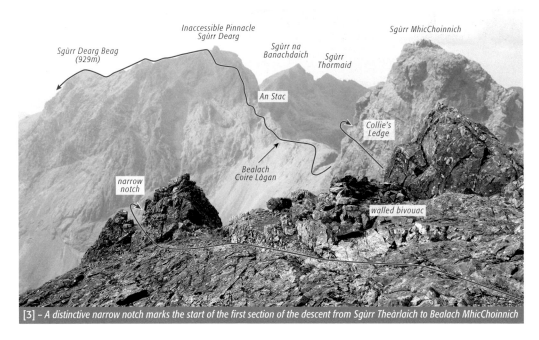

[3] – *A distinctive narrow notch marks the start of the first section of the descent from Sgùrr Theàrlaich to Bealach MhicChoinnich*

[4] – *First section of the descent from Sgùrr Theàrlaich to Bealach MhicChoinnich*

[5] – *First and second sections of the descent from Sgùrr Theàrlaich to Bealach MhicChoinnich*

to the base of the wall and easier ground (Moderate). Follow this up to Bealach MhicChoinnich (*diagrams* **[5]**, **[6]**).

From the bealach, traverse out right on worn rocks and climb a steep little corner-crack which brings you

to the start of Collie's Ledge (named Hart's Ledge in some guidebooks). This is the obvious ledge system leading up and left. It is exposed and tricky in a few places (Grade 2) and leads north below Sgùrr Mhic-Choinnich's summit to join the North-West Ridge at a

[6] – *The loose gully to the black pillar on the second section of the descent to Bealach MhicChoinnich*

[7] – *An Stac from Bealach Coire Làgan*

Traversing Collie's Ledge from Bealach MhicChoinnich to the North-West Ridge of Sgùrr MhicChoinnich. The prominent corner above the climbers is King's Chimney, a Very Difficult grade rock climb

prominent vertical chimney. Climb the chimney (Grade 2) and traverse left on the Coruisk side over slabby boulders to where the ridge narrows again. Scramble up this and ascend broken ledges on the Coire Làgan side to the summit (*diagram* [2]).

Reverse the route to the chimney and continue descending down the ridge to near its end. Scramble down on the Coire Làgan side with some awkward moves (Grade 2) to the foot of the ridge (*diagram p136*).

Follow the path round the corrie rim to Bealach Coire Làgan at the foot of An Stac, the compact buttress forming the lower part of Sgùrr Dearg's East Ridge, below the Inaccessible Pinnacle.

The 'standard' South-East Face of Sgùrr Dearg (Grade 1–2) avoids An Stac to the left (*see p126*), but taking it direct (Grade 3) is more in keeping with the rest of the Coire Làgan Round (*diagram* [7]). From Bealach Coire Làgan, climb straight up a slabby ramp to reach easier stony ground and go up this to a notch below the upper tower. Move left from the notch onto broken ground and climb this to another notch.

Traverse left to gain the ridge crest and follow the line of least resistance up then left, to join the prominent corner-crack of An Stac Chimney. Ascend this to gain ledges which lead left to easy scrambling, the summit, and an unexpected grandstand view of the Inaccessible Pinnacle (*photo p120–1*).

Either ascend the 65m Moderate rock climb of the East Ridge of the pinnacle (you'll need to have brought climbing gear for the 20m abseil, or be prepared to climb back down the route), or ascend the red slab on the left to the lower summit of Sgùrr Dearg.

Descent

The most fitting descent is probably via Sgùrr Dearg's West Ridge (*see p125*). Follow the ridge south-west to where it becomes more defined. Either scramble along the crest (Grade 2) or drop down a cleft on the left (Coire Làgan side) to basalt ledges and follow them below the crest to a col marked by large russet blocks of 'honeycomb' peridotite rock (*photos p128, 133*). In poor visibility the West Ridge requires care as the best line on the crest and on the ledges weaves in and out and up and down.

From the col, it is important to go over Sgùrr Dearg Beag (point 929m on the OS 1:25k map). The prominent path on the right (north) side should be avoided as it leads into a hanging, rocky gully. An awkward and exposed exit can be made back onto the ridge, but the gully is best avoided altogether (*see p114–5, photo p128*).

Instead, continue over Sgùrr Dearg Beag and down its west face to a broad ridge of scree and grass. This leads to a prominent vertical yellow cleft on the western nose, which is descended to the moor and a path to the Glen Brittle Memorial Hut.

It is as quick (and usually much drier) to descend to the road and follow it back to Glen Brittle Campsite, as it is to cut across the moor west of Loch an Fhir-bhallaich to the campsite path and follow that down.

Sgùrr Alasdair above Loch Coire a' Ghrunnda, with Sgùrr Theàrlaich to the right and Sgùrr Sgùmain and Sròn na Ciche to the left

Sgùrr nan Eag & Sgùrr Dubh Mòr

Round of Loch Coire a' Ghrunnda – Sgùrr nan Eag, Caisteal a' Garbh-choire, Sgùrr Dubh Mòr, Sgùrr Dubh an Dà Bheinn

*W*ith Sgùrr Alasdair at its head, upper Coire a' Ghrunnda is one of the most scenic Cuillin corries. A perfect bowl with a beautiful loch, accessible peaks in all directions and less of the fine scree that can make upper Coire Làgan such a grind. Having said that, getting there requires some effort

By the triangular block at the end of the crux footledge traverse, on the South Face of Sgùrr Dubh Mòr

Sgùrr nan Eag & Sgùrr Dubh Mòr

Summits: Sgùrr nan Eag ▲; Sgùrr Dubh Mòr ▲; Sgùrr Dubh an Dà Bheinn ▲;
Optional – Caisteal a' Garbh-choire ▲
Terrain: Grade 1 Scramble (Sgùrr nan Eag); Moderate Grade Rock Climb (Caisteal a' Garbh-choire); Grade 2 Scramble (Sgùrr Dubh Mòr); Grade 1 Scramble (Sgùrr an Dà Bheinn)
Distance: 14km, 8.5 miles
Ascent & Descent: 1135m; 3725ft
Time: 6–7hrs
Start & Finish: Parking before Glen Brittle Campsite (NG 4090 2065)

Sgùrr nan Eag (924m) and Sgùrr Dubh Mòr (944m) are usually climbed together in what is, in effect, a

Round of Loch Coire a' Ghrunnda. It is a round of the loch rather than the corrie, because a full corrie round would necessitate climbing the T–D (Theàrlaich-Dubh) Gap, reversing the South-West Flank of Sgùrr Alasdair (not recommended, especially not without prior knowledge) – or climbing and reversing that route, then traversing Sgùrr Sgùmain to descend the South-West Ridge of Sròn na Cìche or the Sgùmain Stone Shoot! Instead, most take one of three options having completed the two Munros.

The first and fastest is to descend back to Loch Coire a' Ghrunnda. The second is to traverse below Sgùrr Alasdair, climb its South-West Flank (see p148, 157) and descend the Great Stone Shoot into Coire Làgan. The third is to traverse below Sgùrr Alasdair (missing it out), then climb over Sgùrr Sgùmain (a Munro Top) and descend Sròn na Cìche or the Sgùmain Stone Shoot (see p144–5, 157).

Approach

Walk through Glen Brittle Campsite past the toilet block and ascend to a track. Follow this right for a short distance, then turn left back onto the main path. Continue ascending for about 650m to a path junction.

Turn right here onto a well-prepared path and cross over the burn. Continue on the path to reach the wide Allt Coire Làgan which is crossed by boulder-hopping. This can be awkward if there is a lot of water running. About 380m beyond this the path splits at a small cairn (NG 4344 1960). Turn left onto the path into Coire a' Ghrunnda (the right-hand path continues to below Gars-bheinn) and start ascending below the rocky

The route through the headwall into upper Coire a' Ghrunnda

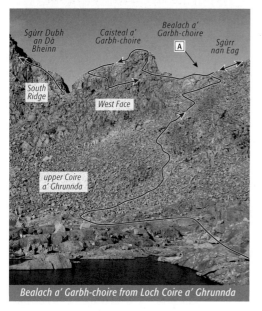

Bealach a' Garbh-choire from Loch Coire a' Ghrunnda

spur of Sròn na Cìche's South-West Ridge, heading for a prominent perched boulder on the skyline.

Pass this and continue east until the path turns north and a rocky section up a worn gully gives access to the corrie. Follow a well-graded zigzag path up the scree below the cliffs. The rest of the route to Loch Coire a' Ghrunnda can be very confusing in poor visibility.

The next objective is a parallel-sided gully on the left side of the slabby headwall of the corrie, left of the Allt Coire a' Ghrunnda. Towards the end of the main cliff face (NG 4474 9175) the path zigzags steeply up towards a rocky gully in the main cliffs, then descends to the parallel-sided gully (*see top left*).

The same point can be gained more directly by leaving the path near the end of the main cliff face. Go straight ahead through large, awkward boulders (no path), then ascend to the parallel-sided gully.

Climb the gully, then up and left to left-slanting grooves which are often wet (Grade 2–3). Above these, the easiest line is to head right to gain the burn and scramble awkwardly beside this to reach Loch Coire a' Ghrunnda. Alternatively, continue at a higher level above the burn over ill-defined terrain.

Go round the right-hand side of the loch to its south-eastern edge (NG 4529 2015), almost directly below Caisteal a' Garbh-choire. Ascend through boulders to a well-worn path, which leads up and left of small

From left following the ridge; Sgùrr Dubh Mòr, Sgùrr Dubh an Dà Bheinn, Caisteal a' Garbh-choire, Sgùrr nan Eag, Sgùrr a' Choire Bhig and Gars-bheinn. To the left in the distance is Blàbheinn

crags, then directly to Bealach a' Garbh-choire [A] (*see diagram & map*).

Ascent

Scramble up the slabby North Ridge of Sgùrr nan Eag (924m) to a path and more bouldery terrain and cross this to the summit, marked by a large cairn on top of a mass of giant boulders. Retrace your steps to Bealach a' Garbh-choire [A]. The small castle-like tower of Caisteal a' Garbh-choire (c820m) can be climbed via a corkscrew line (Moderate), starting on the left side of the South Ridge and taking the least line of resistance on good holds and solid, 'honeycomb' peridotite rock. Traverse almost to the north end, then descend

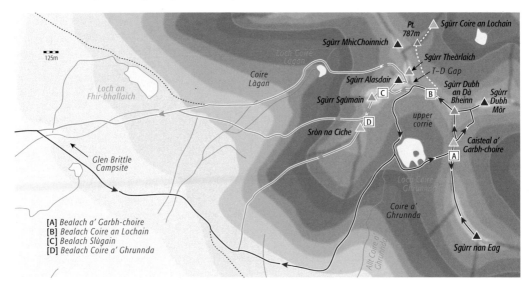

[A] Bealach a' Garbh-choire
[B] Bealach Coire an Lochain
[C] Bealach Slùgain
[D] Bealach Coire a' Ghrunnda

155

Sgùrr Dubh an Dà Bheinn

North-West Ridge to Bealach a' Garbh-choire

East Ridge

col on pinnacled ridge

Sgùrr Dubh Mòr

South Ridge

option 2

rubble gully

route from Dubhs Ridge p159

Caisteal a' Garbh-choire

option 1

slabby wall

yellow scar

from Loch Coire a' Ghrunnda

Bealach a' Garbh-choire

A

An Garbh-choire

The direct route from Caisteal a' Garbh-choire to Sgùrr Dubh Mòr via the rubble gully

a leftwards slanting ramp and corner (Grade 2) on the easier West Face overlooking Coire a' Ghrunnda. The rock is poorer here and can be wet in places (*see p154*). Return south to the bealach, then traverse north round the castle via a path on its east (An Garbh-coire) side.

Sgùrr Dubh an Dà Bheinn (938m) has to be climbed on the return route from Sgùrr Dubh Mòr (944m) to Bealach Coire an Lochain, so there are **two options** from the north end of the castle. (1) If you don't want to climb Sgùrr Dubh an Dà Bheinn twice, a direct route can be made from Caisteal a' Garbh-choire to Sgùrr Dubh Mòr (*diagram above*).

This leaves the main path and heads out right and down over boulders on the An Garbh-choire side, to gain a path which leads above a vertical yellow scar in the rock to an obvious scree ramp leading diagonally up right. Descend the other side and round to the base of a slabby wall guarding access to the wide gully above. Climb the wall (Grade 2) and, with care, follow a rubble-filled gully up then right to join a horizontal path right of the col on the pinnacled ridge between Sgùrr Dubh an Dà Bheinn and Sgùrr Dubh Mòr.

(2) If you don't fancy the direct route, then continue on the main path and climb Sgùrr Dubh an Dà Bheinn's South Ridge (Grade 2). Go up the ridge until it is possible to follow a broad boulder-covered ledge leftwards, then work your way up and back right to the summit. Much variation is possible. A short scramble

starts the descent of the East Ridge towards Sgùrr Dubh Mòr, followed by a rocky path leading to the col on the pinnacled ridge between Sgùrr Dubh an Dà Bheinn and Sgùrr Dubh Mòr, where a path goes horizontally out right.

For both options follow the path out right and round the corner, then up shattered basalt slabs and grooves to grassy ledges. Continue up and right, then up a rocky gully to a col below the South Face of Sgùrr Dubh Mòr.

Scramble up and diagonally right following ledges and the line of least resistance to where a slab (Grade 2)

Ascending the rubble gully below Sgùrr Dubh Mòr

The crux section of the South Face of Sgùrr Dubh Mòr

leads to a large triangular block. Good grassy ledges run leftwards, but accessing them is barred by overhanging rock. Gain a higher, narrow rocky footledge and traverse

Descent into Coire a' Ghrunnda and traverse to the South-West Flank of Sgùrr Alasdair

left (Grade 2) above the overhanging impasse to the grassy ledges and ascend to the summit cairn.

Return to the col on the pinnacled ridge and ascend the East Ridge of Sgùrr Dubh an Dà Bheinn to the summit. It is also possible to bypass the summit via lower ledges on the An Garbh-choire side.

Descent

From the summit, descend the rocky North-West Ridge (Grade 1) to Bealach Coire an Lochain (**[B]** *see map*). Note, this is the obvious bealach immediately below Sgùrr Dubh an Dà Bheinn, **not** the small col further north where the ridge abuts the cliffs leading to the T-D Gap. Cross the bealach and ascend the bouldery continuation ridge for about 120m towards the T-D Gap. From a rocky knoll before a small col, descend diagonally left (Coire a' Ghrunnda side) off the ridge (don't be tempted to leave too early), to a short steep chimney leading to scree, boulders and grass in the corrie below the shear cliffs of Sgùrr Theàrlaich.

From here there are **three options: (1)** The fastest is to descend back into Coire a' Ghrunnda following the burn down to a path which leads south to Loch Coire a' Ghrunnda and the outward route. **(2)** Alternatively, climb the South-West Flank of Sgùrr Alasdair (Grade 3). Gain a path at the cliff base and follow it towards the prominent pinnacles at Bealach Sgùmain (**[C]** *left*).

Ascend, then traverse right to the chimney on Sgùrr Alasdair and climb it and the face above (*see p148 & opposite*). Descend Alasdair's South-East Ridge (Grade 2) to the top of the Great Stone Shoot and descend that to Coire Làgan and the path to Glen Brittle Campsite (*see p139–41*).

(3) For Sgùrr Sgùmain and Sròn na Cìche continue south-west from Bealach Sgùmain and ascend Sgùrr Sgùmain on the Coire Làgan (Grade 2) or Coire a' Ghrunnda (Grade 3) sides (*see p148*). From the top, descend to Bealach Coire a' Ghrunnda (**[D]** *see map*) before Sròn na Cìche and either down the Sgùmain Stone Shoot (*see p145*), or over Sròn na Cìche and down the South-West Ridge to join the outward route.

Sgùrr Coire an Lochain c755m

Although of modest height, this peak (see map p155) has a short but enjoyable summit ridge and a commanding view over Loch Coruisk. From Bealach Coire an Lochain, descend the gully north into Coire an Lochain and contour round the corrie over scree, grass and boulders to a col and climb the ridge to the top. The small summit beyond (729m) requires a Difficult rock climb descent. Pt.787m (OS 1:25k) makes a pleasant extension to the return route (1hr return).

The author descending from the abseil on Sgùrr Dubh Beag's summit tower (photo Rab Anderson)

Sgùrr Dubh Beag, Sgùrr Dubh Mòr & Sgùrr Dubh an Dà Bheinn (Dubhs Ridge)

B ritain's finest scramble is adventurous and amenable, with stunning positions and mountain scenery. The route is very long and quite committing, with an intimidating 'free' abseil from the summit of Sgùrr Dubh Beag. However, the abseil is easily avoided, as it was on the first ascent by Sidney Williams and John Mackenzie in May 1896

The superb curving crack below the summit of Sgùrr Dearg Beag. The abseil bypass goes left, looking up, from below this slab

Dubhs (East) Ridge

Summits: Sgùrr Dubh Beag ▲ ; Sgùrr Dubh Mòr ▲ ;
Sgùrr Dubh an Dà Bheinn ▲
Terrain: Difficult Rock Climb with optional abseil (Sgùrr Dubh Beag); Grade 2 Scramble (Sgùrr Dubh Mòr); Grade 1 Scramble (Sgùrr an Dà Bheinn)
Distance: 11km, 6.75 miles
Ascent & Descent: 1020m; 3347ft
Time: 6–7hrs (add approx 4hrs 30mins from Glen Brittle – see Approach)
Start: Landing stage, Loch na Cuilce (Coruisk)
Finish: Glen Brittle Campsite (NG 4090 2065)

The lower slabs of Sgùrr Dubh Beag (733m) are open and compact with a wide variety of lines at all grades, from walking and gentle scrambling, to more technical climbing, with high or low exposure. Higher up the choices become more limited, the rock quality deteriorates a little and there is more vegetation.

Apart from the sharp crux at the very start, the scrambling is mostly straightforward, providing the line of least resistance is followed. Route-finding skills will help, especially once the East Ridge of Sgùrr Dubh Mòr (944m) is reached. If abseiling, the higher, better anchor requires a 60m rope, the lower 50m.

Approach
The route can be approached in different ways; from Glen Brittle via Coire a' Ghrunnda and An Garbh-coire (*approx 4hrs 30mins*), by going round the coast below Gars-bheinn (*approx 4hrs 30mins*), from the bothy at Camasunary (*see p190–1*) via the 'bad step' and two river crossings (*approx 2hrs*), or from

High on the Dubhs Ridge above Loch Coruisk and Loch Scavaig; Sgùrr na Stri in the background (photo Rab Anderson)

Sligachan (*approx 4hrs 30mins*).

However, coming in by boat from Elgol gives the day a special quality; *www.mistyisleboattrips.co.uk*, or *www.bellajane.co.uk*. If descending to Glen Brittle as described here, then transport will need to be arranged at both ends and this is well worth the effort.

With an early start, a return to Coruisk for a pre-arranged boat back to Elgol is also possible, descending via the rough An Garbh-choire and south of Allt a' Chaoich – the Mad Burn (*approx 2hrs*), or over Sgùrr nan Eag and down Gars-bheinn's North-East Ridge (*approx 3hrs 30mins – see Cuillin Ridge Approaches p18*).

Ascent

From the landing stage, follow the path round the south shore of Loch Coruisk, cross the marshy foot of lower An Garbh-choire and go round the toe of a slabby buttress (NG 4774 2079). The route starts at an obvious grassy gully right of steep slabs and left of stepped roofs, about 100m above the lochside.

Follow a well-worn path to the gully and climb grassy cracks to a terrace. From the terrace, use a leaning block to climb stepped ledges on the slabby frontal face. Make some friction moves out left (Difficult) onto a slab and ascend to easier ground.

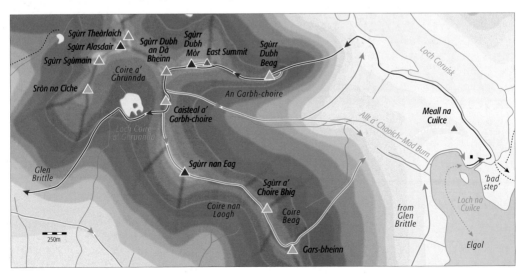

The start of the Dubhs Ridge above the path

The slabs above lead to a steep central overlap, climbed on the left or the right. Follow the line of least (or most!) resistance for some 450m up pleasantly angled slabs and walls to a grass terrace below a broken buttress. Climb this for about 150m to a large grassy saddle below another broken buttress, and ascend a grassy crackline left of water-streaked slabs for about 100m. This leads to a fine slabby wall, split by an impressive 20m curving crack. Climb the crack (Difficult) or the easier cracked slab to its left, then broken ground to the summit of Sgùrr Dubh Beag.

The abseil bypass route starts from the base of the slabby wall, so leave your rucksack here if you don't plan to abseil and return to it after visiting the summit, by descending the grassy terrace to below the curving crack. Having returned to the base of the slab, traverse left and contour horizontally round on the south (An Garbh-choire) side to a cairn at the top of a shallow scree gully. Descend this for about 100m to a grassy terrace and follow it up under the summit cliffs, to the broad arete below Sgùrr Dubh Beag's summit tower.

If abseiling the summit tower, descend the steep West Face for a short distance to a ledge and abseil slings. It is almost 30m to the ground from here. About 5m down another abseil station utilises a jammed boulder, but the security of this has been called into doubt. After the abseil, traverse west a short distance and descend a corner (Grade 2) to a broad arete (*photo p158*).

When the arete ends, descend a steep wall (Grade 3) to reach the col between Sgùrr Dubh Beag and Sgùrr Dubh Mòr. Slabs lead up the crest of the East Ridge to a small tower which is skirted via grassy ledges on its left (An Garbh-choire) side. Above, it is possible to zigzag up on broken ledges and climb steep rock to regain the ridge crest near the East Summit. Alternatively and a lot easier, continue a gentle ascent for about 300m on ledges below the crest of the ridge, until they lead to a final rocky ridge and the summit of Sgùrr Dubh Mòr (*diagram p156*).

From the summit cairn, descend on the west side and follow grassy ledges left (looking down) to a rocky footledge. Traverse this to a triangular block and step down to lower ledges. Descend the diagonal line of least resistance down a slab and rocky steps (Grade 2) to reach a col (*see p156–7*). Follow a path down a broad rocky gully, then right (looking down) over grassy ledges. Descend further shattered basalt slabs and grooves for a short way, until the rocky spur on the right (looking down) can be turned to gain a horizonal ledge leading to the col below Sgùrr Dubh an Dà Bheinn. Climb the East Ridge to the summit.

Descent
Scramble down the South Ridge (Grade 2) to reach Caisteal a' Garbh-choire. Skirt this on its left (east) side to reach Bealach a' Garbh-choire and descend west to Loch Coire a' Ghrunnda (*see p154, 156*).

From the loch, follow the path from the outflow staying well above the burn and keeping right until it is possible to scramble down left-slanting grooves which are often wet (Grade 2–3). Descend to a parallel-sided gully (*see p154*) and follow the path round the scree or directly over boulders, to the main cliff face. Zigzag down scree below the cliffs to leave the corrie by a rocky gully and traverse below the broad South-West Ridge of Sròn na Cìche. Cross the Allt Coire Làgan via boulder-hopping to reach the Coire Làgan path. Turn left and follow this back to Glen Brittle Campsite.

The pleasantly angled slabs of the lower ridge

Meall na Cuilce 183m
This fine viewpoint overlooks the south-west end of Loch Coruisk. The easiest ascent is via the burn just south of the Mad Burn (Allt a' Chaoich), from the landing stage for the Elgol boat at Loch na Cuilce (Coruisk)

Sgùrr a' Choire Bhig and Gars-bheinn from the rocky East Ridge of Sgùrr nan Eag

Sgùrr nan Eag, Sgùrr a' Choire Bhig & Gars-bheinn

*S*gùrr a' Choire Bhig and Gars-bheinn are usually rushed over by climbers at the start or finish of their Cuillin Ridge traverse. But both peaks are fine rocky mountains and reward greater attention. You can even offer encouragement to teams slogging up the Gars-bheinn screes at the start of their ridge traverse.

The slabby North Ridge of Sgùrr nan Eag, with Sgùrr a' Choire Bhig and Gars-bheinn behind

Sgùrr nan Eag, Sgùrr a' Choire Bhig & Gars-bheinn

Summits: *Sgùrr nan Eag* ▲ *; Sgùrr a' Choire Bhig* ▲ *; Gars-bheinn* ▲
Terrain: *Grade 1 Scramble (Sgùrr nan Eag)*
Distance: *15km, 9.25 miles*
Ascent & Descent: *1080m; 3543ft*
Time: *6–7hrs*
Start & Finish: *Parking before Glen Brittle Campsite (NG 4090 2065)*

This route is mostly a hillwalk with lots of easy scrambling on Sgùrr nan Eag and the fine ridge beyond to Sgùrr a' Choire Bhig (875m) and Gars-bheinn (895m). The ridge is scattered with rocks and boulders, so the going is rough in places, while the screes on Gars-bheinn's southern flanks are tedious, but better in descent than ascent. Nevertheless, the situations are fantastic and the sea views even better.

Approach

Walk through Glen Brittle Campsite past the toilet block and ascend to a track. Follow this right for a short distance, then turn left back onto the main path. Continue ascending on this for about 650m to a path junction. Turn right here onto a well-prepared path and cross over the burn. Continue on the path to reach the wide Allt Coire Làgan which is crossed by boulder-hopping. This can be awkward if there is a lot of water running. About 380m beyond this the path splits at a small cairn NG 4344 1960.

Turn left onto the path into Coire a' Ghrunnda (the right-hand path is the return from Gars-bheinn) and start ascending below the rocky spur of Sròn na Ciche's South-West Ridge, heading for a prominent perched boulder on the skyline.

Pass this and continue east until the path turns north and a rocky section up a worn gully gives access to the corrie. Follow a well-graded zigzag path up the scree below the cliffs. The next objective is a parallel-sided gully on the left side of the slabby headwall of

Sgùrr Alasdair and the peaks of Coire a' Ghrunnda from the summit ridge of Sgùrr nan Eag

the corrie, left of the Allt Coire a' Ghrunnda (*see p154*).

Near the end of the main cliff face (NG 4474 9175) the path ascends more steeply, heading towards a rocky gully in the main cliffs, then descends to the parallel gully in the headwall. The same point can be gained more directly by leaving the path near the end of the main cliff face. Go straight ahead through large boulders

(no path), then ascend to the parallel-sided gully.

Climb the gully, then up and left to left-slanting grooves which are often wet (Grade 2–3). Above these the easiest line is to head right to gain the burn and scramble awkwardly beside this to reach Loch Coire a' Ghrunnda. Alternatively, continue at a higher level above the burn over ill-defined terrain.

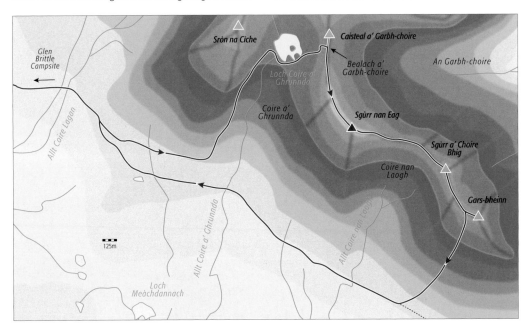

Gars-bheinn from the Coire a' Ghrunnda path

Go round the right-hand side of the loch to its south-eastern edge, almost directly below Caisteal a' Garbh-choire (NG 4529 2015). After an initial ascent over boulders, a well-worn path skirts small crags on the left then ascends more directly to Bealach a' Garbh-choire (*see p154*).

Ascent

It would be easy to ascend Caisteal a' Garbh-choire (Moderate) from here (*see p154, 156*). Otherwise, scramble (Grade 1) up the slabby North Ridge of Sgùrr nan Eag to more bouldery terrain and cross this to the summit, marked by a large cairn on top of a mass of giant boulders. A rocky path leads over the slabs and boulders of the East Ridge to the col below Sgùrr a' Choire Bhig, from where the fine rocky arete of the North-West Ridge leads to the summit. Descend the short South Ridge and follow a grassier path round the rim of Coire Beag to the North-West Ridge of Gars-bheinn. Climb this passing over a small summit and a scree-filled gully, then cross a second top and descend to a col below the final summit. Ascend steeper rocks to the summit. The views are spectacular in all directions, north to the highest peaks in the Cuillin, east over Coruisk to Blàbheinn and south and west to the mainland, Rùm and the Small Isles.

Descent

There are **two options**: (1) Return by the route of ascent. This is the shortest in terms of distance, but involves an extra 100m or so of ascent and descent.

(2) Alternatively, reverse Gars-bheinn's North-West Ridge to about NG 4673 1871. Turn south and make rapid progress down the unrelenting scree trough, then grass and rock to gain the 'coastal' path at about NG 4633 1777 (approx 230m altitude).

Follow the wet path west, crossing over Allt Coire nan Laogh and Allt Coire a' Ghrunnda, beyond which the path ascends to meet the Coire a' Ghrunnda path used on the approach, at the small cairn NG 4344 1960. Retrace the outward route to Glen Brittle.

Shapely Gars-bheinn from the summit of Sgùrr a' Choire Bhig

WESTERN RED HILLS

*Marsco, left, Beinn Dearg Mheadhonach, Beinn Dearg
Mhòr and Glamaig from Garbh-bheinn*

167

Coire na h-Àirighe on the north-eastern flanks of Glamaig/Sgùrr Mhairi, viewed across Loch Sligachan from Peinachorrain

Glamaig

*T*his mountain has an unenviable reputation as a gigantic scree cone and if you approach from Sligachan to the west, then its notoriety is well earned. The North-East Ridge is the most enjoyable route if tackling the mountain by itself and includes an ascent of An Coileach, but it is still breathtakingly steep. If you do fancy the West Face, then the Glamaig Hill Race tackles it every year. The 2012 record stands at 44 minutes and 27 seconds round trip!

An Coileach from the broad ridge leading to the summit of Sgùrr Mhairi, Glamaig's highest point

North-East Ridge from A87

Summits: *Sgùrr Mhairi* ▲ *; An Coileach* ▲
Terrain: *Hillwalk*
Distance: *6km; 3.75 miles*
Ascent & Descent: *795m; 2600ft*
Time: *3hrs 30mins–4hrs 30mins*
Start & Finish: *Layby on A87 (NG 5373 3089)*

The North-East Ridge rises above Gleann Torra-mhichaig and is easily accessed from the A87 south-east of Sconser. The going is steep, but the sea views are magnificent. Glamaig/Sgùrr Mhairi (775m) is often climbed in conjunction with Beinn Dearg Mheadhonach (651m) and Beinn Dearg Mhòr (731m), (see p173).

Approach

Start from the signposted long layby on the east side of the A87, about 150m north of the bridge over the Abhainn Torra-mhichaig (NG 5373 3089).

Ascent

Cross over the road to a gate in the fence and gain the hillside. Ascend in a north-westerly direction for about 550m, over rough moorland and below power-lines, to reach the North-East Ridge where it starts to steepen below the lowest crags.

Keep left of the crags on a path through the heather, close to old fence posts. After an initial steep section the ground eases off and becomes grassier and the path disappears. Above this, further steep ground leads to a second crag which is easily avoided on the left. Grassy slopes then lead to a final zigzag through

Looking towards Sgùrr Mhairi, Glamaig's highest point, from the board ridge beyond An Coileach

rocky ground to gain the top of An Coileach.

Traverse the fine broad ridge linking An Coileach to Sgùrr Mhairi and gain the rounded summit plateau topped by a cairn – a mountain landscape more reminiscent of the Southern Uplands, than Skye.

Descent

Either reverse the ascent route, or continue a circuit via the Bealach na Sgàirde which will bring you into contact with Glamaig's infamous screes.

To make a circuit, retrace your steps south-east over the summit dome for about 150m, then descend in a more southerly direction, initially over grass, to reach the scree slopes and follow them down to the grassy Bealach na Sgàirde below Beinn Dearg Mhòr.

From the tiny lochan at the bealach, head east following the Allt Mòr Doire Mhic-ùin, then pick-up animal tracks contouring the hillside and follow these round into Gleann Torra-mhichaig. Remain on the higher ground and out of the heather for as long as possible, until a diagonal line can be taken across the moorland and back under the powerlines to the start.

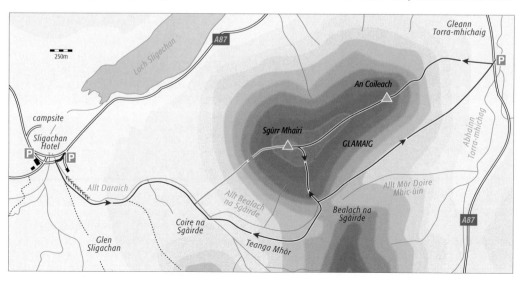

South Face from Sligachan

Summits: *Sgùrr Mhairi* ▲
Terrain: *Hillwalk*
Distance: *10km; 6.25 miles*
Ascent & Descent: *755m; 2475ft*
Time: *4–5hrs*
Start & Finish: *Glen Sligachan car park (NG 4877 2990)*

A direct approach up the West Face is a long hard slog up seemingly never-ending scree. Climbing the South Face via Bealach na Sgàirde is less painful but longer and still involves some ascent on scree.

Approach

From the car park, follow the old road and turn left onto the footpath before the old bridge. Keep immediately left past a circle of boulders with little cairns, to a junction with a gate on the left. Leave the main path, go through the gate and follow a boggy path beside the gorge to reach another gate.

Continue up the south side of the Allt Daraich on a path initially alongside fence posts, to enter Coire na Sgàirde and reach the foot of the shallow spur of the Teanga Mhòr, south of the Allt Bealach na Sgàirde.

Cross the Allt Daraich and go up the crest of the spur, then turn north towards the Allt Bealach na Sgàirde and a final climb up grass and scree to the bealach.

Ascent

From Bealach na Sgàirde, ascend the South Face

Descending the South Face to Bealach na Sgàirde below Beinn Dearg Mhòr

making best use of the large areas of grass to the left of the main scree runs, to gain the plateau and summit of Sgùrr Mhairi. With careful route-finding much of the scree can be avoided.

Descent

It is possible to descend straight down the scree and steep grass of the West Face, cross the Allt Daraich to gain the outward path and follow it back to Sligachan. This is fast but relentless on the knees. Most will elect to return by the route of ascent.

GLAMAIG – Sgùrr Mhairi

South Face

West Face

Bealach na Sgàirde

Allt Bealach na Sgàirde

Teanga Mhòr

Allt Daraich

Approach from Sligachan to Bealach na Sgàirde via the Allt Daraich and Teanga Mhòr

Looking over Bealach Mosgaraidh to Beinn Dearg Mhòr and Glamaig/An Coileach, left, from Beinn Dearg Mheadhonach

Beinn Dearg Mheadhonach & Beinn Dearg Mhòr

These central hills offer enjoyable and elevated ridge walking with fine views. The moorland at the start and finish can be boggy, but once on the tops the going is rocky and firm underfoot. The steep scree descent to Bealach na Sgàirde is short, but requires careful route-finding

Glamaig/Sgùrr Mhairi, Beinn Dearg Mhòr, Beinn Dearg Mheadhonach and Ciche na Beinne Deirge across the Allt Dearg Mòr

Beinn Dearg Mheadhonach & Beinn Dearg Mhòr

Summits: *Beinn Dearg Mheadhonach* ▲ *;*
Beinn Dearg Mhòr ▲ *; Beinn Dearg* ▲ *;*
Terrain: *Hillwalk*
Distance: *11km; 6.75 miles*
Ascent & Descent: *860m; 2820ft*
Time: *4hrs 30mins–5hrs 30mins*
Start & Finish: *Glen Sligachan car park (NG 4877 2990)*

Beinn Dearg Mheadhonach (651m) and Beinn Dearg Mhòr (731m) offer a welcome change to the jagged peaks of the Cuillin and a make fine outing by themselves from Glen Sligachan, although Glamaig is easily included in the round. However, providing transport can be arranged, the best route is a linear traverse starting with Glamaig's North-East Ridge (see p169) and finishing down the Druim na Ruaige of Beinn Dearg Mheadhonach.

Approach

From the car park, follow the old road and turn left onto the footpath before the old bridge. Keep immediately left past a circle of boulders with little cairns to a junction with a gate on the left. Leave the main path, go through the gate and follow a boggy path beside the gorge of the Allt Daraich to reach another gate.

Continue up the right (south) side of the Allt Daraich on a path beside fence posts. Follow the path to NG 4945 2940, then break away from the burn in a south-easterly direction on a vague path over bog and heather towards Druim na Ruaige.

Ascent

At Druim na Ruaige the path becomes clearer and leads over Sròn a' Bhealain and up the crest of the broad ridge, then up a final rocky slope to the main ridge. Follow this south and east to the summit of Beinn Dearg Mheadhonach.

Retrace your steps back along the ridge, descend north over the hump of Beinn Dearg to the Bealach Mosgaraidh, then follow the line of least resistance to the fine summit of Beinn Dearg Mhòr. Glamaig fills the view north across Bealach na Sgàirde. Continue along the ridge overlooking the bealach almost to where it ends in crags, then descend directly down scree to the grassy bealach.

Glamaig/Sgùrr Mhairi: This peak is under 1km from the Bealach na Sgàirde and easily climbed from there if desired (*see p171*). The ascent requires perseverance, but isn't nearly as bad as it looks if care is taken to pick a route to the left (west), where grassy sections of the hillside can be linked to avoid the worst of the scree. From the summit it is possible to descend the West Face, although this is relentlessly steep scree and grass and hard on the knees. Cross over the Allt Daraich to gain the path on its south side. (add 1hr 20mins for ascent from and return to Bealach na Sgàirde).

Descent

From Bealach na Sgàirde, descend right (west) down scree to reach a path beside the Allt Bealach na Sgàirde. Follow this to the spur of Teanga Mhòr and descend it to reach and cross over the Allt Daraich. The path on the left (south) side of the burn leads round the moorland to meet the outward route which is followed back to the start.

On the broad spur of Druim na Ruaige, below Beinn Dearg Mheadhonach

Approaching the summit of Beinn Dearg Mheadhonach, Garbh-bheinn and Blàbheinn in the distance

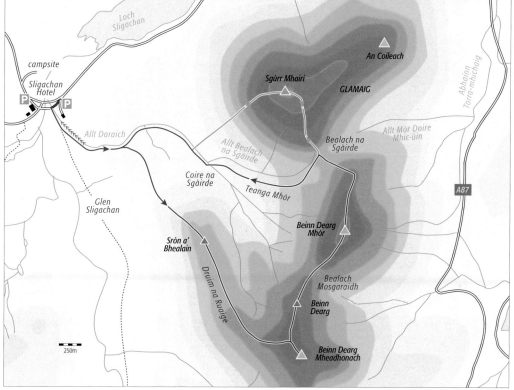

Marsco South Summit and South-East Ridge, with the main summit behind, viewed across An Fraoch-choire from Ruadh Stac

Marsco & Ruadh Stac

*V*iewed from the Sligachan Hotel, the granite bulk of Marsco provides one third of the classic 'shortbread tin' photograph looking down Glen Sligachan, balanced by Sgùrr nan Gillean and the old bridge in the foreground. It's a peak that totally delivers with a dramatic summit ridge and stunning views

Approaching Marsco from Glen Sligachan; the North-East Ridge faces the camera. The distant pointed peak is Sgùrr Hain

From Sligachan

Summits: *Marsco* ▲ *; North Summit* ▲ *;*
South Summit ▲
Terrain: *Hillwalk*
Distance: *14km; 8.5 miles*
Ascent & Descent: *725m; 2380ft*
Time: *4hrs 30mins–5hrs 30mins*
Start & Finish: *Glen Sligachan car park*
(NG 4877 2990)

The North-East Ridge of Marsco (736m) has some steep ground at the top and offers a challenging ascent. It will suit the enthusiast, but others may be content to ascend and descend via Coire nan Laogh. Whichever the route, Marsco is quite a different experience to its northern neighbours and Glamaig.

Approach
From the car park, follow the old road and turn left onto the footpath before the old bridge. Keep immediately left past a circle of boulders with little cairns and go past a junction on the left with a gate. Follow the path down Glen Sligachan for about 3km

to reach the Allt na Measarroch, which drains from the Màm a' Phobuill. Turn left and follow the path up the left (north) side of the burn for about 1.5km, then cross over the burn to gain the North-East Ridge.

Ascent
The grassy ridge steepens significantly as height is gained and a short rocky band is passed through to reach the summit ridge. Follow this over the North Summit to a precariously perched cairn marking the highest point. Descend the spectacular arete, then a broad grassy slope to the col between the main and south summits. The South Summit is well worth visiting for its magnificent views of Garbh-bheinn, Clach Glas and Blàbheinn (*photo p180–1*).

Descent
Return to the col between the main summit and the South Summit, then descend north-west into Coire nan Laogh beside the old fence to gain a path (*diagram p185*). Cross over the Allt Màm a' Phobuill draining the corrie to gain the Màm a' Phobuill.

Follow the path on the right (north) side of the Allt na Measarroch back to Glen Sligachan and the outward route.

The granite screes of Ruadh Stac from the head of Am Fraoch-choire, looking over Glen Sligachan to Sgùrr nan Gillean

From Loch Ainort

Summits: *Ruadh Stac* ▲; *Marsco* ▲;
South Summit ▲
Terrain: *Hillwalk*
Distance: *13km; 8 miles*
Ascent & Descent: *1020m; 3355ft*
Time: *5–6hrs*
Start & Finish: *Layby on A87 above Loch Ainort
(NG 5344 2673)*

*Approaching from Glen Sligachan is the most
popular way to climb Marsco, but the route from
Loch Ainort gives easy access to the fine and rocky
South-East Ridge and facilitates an ascent of the red
granite dome of Ruadh Stac (493m), with its
panoramic view of the Cuillin Ridge.*

Approach

From the parking, follow the crash-barrier downhill
then cross over the road to the path on the right
(north) side of the Allt Coire nam Bruadaran, which
leads towards the Eas a' Bhradain waterfall. Don't
drop down to the waterfall, but keep high on a rough
and often muddy path and pass above the falls.

Continue beside the Allt Coire nam Bruadaran. The
going can be marshy in places, but the corrie starts to
steepen after about 2km and grassier ground is
ascended south-west then south to the 323m col
between Marsco and Druim Eadar Dà Choire.

It is possible to reach the same point by crossing
the moorland east of the Allt Coire nam Bruadaran to
gain the Druim Eadar Dà Choire spur, the approach
for the North Ridge of Garbh-bheinn (*see p195*), then
contouring west and south below the rocky top of
Druim Eadar Dà Choire. However the moorland path
is indistinct at the start, the ground can also be wet
and the Allt Coire nam Bruadaran path will still have
to be tackled on the return.

Ascent

From the 323m col, pick up a path which makes a
contouring descent round the head of Am Fraoch-
choire below Garbh-bheinn, cross the shallow gorge
of the Allt nam Fraoch-choire at about 270m, then
ascend to the 337m col between Ruadh Stac and
Garbh-bheinn. Ascend the broad East Ridge of Ruadh
Stac to the grassy summit and panoramic view.

Return to the 323m col below Marsco and climb the
broad South-East Ridge over granite boulders and slabs,
in the vicinity of an old fence and wall. Grassier and
steeper ground leads to the 643m South Summit.

Cross the col beyond and ascend a broad slope to
the even more spectacular summit arete of Marsco
and a perched summit cairn.

Descent

Return to the col between the main summit and the
South Summit, then descend north-west into Coire
nan Laogh beside the old fence to gain a path
(*diagram p185*). Cross over the Allt Màm a' Phobuill
draining the corrie to gain the Màm a' Phobuill. Follow
the north side of the Allt Màm a' Phobuill into Coire
nam Bruadaran to meet the Allt Coire nam Bruadaran
and return to the start.

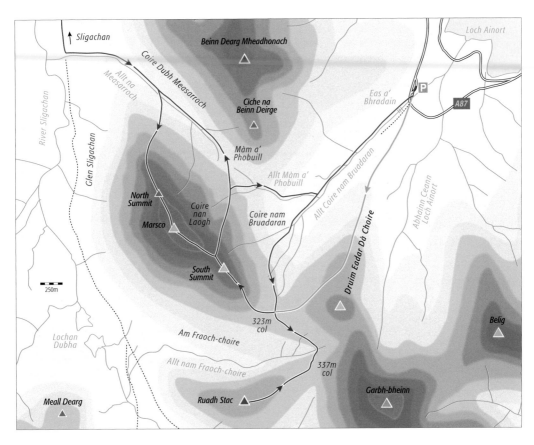

The rocky South-East Ridge and South Summit of Marsco with the main summit behind, from Druim Eadar Dà Choire

The South Summit of Marsco, framed by Garbh-bheinn, Clach Glas, the tops of Blàbheinn and Ruadh Stac

Marsco and the broad col of Màm a' Phobuill, left, from the Allt Dearg Mòr at sunset. Garbh-bheinn is on the left

Round of the Western Red Hills
Marsco, Ciche na Beinne Deirge, Beinn Dearg Mheadhonach, Beinn Dearg Mhòr, Glamaig

A traverse of all the Western Red Hills is easily achieved from Sligachan and offers an interesting and varied circuit. There's a reasonable amount of granite scree involved, but that is par for the course, whichever way these hills are tackled

The surprisingly sharp summit ridge of Marsco. In the distance are Macleod's Tables, left, and The Storr, right

Round of the Western Red Hills

Summits: *Marsco ▲ ; North Summit ▲ ; South Summit ▲ ; Ciche na Beinne Deirge ▲ ; Beinn Dearg Mheadhonach ▲ ; Beinn Dearg ▲ ; Beinn Dearg Mhòr ▲ ; Glamaig/Sgùrr Mhairi ▲ ; Optional – Glamaig/An Coileach ▲*
 Terrain: *Hillwalk*
Distance: *18.5km; 11.5 miles*
Ascent & Descent: *1725m; 5665ft*
Time: *7hrs 30mins–8hrs 30mins*
Start & Finish: *Glen Sligachan car park (NG 4877 2990)*

If desired, this route could be extended to include An Coileach (673m), the eastern summit of Glamaig, adding an extra 2.5km to the day and about 200m extra ascent and descent.

Approach
From the car park, follow the old road and turn left onto the footpath before the old bridge. Keep immediately left past a circle of boulders with little cairns and go past a junction on the left with a gate. Follow the path down Glen Sligachan for about 3km to reach the Allt na Measarroch, which drains from the Màm a' Phobuill. Turn left and follow the path up the left (north) side of the burn for about 1.5km, then cross over the burn to gain the North-East Ridge.

Ascent
The grassy ridge steepens significantly as height is gained and a short rocky band is passed through to reach the summit ridge. Follow this over the North Summit to a precariously perched cain marking the highest point. Descend the spectacular arete, then a broad grassy slope to the col between the main summit and the South Summit.

The South Summit offers a fine view over Garbh-bheinn, Clach Glas and Blàbheinn and is worth visiting. Return to the col and descend north-west near fence posts, down a steep spur forming the eastern side of Coire nan Laogh (*diagram p185*). Cross over the Allt Màm a' Phobuill draining the corrie to gain the Màm a' Phobuill.

Facing the screes of Ciche na Beinn Deirge's South Face, leave the main path and ascend to gain an animal path and traverse east at the base of the scree.

Although a little faint in places, the path takes you round to the south-east side of the peak, with views north-east to Loch Ainort, from where heathery and rocky sections in the scree make for easier upward progress. Go over Ciche na Beinn Deirge and follow the broad ridge beyond to a col, then straight up to the summit of Beinn Dearg Mheadhonach.

Traverse rocky Beinn Dearg Mheadhonach and the bump of Beinn Dearg and descend to the Bealach Mosgaraidh. From there, follow the line of least resis-

tance to the fine summit of Beinn Dearg Mhòr (*see p173–5*). Continue along the ridge overlooking the Bealach na Sgàirde almost to where it ends in crags, then descend scree directly to the grassy bealach.

The ascent from Bealach na Sgàirde to Sgùrr Mhairi, Glamaig's highest summit, requires perseverance, but isn't nearly as bad as it looks if care is taken to pick a route to the left (west), where grassy sections of the hillside can be linked to avoid the worst of the scree. Once grass is gained, follow the broad grassy plateau to the summit. The rocky peak of An Coileach, Glamaig's second summit, lies to the east and is easily reached via an out and back route along the linking ridge, adding about 1hr to the day.

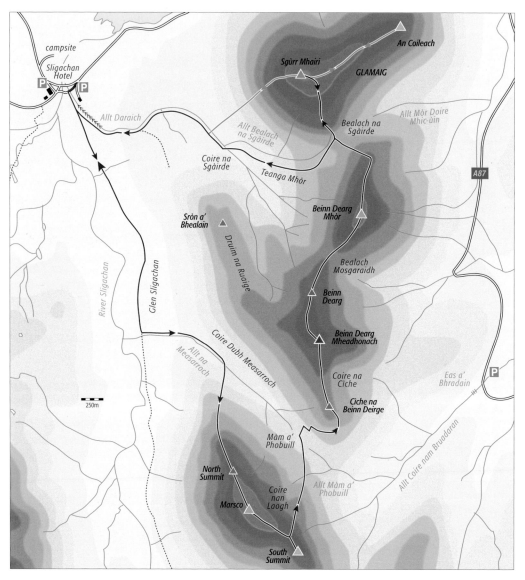

Coire nan Laogh and the route onto Ciche na Beinn Deirge, from Marsco

Descent

From the summit of Glamaig it is possible to descend the West Face, although this is relentlessly steep scree and grass and hard on the knees. In addition, the Allt Daraich will need to be crossed to return to the path on its south side. Alternatively, return to Bealach na Sgàirde. From Bealach na Sgàirde, descend right (west) from the bealach down scree to reach a path beside the Allt Bealach na Sgàirde (*see p171*). Follow this to the spur of Teanga Mhòr and descend it to reach and cross the Allt Daraich. A path on the left (south) side of the Allt Daraich leads round the moorland to a gate.

Go through this and follow a boggy path down beside the gorge to another gate, beyond which the Glen Sligachan path is joined and followed back to the start.

Glamaig/Sgùrr Mhairi, left, Beinn Dearg Mhòr, Beainn Dearg Mheadhonach and Marsco from the Allt Dearg Mòr

185

GABBRO OUTLIERS

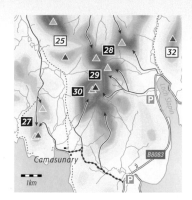

*Traversing left to the stubby pinnacle on the steep west facing
wall of the Summit Tower on the North Ridge of Clach Glas*

Approaching the rocky defile separating the main summit of Sgùrr na Stri, left, from the lower West Summit, right

Sgùrr Hain & Sgùrr na Stri

*S*gùrr Hain is a pleasant little hill, but Sgùrr na Stri is a perfect gem. Located at the southern end of the mountain mass between the Cuillin and Blàbheinn, it has stunning views west over Loch Coruisk to the Cuillin Ridge and south to the Small Isles of Rùm and Eigg

Captain Maryon's Memorial Cairn above the south end of Loch a' Choire Riabhaich

From Sligachan

Summits: *Sgùrr Hain ▲ ; North Summit▲ ; Sgùrr na Stri▲ ; West Summit ▲*
Terrain: *Hillwalk*
Distance: *24km; 15 miles*
Ascent & Descent: *570m; 1875ft*
Time: *6hrs 40mins–7hrs 40mins*
Start & Finish: *Glen Sligachan car park (NG 4877 2990)*

The approach from Glen Sligachan makes for a long day, but the path is fairly flat and there is little loss of height. Sgùrr Hain (418m) and Sgùrr na Stri (495m) are both visible at the head of the glen from the start and the scenery is better than the shorter approach from Kirkibost (see p191).

Approach

From the car park, follow the old road and turn left onto the footpath before the old bridge. Keep immediately left past a circle of boulders with little cairns and go past a junction on the left with a gate.

Follow the path down Glen Sligachan for about 7km, fording the Allt na Measarroch at the foot of Marsco and continuing beyond on a slightly rougher path to reach the watershed at the twin pools of Lochan Dubha in the base of the glen. The path descends for about 350m to a junction with a cairn (NG 5018 2402). Turn right off the main path and follow a clear path across the head of Srath na Crèitheach.

Ascend past a lochan to the col on the rocky shoulder of Druim Hain and a junction of paths, north of Sgùrr Hain. The right-hand path descends to Loch Coruisk. The left-hand contours below Sgùrr Hain to Sgùrr na Stri.

Ascent

Ignore both paths and scramble up Sgùrr Hain's North Ridge via the line of least resistance, to gain the North Summit marked by a small cairn, then go south along the ridge with fine views east over Loch na Crèitheach to Garbh-bheinn and Blàbheinn, to reach the high-point. From the summit, weave south then west down rocky ground to meet the path to Sgùrr na Stri, which contours below Sgùrr Hain.

Follow the path for about 180m until Captain Maryon's Memorial Cairn comes into view overlooking

The approach from Camasunary to Sgùrr na Stri and the path round the south end of Loch na Crèitheach

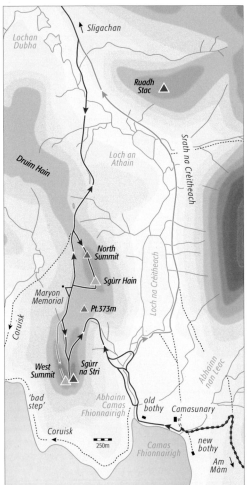

the south end of Loch a' Choire Riabhaich, some 100m below the path to the west. Maryon disappeared in July 1946 while walking in the Cuillin and the stone cairn and plaque mark the spot where his body was found two years later.

Return to the path and descend slightly for about 250m, to reach an unnamed burn in a distinct open gully which rises up the north face of Sgùrr na Stri, splitting it into two summits. Following a recent survey, the east summit was found to be higher by nearly 1m, but the West Summit has a more dramatic view.

Remain on the left (east) side of the burn and follow the path into the upper reaches of the open gully. Continue in the gully to pass through a narrow, rocky gap between the main east summit (on the left) and the lower West Summit (on the right).

From the gap, scramble up on the left and along a wide ledge leading to the summit. Admire the fine views north-east to Garbh-bheinn and Blàbheinn and east to Camasunary, then return to the rocky gap. Make a zigzag scramble up shelves and slabs on the right-hand side of the gap to gain the West Summit and spectacular views over Loch Coruisk to the Cuillin Ridge and over the sea to Rùm and Eigg.

Descent

There are **three options**: (1) Return to the gap, then by the route of ascent, utilising the path below Sgùrr Hain. (2) Down the North Ridge of the West Summit. (3) Descend to the Abhainn Camas Fhionnairigh (*see route opposite*) and cross over. A path leads round the south end of Loch na Crèitheach to reach the main path through Srath na Crèitheach, which is followed north to Glen Sligachan (*27km/16.5 miles; 590m; 1935ft ascent & descent; 7hrs 30mins*).

From Kirkibost

Summits: *Sgùrr na Stri* ▲ *; West Summit* ▲
Terrain: *Hillwalk*
Distance: *15km; 9.25 miles*
Ascent & Descent: *640m; 2100ft*
Time: *4hrs 30mins–5hrs 30mins*
Start & Finish: *Parking on B8083, south-west of Kirkibost & Kilmarie (NG 5452 1717)*

This route offers a much shorter approach than Glen Sligachan, although the vehicle track over Am Màm to Camasunary involves the loss of about 175m at the start of the day, all of which needs to be regained on the return. In spate or high tide and rough sea, it may be difficult to cross the Abhainn Camas Fhionnairigh without wading.

Approach

This is the same approach as for the South Ridge of Blàbheinn (*see map p212*). From the parking, follow the signposted track north-west to the Am Màm and views over Camasunary to Sgùrr na Stri. Descend the other side to the farmhouse at Camasunary.

There is a newly built and always open bothy to the south of the main house, which replaces the now closed bothy on the seashore to the west.

Cross the bridge over the Abhainn nan Leac and follow the seashore west past Camasunary and the former bothy, to the bank of the Abhainn Camas Fhionnairigh. How the river is crossed will depend on

the tide and water flow. There are stepping stones about 100m up the river bank and other crossing places further north.

A crossing is also possible at a section of slabby rock (NG 5084 1950) and at stepping stones where the river divides (NG 5097 1969). Alternatively, it may be necessary to wade.

Ascent

Either way, gain a faint path which starts west of the burn draining the corrie below Pt.373m on the ridge between Sgùrr na Stri and Sgùrr Hain. The path climbs away from the burn up the south side of the corrie, then turns north to cross the burn and ascends towards the col left of Pt.373. Turn left below the col to gain a grassy rake and follow it up onto the rocky ridge leading south towards Sgùrr na Stri (*see top left*).

Once on the ridge, traverse round westwards to meet the path beside the burn draining the gully between Sgùrr na Stri's two summits. Pass through a narrow, rocky gap between the West Summit and the main east summit. From the gap, scramble up on the left and along a wide ledge leading to the summit.

Admire the fine views north-east to Garbh-bheinn and Blàbheinn and east to Camasunary, then return to the rocky gap. Make a zigzag scramble up shelves and slabs on the right-hand side of the gap to gain the West Summit and spectacular views over Loch Coruisk to the Cuillin Ridge and over the sea to Rùm and Eigg.

Descent

Reverse the route of ascent.

Descending the corrie below Pt.373m towards the Abhainn Camas Fhionnairigh, the beach at Camasunary and the track over the Am Màm to Kirkibost

One of the great mountain views of the world: Loch Coruisk and the Cuillin Ridge from Sgùrr na Stri

The North Ridge of Garbh-bheinn, looking north to Druim Eadar Dà Choire, Beinn Dearg Mheadhonach & Beinn Dearg Mhòr

Garbh-bheinn & Belig

*W*hether approached from Loch Ainort to the north or Loch Slapin to the east, combining these two mountains creates a high-level circuit characterised by rocky ridges and impressive views. Both rounds have their highlights, but of the two, the Loch Slapin route is probably the more scenic

Belig, left, and Garbh-bheinn from the ridge of Druim Eadar Dà Choire. Garbh-bheinn's North Ridge is on the right

From Loch Ainort

Summits: *Druim Eadar Dà Choire* ▲ *;*
Garbh-bheinn ▲ *; Belig* ▲
Terrain: *Hillwalk*
Distance: *10km; 6.25 miles*
Ascent & Descent: *1090m; 3585ft*
Time: *4hrs 40mins–5hrs 40mins*
Start & Finish: *Layby on A87 above Loch Ainort*
(NG 5344 2673)

The North Ridge of Garbh-bheinn (808m) is rockier than the South-East Ridge climbed from Loch Slapin, but the walk over the moor and road noise from the busy A87 can create an austere ambiance.

Approach

From the parking, follow the crash-barrier downhill, cross over the Allt Coire nam Bruadaran then cross to the other side of the road. Go through the fence following a path left (south) of the Eas a' Bhradain waterfall for a very short way, then break out south onto the open heather moorland, aiming south-west for the prominent broad spur of Druim Eadar Dà Choire.

The going improves as height is gained and after about 700m, a path starts to develop on the left (east) side of the broad ridge overlooking the Abhainn Ceann Loch Ainort, in the vicinity of some large granite boulders (NG 5309 2589). The terrain starts to steepen and

the ridge, initially grassy then scattered with angular pink granite boulders, becomes better defined.

Weave in and out of the granite to reach the top of Druim Eadar Dà Choire, with fine views west to Marsco, Sgùrr nan Gillean and the Cuillin Ridge and south to Clach Glas and Blàbheinn, with Rùm and Eigg beyond. Follow the old fence posts south-east, down to the col at the start of Garbh-bheinn's North Ridge, where the pink granite turns to black gabbro.

This old boundary is part of a 12km fence and wall running from Glen Sligachan to Luib on Loch Ainort and followed in part on the ascent of Marsco from Màm a' Phobuill via the South Ridge (*see p178*) and Garbh-bheinn's North Ridge. It is at its best as a wall on Belig's West Ridge and on Glas-Bheinn Mòr (*see p219*), which it traverses the length of.

Ascent

The rocky path leads up and left onto the grassy ridgeline, which is followed until the ground becomes rockier and starts to steepen. Zigzag up scree paths with occasional rocky sections, to where the ridge levels out and becomes grassier again, then traverse round the rim of Coire na Seilg. The grassy ridge ends and steeper rocky ground can be tackled via scrambling on the crest to the left, or scree to the right, with increasingly good views south across Coire Dubh to Clach Glas and Blàbheinn.

Zigzag through broken rocks to a final section of solid rock which offers pleasant, easy scrambling leading to

195

Tthe final section of scrambling on the North Ridge of Garbh-bheinn

the craggy summit, which can be taken direct or avoided on the right. The views from the summit of Garbh-bheinn are spectacular (*photo 166–7*).

The next section is common to both the Loch Ainort and the Loch Slapin routes and involves descending the North-East Ridge to the Bealach na Bèiste, then ascending Belig's South-West Ridge. The initial descent from the summit of Garbh-bheinn to the top of the North-East Ridge is steep with some rubble and moss and requires care, especially in poor visibility.

From the summit, descend east for about 6m then drop steeply north following a worn path to gain rocky pinnacles on the North-East Ridge. Zigzag through and round the pinnacles to gain the grassier ridge beyond and follow this to rocky steps and scree overlooking Bealach na Bèiste. Zigzag down the scree, swing right to grassy and rocky outcrops and weave down through them to the bealach below Belig.

Ascend directly from the bealach to the worn line through the rock and scree band and climb this keeping slightly to the right, avoiding most of the scree via grassy runnels and scrambling up the rocky ribs.

A less steep section of rock and grass leads north to a stone wall, part of the boundary described earlier. When the way ahead is barred by steep rock, cross over the wall and follow it to the summit of Belig (702m).

Descent

There are **two options**: **(1)** The nose of Belig's North Ridge terminates in crags, which are avoided on their left (west) side. Descend the ridge over scree and grass, to about NG 5435 2454, then cut diagonally north-west from the ridge down steep tedious scree paths, to skirt below the crags and gain easier grassy ground. Below the crags, head north into Coire Chòinnich to reach the Allt a' Mheadhoin and cross over.

(2) Return over Pt.637m and down to the col between Belig and Glas-Bheinn Mhòr. Descend north and north-west to the Allt a' Mheadhoin.

Both routes now follow the green right (east) bank of the Allt a' Mheadhoin to the Abhainn Ceann Loch Ainort, which leads to a gate in the fence before the bridge over the A87. Follow the road west to the road cutting, then cross to the other (north) side of the road and follow a path over the top of the cutting back to the road and the start.

Nearing the summit of Garbh-bheinn on the North Ridge

From Loch Slapin

Summits: *Garbh-bheinn* ▲ *; Belig* ▲ *; Pt.637m* ▲
Terrain: *Hillwalk*
Distance: *10.5km; 6.5 miles*
Ascent & Descent: *1130m; 3700ft*
Time: *5–6hrs*
Start & Finish: *Blàbheinn car park on Loch Slapin (NG 5608 2156)*

Encircled by mountains of jagged gabbro on one side and rounded granite on the other, the head of Loch Slapin is one of the most beautiful places on Skye.

Approach

The corrie of the Allt Aigeinn, east of Garbh-bheinn and south of Belig could be used to start or finish this route. However, this corrie is rough and bouldery in its upper reaches and generally pathless, compared with Choire a' Càise to the south. The route could also be started with an ascent of Sgùrr nan Each, but the

Grade 2–3 scrambling on this peak is, perhaps, better matched with an ascent of the Clach Glas – Blàbheinn traverse. The ascent of Sgùrr nan Each is described as part of that route (*see p201*).

From the parking, return to the road and walk north to the bridge over the Allt na Dunaiche. Turn left onto the Blàbheinn path and follow it into lower Choire a' Càise, to meet the Allt na Dunaiche. After about 2km, the Blàbheinn path crosses the burn towards Coire Uaigneich. Do not cross, but continue towards the back of the corrie on a minor path which is ill-defined in places, on the right (north) side of the burn.

Upper Choire a' Càise lies directly below Bealach Clach Glas and the cliffs between Clach Glas and Sgùrr nan Each and is separated from the wider lower corrie by a craggy spur, defined on its left by the deep cleft of the burn draining the upper corrie, and on its right by a smaller ravine with a burn, hidden from below. Both burns join below the spur (*diagram p199*).

Continue beside the Allt Dunaiche to arrive at a short section of wall on the left (west) bank and a couple of blocks on the right (east) bank (NG 5425

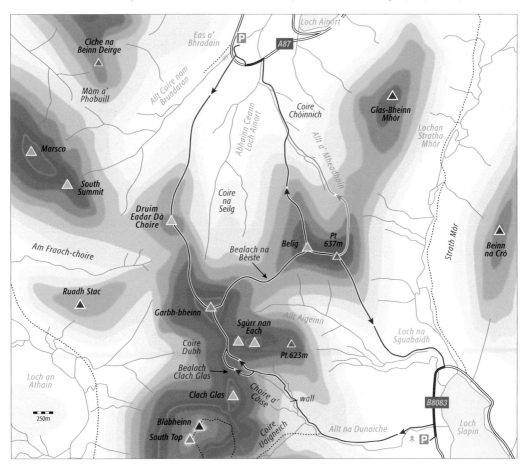

2201). Cross the burn just before the wall and follow the broad spur between the two burns on an initially ill-defined path, which becomes much clearer with height. The path leads almost to the mouth of the deep cleft, then cuts up and right. Zigzag up to a grassy ramp and rock slabs leading left into the upper corrie.

At the top, exit right or left up scree and boulders to the ridge. The left exit leads to Bealach Clach Glas and is shorter, but is further away from Garbh-bheinn. On this exit, much of the scree can be avoided via a rough path at the base of the Clach Glas cliffs.

Ascent
Turn north, traverse scree and grass on the left (west) flank of the ridge round the base of Sgùrr nan Each to Garbh-bheinn's South-East Ridge and ascend near its crest to the summit. From there, descend the North-East Ridge to the Bealach na Bèiste, then ascend Belig's South-West Ridge to the summit, as described in the Loch Ainort route *(see p195)*.

Descent
From Belig's summit descend onto Pt.637m. From its very south-east aspect, start a steep descent down the South Ridge on rock and grass, with some small sections of scrambling. The ridge is steep and exposed in places, although the difficulties can all be turned with careful attention to route-finding.

Continue beyond the base of the ridge to the Allt Aigeinn and follow it to where it merges with gravel beds before Loch na Sguabaidh. Cross over and head east then south to the road, which is followed south for 750m back to the parking *(map p197)*.

The rocky but easy South-East Ridge of Garbh-bheinn

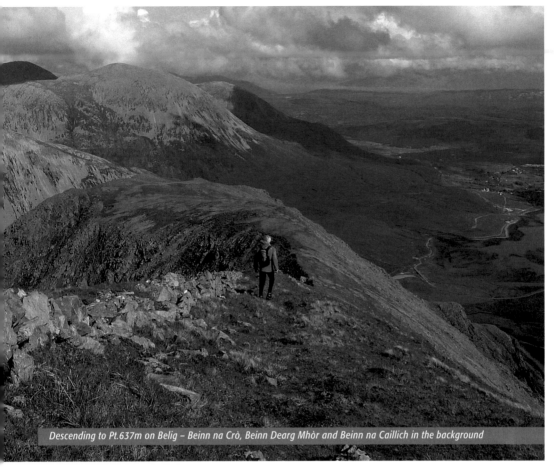

Descending to Pt.637m on Belig – Beinn na Crò, Beinn Dearg Mhòr and Beinn na Caillich in the background

Looking up the Allt na Dunaiche to the route into upper Choire a' Càise

Looking down the steep wall from the recess below the parallel-sided chimney of the Summit Tower on the North Ridge of Clach Glas (see p205). The climber below is on the platform rib. In the background are Marsco, left, and Garbh-bheinn, right

Sgùrr nan Each, Clach Glas & Blàbheinn (Clach Glas Traverse)

*C*omparable in quality to the Cuillin Ridge, this extended traverse is a major undertaking requiring confidence and ability in equal measure, along with good route-finding skills. Many will find a rope useful as some sections are exposed and the rock is poor in places. The route is committing and while escape may be possible, it will never be straightforward

About to skirt the rock fins before the steep slabby wall on the West Ridge of Sgùrr nan Each. The West Summit lies beyond and Garbh-bheinn to the right

Sgùrr nan Each – Blàbheinn

Summits: Pt.623m ▲ ; Sgùrr nan Each ▲ ;
West Summit ▲ ; Clach Glas ▲ ; Blàbheinn ▲ ;
South Top ▲ ; Optional – Garbh-bheinn ▲
Terrain: Grade 2–3 Scramble (Sgùrr nan Each);
Moderate Grade Rock Climb (Clach Glas);
Difficult Grade Rock Climb (5m Wall & 20m
Chimney) Blàbheinn
Distance: 10km; 6.25 miles
Ascent & Descent: 1150m; 3775ft
Time: 6hrs 30mins–7hrs 30mins
Start & Finish: Blàbheinn car park on Loch
Slapin (NG 5608 2156)

This route extends the traverse of Clach Glas (786m) by starting up Sgùrr nan Each (720m) and finishing up the 20m chimney on Blàbheinn's North-East Face. This involves a few places with climbing to the grade of Difficult, but only for a couple of moves. However,

there is much exposure and many may require the reassurance of a rope and climbing kit. A major stumbling block on the route (and there are a few thought-provoking sections), is the exposed 5m Wall between Clach Glas and Blàbheinn. After rain this can be dauntingly wet and greasy for anyone without climbing equipment. However, it could be avoided by descending north-west down the gully to its right and climbing broken walls to the terrace above (see p208).

If the full traverse doesn't appeal, then Sgùrr nan Each (an easier section) can be avoided by ascending via Choire a' Càise (see diagram p199). Blàbheinn can also be left out by descending south before the 5m Wall and following the rough and tedious scree down below the North-East Face of Blàbheinn.

The traverse can also be tackled in a 24km day from Sligachan by ascending to the Màm a' Phobuill on Marsco (see p177), traversing rough terrain south round Coire nam Bruadaran to Druim Eadar Dà Choire, ascending Garbh-bheinn's North Ridge (see p195), then descending the South-East Ridge to Clach Glas.

For the return to Sligachan, descend the scree-filled Dogleg Gully with care into Coire Dubh. It is important to keep high in the corrie to clear the deep-cut gorges of the upper burns, after which the south side of the main burn can be followed to Loch an Athain and the Glen Sligachan path (see below, opposite & map p190).

Approach

From the car park, return to the road and walk north to the bridge over the Allt na Dunaiche. Turn left onto the Blàbheinn path and follow it up past two water-falls linked by a gorge. A bit beyond the second water-fall, leave the path for the hillside on the right and climb the broad and initially boggy ridge towards the rocky prow of the South-East Ridge of Sgùrr nan Each.

Ascent

Climb the prow direct, heading slightly left of centre following ill-defined faultlines, scrambling and weaving in and out of crags on stones and grass, to reach the cairned summit of Pt.623m. The route is quite worn and less precipitous than it appears from below.

Ascend the grassy ridge beyond, then weave up through boulders and short scrambles to a rocky crest leading to the main summit and cairn. Scramble down the West Ridge on slabby rocks to a grassy top, then go left round the fins of rock on the ridge to regain the crest (*see p201 & opposite*). Continue to the top of a steep slabby wall, barring access to the col below.

There are **two ways down**: **(1)** Descend the slabby wall near its left edge (looking down) to reach a wide crack and descend it to the col (Grade 2–3).

The steep slabby wall forming the crux of the West Ridge of Sgùrr nan Each

(2) Further to the left, descend left then diagonally right down an easier angled and more fractured slab to reach the col (Grade 1–2).

From the col, scramble up to the ridge and follow it over the grassy West Summit and a step over a chockstone where the ridge narrows, to reach easier ground above the col between the West Summit of Sgùrr nan Each and Garbh-bheinn's South-East Ridge. Turn south and follow the rim of upper Choire a' Càise

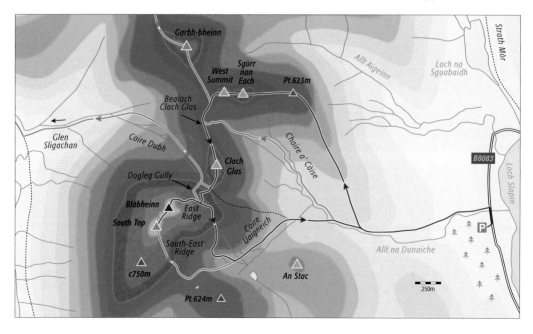

The traverse of Sgùrr nan Each to Clach Glas and Blàbheinn, viewed from Garbh-bheinn's South-East Ridge

round over rocks and grass on ill-defined paths to Bealach Clach Glas, at the foot of the North Ridge of Clach Glas. This bealach is the left-hand exit from upper Choire a' Càise, the approach for anyone not wishing to climb Sgùrr nan Each first (*diagram p199*).

While some of the difficulties on the North Ridge of Clach Glas can be avoided by ledges and gullies on the right (Coire Dubh side), the generally loose terrain can be more effort than it is worth. Sticking on or near to the crest is often the best tactic and usually involves the best rock. The scrambling is in the Grade 2–3 range, with easier sections in between.

From **Bealach Clach Glas**, climb a short wall and ascend easier ground to the foot of a stepped slab. Climb it without difficulty on the left and continue up easier ground to reach a rocky crest. Climb this directly or via slabbier rock to the right.

Descend to a small col then climb a brown slab. A short step down leads to a grassy section. Follow the line of least resistance over some small pinnacles to a steeper descent of the crest, to arrive above a col with a chockstone and scree gullies on either side. Descend to the left then cut back right to the col.

Regain the ridge and follow a section of path to a mossy-topped pinnacle. Pass this on the right, or climb over it with some precarious finishing moves on blocks forming the top of a hole in the pinnacle.

The start of the North Ridge of Clach Glas

Small pinnacle with a hole through it on the North Ridge of Clach Glas, Garbh-bheinn in the distance

An open corner gives access to the platform rib below the Summit Tower on the North Ridge of Clach Glas

Another section of path is followed right of a small pinnacle with a hole through it, then before the path ends, ascend to regain the ridge crest and arrive at a constricted notch with a small chockstone in it.

A chimney dyke leads straight up from this but looks very unattractive, so descend slightly until you can traverse out right to gain easier ground. Climb straight up gabbro slabs to regain the ridge crest. Continue over and round small pinnacles, until it is possible to traverse down and right into the scree gully below the impressive **Summit Tower**.

The right-hand side of the tower has a large open corner which is the line of the route. Start up the corner but quit it early on for a groove in its right edge and follow this to a platform rib below a steep slabby west-facing wall, characterised by a diamond-shaped roof in its lower left-hand section and a dark parallel-sided hanging chimney in its upper right. This wall is exposed and sustained climbing (Moderate) and many may need the reassurance of a rope.

Climb straight up towards the diamond-shaped roof, then traverse diagonally right below it (sometimes wet) to ledges in a recess below the parallel-sided chimney (about 10m, belay possible). Now traverse left below roofs to pass behind a stubby pinnacle on the edge and gain its top (*photo p186–7*).

The steep west-facing wall of the Summit Tower, directly above the platform rib on the North Ridge of Clach Glas

Scramble a short way up slabby rock in a highly exposed position, then move right into the relative security of the upper part of the parallel-sided chimney, taking care with gravel and stones underfoot. A massive pyramidal block further right provides a belay (10m). Climb the chimney then a right-slanting fault to gain easier ground. The slabby summit ridge narrows to a transverse cleft, then widens again to the mossy rocks of the summit (*see p206*).

From the summit, the upper section of the South

Ridge leads down to **The Imposter**, a steep blocky step where the Summit Tower joins the continuation of the South Ridge below. It was named by the first ascensionists who found it easier in ascent than it looked!

There are **three ways to tackle the step: (1)** The first completely avoids it via a chimney on the East Face of the Summit Tower, overlooking Loch Slapin (*see diagrams following page*). Return a short distance back to the transverse cleft splitting the summit ridge and scramble down the mossy break on the east (Loch

Descent to the square-cut chimney avoiding The Imposter

Square-cut chimney on Loch Slapin side, avoiding Imposter

Descending the South Ridge to The Imposter on the Summit Tower of Clach Glas. A steep step down utilising a dubious cracked block, gains the horizontal continuation of the South Ridge, below the person. Stac Ruadh and Marsco in the background with Sgùrr nan Gillean and the Cuillin Ridge beyond and flat-topped MacLeod's Tables in the distance

Slapin) side to grassy ledges. Cross these to an old cairn marking the top of a wide square-cut chimney. Descend the chimney then follow grassy ledges right (looking down) to emerge at the foot of the Summit Tower, on the horizontal continuation of the South Ridge below the *The Imposter* and the blocky step.

The other two ways necessitate descending the upper South Ridge of the Summit Tower directly to *The Imposter*. **(2)** From the summit, descend slabby rock to a trough on the arete leading to the final step of *The Imposter,* which is formed by a dubious cracked block. Using the block, make some steep and exposed moves down to a basalt dyke on the horizontal continuation South Ridge. A lightning strike has made the rock very unstable hereabouts.

(3) Alternatively, descend as for (2) to the cracked block, but then down slabby rock on the left (looking down) diagonally away from the arete, to reach the ledge utilised by the chimney descent (1) and follow it right (looking down) to below the cracked block. Great care should be taken on these exposed routes and the reassurance of a rope is strongly recommended.

Having gained the easier horizontal continuation of the South Ridge below, follow the line of least resistance down the fractured arete to a slab on the left (Loch Slapin side) and descend this to broken ground, then a small col, from where the path swings right on easier ground following the line of the ridge.

The path then merges into stony slabs which are descended to broken ground and a ledge which leads round left to a slabby rampline and short chimney on the Loch Slapin side (*see diagram following page*).

Traverse rocky ledges back right to the ridge crest and descend to a col. Ahead is the **Bealach Tower**. Ascend the ridge to just short of the tower's summit and turn it on the Loch Slapin side, by a path traversing round to the left. The path becomes a rocky ledge which skirts the tower and leads to a col spanned by an impressive rock-bridge, before a minor pinnacle. Traverse horizontally right to gain a grassy and stony arete leading to a grassy col known as the **'Putting Green'**.

It is possible to exit here without including Blàbheinn, by descending the rocky gully on the left (Loch Slapin side), then down tedious scree below Blàbheinn's

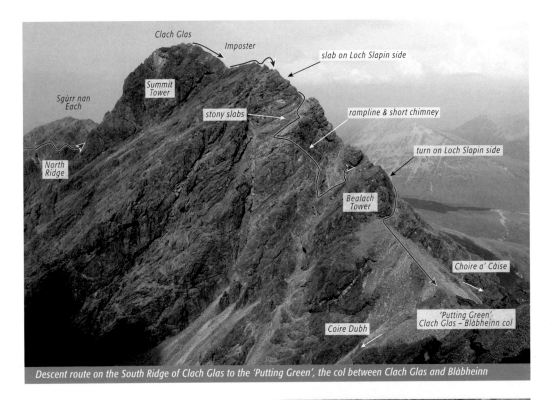

Clach Glas

Imposter

slab on Loch Slapin side

Summit
Tower

Sgùrr nan
Each

stony slabs

rampline & short chimney

North
Ridge

turn on Loch Slapin side

Bealach
Tower

Choire a' Càise

Coire Dubh

'Putting Green'
Clach Glas – Blàbheinn col

Descent route on the South Ridge of Clach Glas to the 'Putting Green', the col between Clach Glas and Blàbheinn

East Ridge

20m Chimney

Blàbheinn
North-East Face

blocky fault

upper
gully
hidden

5m
Wall

gully

possible
alternatives
to 5m Wall

'Putting Green'
Clach Glas – Blàbheinn col

Dogleg Gully

Coire Dubh

Ascent route from the 'Putting Green' to the 5m Wall and 20m Chimney on the North-East Face of Blàbheinn

Passing the chockstone in the 20m Chimney. The rock is well-worn, but the holds are good and the line is obvious

North-East Face to the path into Choire a' Càise. The scree on the right (Coire Dubh side) leads to the foot of Dogleg Gully and a route down the north side of the corrie to Srath na Crèitheach and Glen Sligachan.

Cross the 'Putting Green' and ascend to a narrow notch below a steep little wall which bars further progress. This is the **5m Wall** (Difficult) which can be wet and slimy. The wall ends on a shifting scree slope and needs a gentle exit. There is protection and a belay at the top. A large terrace then leads right.

Nearing the top of the awkward 5m Wall

If the wall proves unclimbable then descend the gully on the right (Coire Dubh side) for about 12m. Above a terrace on the Blàbheinn side, a boulder-filled gully or a slanting groove could be climbed to reach the terrace beyond the 5m Wall. Another alternative would be to return to the 'Putting Green', descend left into Coire Dubh to the start of Dogleg Gully, then scramble up that (Grade 1–2) to the East Ridge of Blàbheinn (*diagrams p203, 208*).

From the 5m Wall, traverse up and right on a terrace, then back left up a blocky fault to large bay below a wide chimney with a chockstone halfway. Climb the **20m Chimney** (Moderate), polished in places, to surmount the chockstone and finish up a cracked corner. The chimney can be protected and there is a belay at the top. Scramble over blocks to the top of Dogleg Gully and the East Ridge of Blàbheinn at NG 5327 2176.

Turn right and ascend the rocky path to the summit of Blàbheinn, just 330m and about 15mins further on. After all the effort, it is worthwhile including Blàbheinn's South Top in this route (*see p213*).

Descent

From the main summit of Blàbheinn descend east, then south back down the East Ridge (*diagram p212*) to Coire Uaigneich. Continue down towards Choire a' Càise, crossing the Allt Coire Uaigneich near the bottom to reach and cross the Allt na Dunaiche and join the approach route.

If including Blàbheinn's South Top (926m), then either return back to the main summit and descend the East Ridge, or descend the South-East Ridge to the col below Pt.624m (*diagram p213*), then descend left (east) into Coire Uaigneich to reach Choire a' Càsie.

High on Blàbheinn's South Ridge – 2km of steep paths and pleasant scrambling, with little scree until the very top

Blàbheinn

L ike Sgùrr nan Gillean, Blàbheinn's proximity to the road and picturesque setting makes it one of the most photographed mountains on Skye. There the similarities end, as the ascent of Blàbheinn by its East Ridge is a straightforward and popular hillwalk. For anyone wanting more of a challenge, the South Ridge offers some enjoyable scrambling and stunning views

Blàbheinn, left, and Clach Glas from Loch Slapin. Blàbheinn's East Ridge follows the left to right line of weakness across the main face, right of Central Gully which divides the summits. The left-hand skyline is the broad South-East Ridge

East Ridge

Summits: *Blàbheinn* ▲ *; South Top* ▲
Terrain: *Hillwalk*
Distance: *8.5km; 5.25 miles*
Ascent & Descent: *919m*
Time: *4–5hrs*
Start & Finish: *Blàbheinn car park on Loch Slapin (NG 5608 2156)*

The most popular route on Blàbheinn (929m) offers an easy but rather laborious ascent. There is a lot of scree in places and the route is ill-defined in its lower reaches, so it requires effort and route-finding skills in poor visibility. Nevertheless, the mountain scenery is impressively atmospheric, especially in the mist.

Approach

From the car park, return to the road and walk north to the bridge over the Allt na Dunaiche. Turn left onto the Blàbheinn path and follow it into lower Choire a'

Càise, to where it crosses over the burn. Continue ascending west to reach the burn draining Coire Uaigneich below Blàbheinn's South Face. Cross this to its right (west) side and ascend more steeply on the well-defined path to enter upper Coire Uaigneich, where the path levels out at a grassy alp (NG 53675 21226), left of the steep lower buttresses of the East Ridge and some 150m before a massive boulder.

At this point the path meets a series of burns draining the south-eastern flanks of Blàbheinn, which culminate in a prominent parallel-sided cleft, some 30m above the path, with a wide eroded path on the hillside below and to its left.

Ascent

Follow the eroded path, swing left round a craggy spur, then cross right over a scree-fan and up a small grassy spur to the base of a shallow scree-filled gully. This point can also be gained more directly via a steeper path right of the prominent parallel-sided cleft.

Scramble up the scree-filled gully, using the rock on either side to speed progress, to reach grassy slopes

From Upper Coire Uaigneich, the start of the route to the East Ridge is largely hidden from below and ill-defined

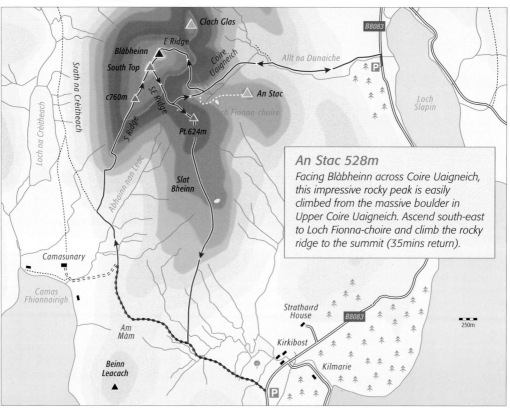

An Stac 528m

Facing Blàbheinn across Coire Uaigneich, this impressive rocky peak is easily climbed from the massive boulder in Upper Coire Uaigneich. Ascend south-east to Loch Fionna-choire and climb the rocky ridge to the summit (35mins return).

to South Top

terrace

steep
loose
chimney

rocky
prow

Great Gully

col between
summits

*Possible routes to the South Top from the col at the top of
Great Gully, between the main summit and the South Top*

then scree and finally, the crest of the East Ridge
above the buttresses and towers of the impressive
North-East Face. Follow the ridge round the edge of
the cliffs in a north-west and westerly direction,
through a section of slabby rock with some easy

scrambling (and assorted paths) to the final grassy
path leading to the summit.

Descent

It is possible to descend Great Gully, the wide gully
dividing the summits on the Loch Slapin side, but this
is filled with tiring scree and not recommended.

There are **two options**: (1) Reverse the line of
ascent on the East Ridge. Alternatively, climb the
South Top (*see below*), then return to the main
summit and descend the East Ridge. (2) Climb the
South Top, then descend the South-East Ridge. From
the main summit, descend south-west to the col at
the top of Great Gully and below the rocky prow of
the South Top. Climb the prow directly or via a narrow
terrace on the left (Loch Slapin) side (both Grade 2) to
a short ridge and follow it to the South Top (926m). It
is also possible to climb the steep chimney further left
but this is unpleasant and loose.

From the South Top cairn, descend on a cairned path
through scree and boulders in a southerly direction
passing below a small crag on the crest. This requires
careful route-finding in poor visibility. Keep right where
the path becomes ill-defined and descend to the col
and lochan below Pt.624m. On the descent there are
loose stones and gravel and some simple scrambling
(Grade 1–2) requiring care. Turn left (east) and
descend into Upper Coire Uaigneich, passing the
massive boulder, to gain the approach path and
follow it back to the start.

small crag on crest

South Top

col between
summits

Blàbheinn
summit

South Ridge

no!

South
Buttress

South-East
Ridge

Great
Gully

Upper Coire Uaigneich

Pt.624m &
Slat Bheinn

From the South Top, the broad South-East Ridge can be used to descend to Kirkibost or Coire Uaigneich and Loch Slapin

Loch na Crèitheach and Blàbheinn from Sgùrr na Stri. The South Ridge is on the right with Pt.624 lower right

South Ridge

Summits: *Blàbheinn* ▲ *; South Top* ▲ *; Pt.624m* ▲
Terrain: *Hillwalk to the lower South Top. Gaining the higher Main Summit is a Grade 2 Scramble*
Distance: *13.5km; 8.25 miles (Main Summit)*
Ascent & Descent: *995m; 3270ft (Main Summit)*
Time: *5hrs 40mins–6hrs 40mins (Main Summit)*
Start & Finish: *Parking on B8083, south-west of Kirkibost & Kilmarie (NG 5452 1717)*

This route is the best on the mountain and offers a 2km mix of grassy paths and easy scrambling in a magnificent situation. There is some scree, but it is limited to the very top.

The mountain ambiance is first class, with panoramic views through the pinnacled gullies of the West Face to the Small Isles of Eigg and Rùm, the pasture of Camasunary, jagged tops of the Cuillin Ridge, gunmetal lochs of Srath na Crèitheach and the pink granite monoliths of Stac Ruadh and Marsco.

However, it's a lot less popular than the East Ridge, as it's longer and the main Munro summit can only be gained by descending a short steep Grade 2 scramble from the South Top (926m and a Munro Top), which needs re-ascending to return to the starting point.

Approach
This is the same approach as for Sgùrr na Stri from Kirkibost and the B8083 (*see p191*). From the parking, follow the signposted track north-west to the Am Màm and views over Camasunary to Sgùrr na Stri, then descend the other side towards the farmhouse at Camasunary. Just before a sharp left-hand bend leave the track for a cairned path on the right and traverse the hillside towards the grassy base of the South Ridge. The path is boggy in places and is marked with occasional red paint spots.

Cross a couple of small burns and descend slightly to cross the Abhainn nan Leac below a picturesque small waterfall. Continue on the traversing path to about NG 5214 1942, where it cuts through a line of large gabbro boulders on the vague grassy spur below the rocky prow of the lower South Ridge (*map p212*).

Ascent
Climb the spur on an initially ill-defined path to below the crag forming the rocky prow of the main ridge. Turn this on the right and traverse the right side of the ridge for a short distance, then zigzag steeply straight up on a rough path, to gain a col on the ridge at about 370m. Just west of the col there is a spectacular panorama over Camasunary.

From the col, a grassy ridge develops into rocky steps interspersed with grassy cols. At about 550m, the ridge starts to level off after a short scramble above a col and some spectacular views can be had down through the rocky clefts of the West Face.

A top at c760m turns out to be a false summit, but

the South Top can be seen from here and the path now weaves up through boulders and grass, to boulders and scree and the summit cairn. The main summit of Blàbheinn is clear to the north-east and can only be reached by scrambling.

There are **two ways to the main summit** (*diagram p213*): **(1)** Stick to the crest of the ridge. Scramble down, initially on the left (west) side, then on the right (east) side, to where a few steep moves (Grade 2–3) down the awkwardly undercut rocky prow gain the col. A rope might be reassuring here.

(2) Alternatively, follow the path on the crest of the ridge for about 37 paces then break off right (east) on an earthy path leading down to the top of a steep, loose chimney. From the top of the chimney, gain a narrow terrace of orange rock on the left and traverse carefully across the wall to the col (Grade 2). The loose chimney can be descended, but is unpleasant.

Ascend the ridge to the main summit. It is necessary to return to the South Top to descend. Climbing the prow direct (1), feels easier in ascent.

Descent

From the South Top cairn, descend in a southerly direction on a cairned path through scree and boulders, passing below a small crag on the crest. This requires careful route-finding in poor visibility. Keep right where the path becomes ill-defined and descend to the col below Pt.624m. On the descent there are loose

Looking back to Blàbheinn from Slat Bheinn. The South Ridge is on the left

stones and gravel and some simple scrambling (Grade 1–2) requiring care (*diagram p213*).

From the grassy col and lochan, ascend Pt.624m then cross the broad grassy ridge of Slat Bheinn, weaving between crags and lochans and heading for the road which can be seen in the distance. At the end, overlooking Kirkibost and Strathaird, descend in a south-westerly direction and cross the moor above the fence to reach the track just before it descends to the gate and the burn. Follow the track back to the start.

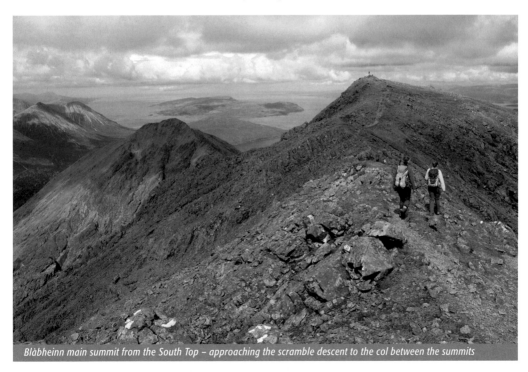

Blàbheinn main summit from the South Top – approaching the scramble descent to the col between the summits

EASTERN RED HILLS

*Looking east to Beinn na Caillich and the mainland
from the East Ridge of Beinn Dearg Mhòr*

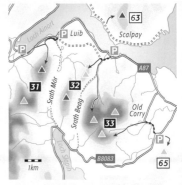

The North Ridge of Glas-Bheinn Mhòr from the shore of Loch Ainort, north of Luib

Glas-Bheinn Mhòr & Belig

*T*he most westerly of the Eastern Red Hills, Glas-Bheinn Mhòr appears little more than a tedious granite scree lump when viewed from the zigzags on the A87 down to Loch Ainort. However, make the effort to look up when passing Luib and its mountain credentials are revealed; an impressively steep North Ridge with extensive sea views, that's well worth the effort

The wall on Glas-Bheinn Mhòr, looking down to Luib and the Isle of Raasay in the distance

From Loch Ainort

Summits: *Glas-Bheinn Mhòr* ▲*; Pt.637m* ▲*;*
Belig ▲
Terrain: *Hillwalk*
Distance: *9.5km; 6 miles*
Ascent & Descent: *890m; 2920ft*
Time: *4–5hrs*
Start & Finish: *Start of the old road to Moll (NG 5436 2684) or the layby on Loch Ainort at (NG 5490 2711)*

Climbed in isolation, Glas-Bheinn Mhòr (569m) gives a 3hr up and down ascent, which makes it great for a short day. Combining it with higher Belig (702m) to the south makes for a more satisfying outing, but one that's not much longer. The only downside is the fast moving traffic on the A87 beside Loch Ainort.

Approach
Whichever parking you choose involves walking beside the A87 at the start and finish. Follow the lochshore

north-east until forced onto the road verge by the trees at Aricharnach. Follow the verge to an access road on the left leading down to a lochside house. On the opposite (south) side of the road is a gate in a new fence, before a green cattle shed on the lower flanks of Glas-Bheinn Mhòr. Cross the road and the ditch and go through the gate. The route from Luib (*see following pages*) gains the same access point via the upper old road, which leads to the barn.

Ascent
Ascend beside the fence to gain the open hillside. Move left to the grassy North Ridge and climb this following fence posts and the scattered traces of an old boundary wall of granite boulders.

The wall becomes more prominent as height is gained, with sea views over Loch Ainort and Loch na Cairidh and north to Scalpay and Raasay. The steep start eases off after about 1km and the wall leads to the summit, marked with a large cairn and great views south-west to Belig and Garbh-bheinn.

Go over the top and down the South-West Ridge to

Looking north to Glas-Bheinn Mhòr and its capping wall, from Pt.637m on Belig. To the left is the prominent summit cone of Dùn Cana on the Isle of Raasay. The small hill in shade on the mainland below is Meall a' Mhaoil. To the left are the double summits of Glamaig with Meall Dearg Mheadhonach to their left. Right of these on the coast in the near distance is Ben Tianavaig, with The Storr above it in the far distance

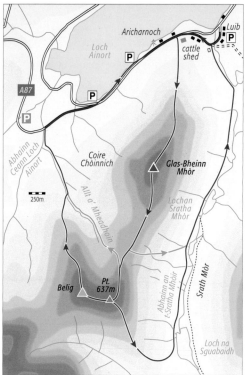

the col below Belig. Ascend the stubby rocky spur on the left side of the corrie, starting up scree then grass to the right of the craggy nose, to gain the ridge and follow it to the top of Pt.637m, Belig's eastern summit. Swing round the rim of upper Coire Chòinnich to the main summit.

Descent

There are **two options**: (1) The nose of Belig's North Ridge terminates in crags, which are avoided on their left (west) side. Descend the ridge over scree and grass, to about NG 5435 2454, then cut diagonally north-west from the ridge down steep, rough and tedious scree paths, to skirt below the crags and gain easier grassy ground. Below the crags, head north into Coire Chòinnich to reach the Allt a' Mheadhoin and cross over.

(2) Return round the rim of upper Coire Chòinnich , go over Pt.637m and back down to the col between Belig and Glas-Bheinn Mhòr. Descend north and north-west to meet and follow the right (east) bank of the Allt a' Mheadhoin.

Both routes now follow the green right (east) bank of the Allt a' Mheadhoin to the Abhainn Ceann Loch Ainort, which leads to a gate in the fence before the bridge over the A87. Turn right along the road verge back to the parking.

From Luib

Summits: *Glas-Bheinn Mhòr* ▲ *; Pt.637m* ▲ *; Belig* ▲
Terrain: *Hillwalk*
Distance: *13km; 8 miles*
Ascent & Descent: *890m; 2920ft*
Time: *5–6hrs*
Start & Finish: *Luib old road (NG 5644 2785)*

This is a more attractive route than that from Loch Ainort. It is longer, but the walk through Strath Mòr opens up what for many, will be a previously unexplored part of Skye's mountain landscape.

Approach
Turn off the A87 at Luib and park on a section of the old road at the start of the village. Parking is limited and some is private, so make the most of available space. Continue on the loop of the old road south then north-west, up and over to reach the A87 at a green cattle shed. Follow the road verge past the barn, then cross a ditch to a gate in the fence and go through.

Ascent
Ascend beside the fence and wall to the summit of

Glas-Bheinn Mhòr, as for the route from Loch Ainort (see *p219*). Descend south to the col below Belig, then ascend to Pt.637m and the summit of Belig.

Descent
There are **two options**: (1) Return to the top of Pt.637m and from its very south-east aspect start a steep descent down the South Ridge on rock and grass with some small sections of easy scrambling. The ridge is steep and feels exposed in places, although the difficulties can all be turned with careful attention to route-finding.

At the base of the ridge swing round north to gain animal tracks on the west side of Loch na Sguabaidh and follow them north to join the path beside the Abhainn an t-Sratha Mhòir. Continue north on this path past Lochan Sratha Mhòr to reach the old road at Luib and the parking. This route is both steeper rockier and longer than the alternative below, however the South Ridge is spectacular and walking the length of Srath Mòr gives a refreshing remoteness.

(2) Alternatively, retrace your steps to the col between Pt.637m and Glas-Bheinn Mhòr and descend steeply east to reach the path on the left (west) side of the Abhainn an t-Sratha Mhòir and follow it to Luib as described above. This alternative descent is about 1.5km shorter than descending Belig's South Ridge.

The southern aspect of Beinn na Crò presents an impressive profile when viewed from the west shore of Loch Slapin

Glas-Bheinn Bheag
& Beinn na Crò

*L*ike Glas-Bheinn Mhòr, Beinn na Crò's north-south orientation gives it an
impressive profile when viewed from either end. Its north end is largely hidden
from the A87, but the southern aspect when viewed from west Loch Slapin, does
the mountain justice. But with the Blàbheinn massif such a close neighbour,
Beinn na Crò is easily missed. That is a shame. It's a superb peak in a fine
location and a worthy objective for any mountain climber

Approaching the bridge over the Allt Strollamus on the old Luib road below Glas-Bheinn Bheag

From Strollamus

Summits: Beinn na Crò ▲ ; Glas-Bheinn Bheag ▲
Terrain: Hillwalk
Distance: 9.5km; 6 miles
Ascent & Descent: 650m; 2105ft
Time: 3hrs 30mins–4hrs 30mins
Start & Finish: Layby on the south side of the
A87 south-east of Strollamus (NG 5987 2670)

*When climbed from the north, the grassy but
surprisingly steep and well-defined summit ridge of
Beinn na Crò (572m), contrasts with the flat-topped
and the much lower Glas-Bheinn Bheag (350m).
The best access point is the old road between
Luib and Strollamus, with a return along the well-
established path through Srath Beag and An Slugan.*

Approach
The starting point for this route is a layby below a
ruined cottage with a prominent dark green cattle
shed above it. This is easily seen when approaching
on the A87 from the west, but is slightly hidden by
roadside trees when coming from the east. There
is also signposted parking about 250m further
west on the east side of the A87, just before the
bridge over the Allt Strollamus.

Go through the gate below the ruin and follow
animal paths through the bracken on the ruin's left
side. Head straight up towards the cattle shed to
reach a gate, which gives access to a track – the old
road between Strollamus and Luib.

Turn right and follow the track slightly uphill towards
Glas-Bheinn Bheag and cross the bridge over the Allt
Strollamus. Just after this, a path leaves the track on
the left and follows the Allt Strollamus down An

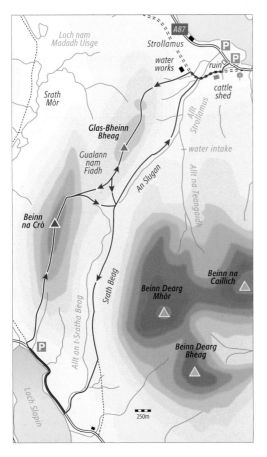

Slugan to Srath Beag and Loch Slapin; the return route. Continue on the track to just short of a fenced enclosure round the small Strollamus Water Treatment Works on the eastern flanks of Glas-Bheinn Bheag.

Ascent
Starting about 60m south of the works, climb the grass and heather hillside, scattered with round granite boulders, to reach a burn. Continue beside it making the most of grassy areas, to reach the broad North Ridge and fine views south to Beinn Dearg Mhòr and Beinn na Caillich.

Follow the open ridge over rock and grass, dotted with tiny lochans, with Beinn na Crò rising steadily ahead. A line of old fence posts lead to the cairned summit of Glas-Bheinn Bheag.

Descend to the Gualann nam Fiadh, the col between Glas-Bheinn Bheag and Beinn na Crò, cross over, and make a short ascent to gain Beinn na Crò's grassy North Ridge. This proves to be unexpectedly well-defined and steepens as it becomes rockier. The ridge then levels out and an old circle of rocks is passed to reach the cairned summit.

Descent
Retrace your steps down the North Ridge, then go due east below the Gualann nam Fiadh col. Descend steeply to a path at the watershed between Srath Beag to the south and An Slugan to the north. Turn left and follow the path north beside the Allt Strollamus to the bridge and the track.

Descending the North Ridge; Loch nam Madadh Uisge and Luib to the left with Dùn Cana and Raasay beyond

Approaching the summit on the South Ridge of Beinn na Crò

From Loch Slapin

Summits: *Beinn na Crò* ▲ *; Glas-Bheinn Bheag* ▲
Terrain: *Hillwalk*
Distance: *10km; 6.25 miles*
Ascent & Descent: *650m; 2130ft*
Time: *3hrs 40mins–4hrs 40mins*
Start & Finish: *North end of Loch Slapin at foot-path through Strath Mòr (NG 5653 2238)*

Loch Slapin provides a magnificent backdrop for an ascent from the south. A return back down the South Ridge makes a pleasant if short route. A longer and more interesting round descends the North Ridge, then goes east to the path in Srath Beag. This gives a direct if rough descent to Loch Slapin.

Ascent

From the parking, follow the Srath Mòr footpath for about 120m to where the fence turns up the hillside and ascend its left side to reach the obvious incut burn.

Keeping to the burn's left, climb the steep spur, initially on heather and grass, then over rockier ground to reach the summit cairn. Follow the grassy ridge north, then more steeply down the rocky North Ridge to an altitude of about 420m, where it starts to level out. Drop down to the Gualann nam Fiadh col. Glas-Bheinn Bheag can be climbed from here via its South Ridge.

Descent

From the Gualann nam Fiadh col, descend east to the watershed between Srath Beag and An Slugan and the through path. Turn right and descend Srath Beag to the road. The path is quite rough and boggy in places. Walk back along the road to the start.

The South Ridge above Loch Slapin

225

Beinn na Caillich from picturesque Loch Cill Chriosd in Strath Suardal. The East Face is in shade on the right

Beinn Dearg Bheag, Beinn Dearg Mhòr & Beinn na Caillich

"Walk up Beinn-a-caillich, or, the hill of the old hag; one of those picturesque mountains that made such a figure from the sea. After ascending a small part, find its sides covered with vast loose stones, like the paps of Jura, the shelter of ptarmigans: the top flat and naked, with an artificial cairn, of a most enormous size, reported to have been the place of sepulture of a gigantic woman in the days of Fingal. The prospect to the West was that of desolation itself; a savage series of rude mountains, discoloured black and red, as if by the rage of fire."

Thomas Pennant: A Tour in Scotland, 1772

Beinn Dearg Bheag, left, Beinn Dearg Mhòr and Beinn na Caillich, from Strath Suardal

From Strath Suardal

Summits: *Beinn Dearg Bheag* ▲ *; Beinn Dearg Mhòr* ▲ *; Beinn na Caillich* ▲
Terrain: *Hillwalk*
Distance: *11km; 6.75 miles*
Ascent & Descent: *975m; 3200ft*
Time: *4hrs 30mins–5hrs 30mins*
Start & Finish: *North side of the B8083, before steep descent to Strath Suardal (NG 6278 2198)*

Pennant made his ascent from the now ruined house at Coire-chat-achan (Coriatachan), which also hosted Johnson and Boswell on their tour the following year; they declined to climb the hill, discouraged by poor weather and the steepness. Whether you tackle Beinn na Caillich's East Face in ascent or descent as here, is a matter of preference. Either way, as Pennant observed, there's lots of scree and boulders to negotiate.

Approach

A small parking area near a chambered cairn serves the path on the south side of Strath Suardal. This path follows the line of the small railway which transported Skye Marble from quarries at the south end of the strath to Broadford. From the parking, follow a path on the right (north) side of the road towards the Broadford River to reach a footbridge. Cross over the river and continue on a track through the farmyard and past the ruined walls of Coire-chat-achan on the right, to a point where the fence on the left ends, just before the new house and the tarmac road.

Leave the track here and head left over heather and grass towards the East Ridge of Beinn Dearg Bheag. Cross the Allt Beinn Deirge to gain the base of the ridge.

Ascent

Follow a path up onto Beinn Dearg Bheag (582m) to gain the small cairn on the summit. From there, make a rocky descent round the rim of Coire Odhar to

227

Pennant's view to Beinn Dearg Mhòr, Blàbheinn and The Cuillin, from the West Ridge of Beinn na Caillich

Bealach Coire Sgreamhach. The ascent ahead looks like steep and unpleasant scree, but is not as bad as it appears (and certainly no worse than it is in descent), providing sufficient effort is put into zigzagging to make the most of the grass patches. The slope leads directly to the tall cairn on the rocky summit of Beinn Dearg Mhòr (709m) and fine views west to Pennant's fire-baked black and red mountains.

Descend the North-East Ridge round the rim of Coire Rèidh (*photo 216–7*) to gain the foot of the West Ridge of Beinn na Caillich (732m) and ascend to the large summit cairn, trig point and spectacular sea views.

Descent

From the summit, go down the broad East Face on grass and assorted paths through the boulders (*photo p10*) to reach a better defined path on the right (south) bank of a burn at about NG 6133 2307 and follow it down to the road. Gain the track and follow the outward route back to the parking.

Beinn Dearg Bheag and the Bealach Coire Sgreamhach from the southern flanks of Beinn Dearg Mhòr

The summit cairn on Beinn na Caillich – "reported to have been the place of sepulture of a gigantic woman in the days of Fingal"

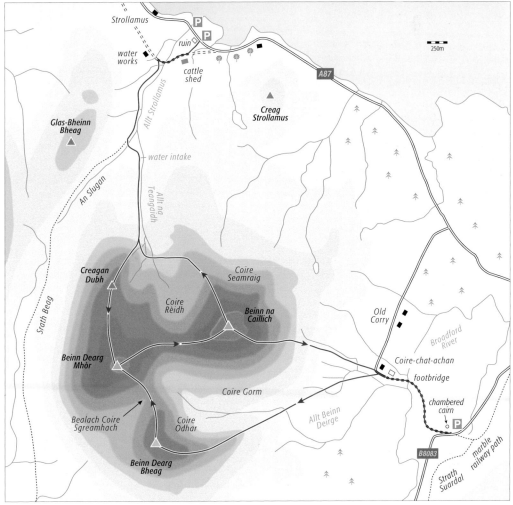

From Strollamus

Summits: *Creagan Dubh* ▲ *;*
Beinn Dearg Mhòr ▲ *; Beinn na Caillich*▲
Terrain: *Hillwalk*
Distance: *10.5km; 6.5 miles*
Ascent & Descent: *885m; 2900ft*
Time: *4hrs 15mins–5hrs 15mins*
Start & Finish: *Layby on the south side of the
A87 south-east of Strollamus (NG 5987 2670)*

*This circuit is very different, but every bit as good as
the route from Strath Suardal to the east. The main
differences are that Beinn Dearg Beag isn't included
and descending the North-West Ridge is a lot less
tiresome than the scree and boulders of the East
Face. However, following the Allt na Teangaidh might
be awkward when the water is high. The route is less
travelled than that from Strath Suardal (map p229).*

Approach
The starting point is a layby below a ruined cottage
with a prominent dark green cattle shed above it. This
is easily seen when approaching on the A87 from the
west, but is slightly hidden by roadside trees when
coming from the east. There is also signposted
parking about 250m further west on the east side of
the A87, just before the bridge over the Allt Strollamus.

Go through the gate below the ruin and follow
animal paths through the bracken on the ruin's left
side. Head straight up towards the cattle shed to
reach a gate, which gives access to a track – the old
road between Strollamus and Luib.

Turn right and immediately after the bridge over the
Allt Strollamus, turn left onto the Srath Beag footpath to
Loch Slapin. Follow this for about 700m to a concrete
block with a manhole cover (NG 5907 2592) and two
concrete posts, one with the letters WOV and one SV.
About 250m beyond is another manhole cover and a
blue concrete post with AV on it (NG 5900 2569).

Break left off the main path here and follow an
intermittent path down to the Allt Strollamus and
some large boulders at the bank. Cross the burn and
go left to a concrete post with the word WATER on it.
A rough path leads round to a weir and water intake
on the Allt na Teangaidh.

Follow the fence around the scheme and continue
on good animal paths on the right (west) side of the
burn, sticking to the grassy edge by the water where
there are animal paths and the going is generally
easiest. Shortly after a small stand of birch and rowan
trees on the opposite bank (NG 5911 2540), cross
the burn left then back right on boulders to avoid a
small erosion scar in the bank. Continue beside the
burn and ascend a path between it and the black crags
of Creagan Dubh on the right, to gain lower Coire Rèidh,
below the prominent North Ridge of Creagan Dubh.

Beinn na Caillich and Beinn Dearg Mhòr from Creagan Dubh; Beinn na Caillich and Sgùrr na Còinnich, Kylerhea, in the background and the mainland in the distance

Ascent

The grassy runnel in the centre of the North Ridge of Creagan Dubh gives easy access to the top, from where a bouldery ridge leads to the tall cairn on Beinn Dearg Mhòr (709m). Descend the North-East Ridge round the rim of Coire Rèidh to the foot of Beinn na Caillich's West Ridge and ascend to the large summit cairn, trig point and extensive sea views.

Descent

From Beinn na Caillich's summit, go down the North-West Ridge on scree and grass to reach the foot of the ridge, then contour down and west round boulder-strewn Coire Rèidh to the Allt na Teangaidh. Cross over the burn and continue descending to the foot of the North Ridge of Creagan Dubh, to regain the approach path and follow this back to the start.

The weir and water intake on the Allt na Teangaidh with Beinn na Caillich, Beinn Dearg Mhòr and Creagan Dubh, beyond

KYLERHEA

Beinn na Caillich from Sgùrr na Còinnich. Kyle of Lochalsh and the Skye Bridge can be seen to the left with the mountains of Applecross in the distance and Loch Alsh to the right

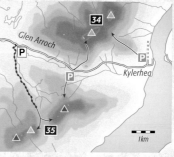

Beinn na Caillich, left, and Sgùrr na Còinnich above Kyleakin, viewed from the Skye Bridge

Beinn na Caillich
& Sgùrr na Còinnich

*D*espite being the first Skye mountains visitors will see up close, the peaks
*overlooking the Skye Bridge are usually passed by en route for the main
massifs further west. Beinn na Caillich is the lower of the two hills by a few
metres, but is a lot rockier and gives a more interesting ascent*

The trig point on the top of Sgùrr na Còinnich, Beinn na Caillich in shade behind

From Kylerhea

Summits: *Beinn Bhuidhe* ▲ ; *Beinn na Caillich* ▲ ;
Sgùrr na Còinnich ▲
Terrain: *Hillwalk*
Distance: *8km; 5 miles*
Ascent & Descent: *840m; 2760ft*
Time: *3hrs 40mins–4hrs 40mins*
Start & Finish: *Kylerhea Otter Hide car park
(NG 7866 2112)*

*In the mid-18th century some 7,000 cattle passed
over the Bealach Udal every year to the narrow strait
of Kyle Rhea, where they were tied head to tail and
swum across to the mainland, en route to market.
Today the strait is plied by a tiny vehicle ferry.*

Approach
From the south end of the car park, gain the hillside
and ascend tufted grass and heather. Initially the
going is quite rough and steep, so picking the

grassiest looking line may prove worthwhile. The
views east and south-east across Kyle Rhea to
Glenelg, the impressive bulk of Beinn Sgritheall and
Knoydart beyond, and the vehicle ferry, all prove a
welcome distraction.

After about 350m the terrain becomes grassier and
the going improves. The rounded summit of Beinn
Bhuidhe (488m) is reached after 1.5km and gives a
view north to Sgùrr na Còinnich (739m) and Beinn na
Caillich (732m), separated by Bealach nam Mulachag.
A short descent gains the foot of Sgùrr na Còinnich's
broad South-East Ridge, which is ascended for a short
way before cutting off right round the top of Coire
Buidhe to gain Bealach nam Mulachag.

Ascent
Beinn na Caillich is climbed first via the lower of two
stony ramplines on the right-hand side of its craggy
South Ridge. From the right edge of the bealach overlooking the corrie, follow a stony path to the lowest
rocks and skirt them on the right to gain the rampline.

Ascend this on grass and scree runnels, to where

Beinn na Caillich

Bealach nam Mulachag

The stony ramp on the right-hand side of the South Ridge of Beinn na Caillich

the ramp breaks out onto the better defined ridgeline. Follow this, initially grassy then rockier, with great sea views to the summit.

Return to the bealach, then ascend the grassy East Face of Sgùrr na Còinnich weaving in and out of small rocky buttresses, to reach a saddle with a tiny lochan between two knolls. Beyond these a broad ridge and final slopes lead to a large cairn and a circular trig point.

Descent

Return east to the broad ridge and follow its crest to the right-hand and more pronounced of the two knolls. From here, go east then south and south-east making the best of the grassy sections between the scree and rocks of the broad South-East Ridge, to gain the broad col before Beinn Bhuidhe. From there, go over Beinn Bhuidhe and follow the ascent line back to the start.

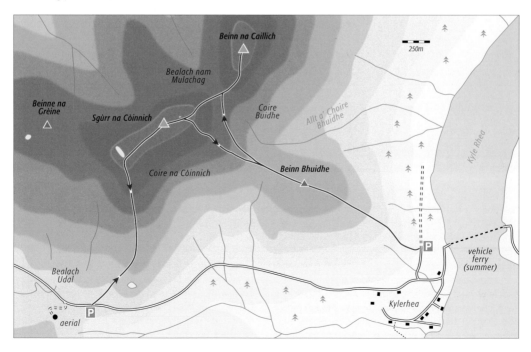

Beinn na Caillich

Bealach nam Mulachag

Beinne na Grèine

Sgùrr na Còinnich

Coire Buidhe

Allt a' Choire Bhuidhe

Coire na Còinnich

Beinn Bhuidhe

Kyle Rhea

250m

P

vehicle ferry (summer)

Bealach Udal

P

aerial

Kylerhea

The summit of Sgùrr na Còinnich from the large lochan to the south-west

From Bealach Udal

Summits: *Sgùrr na Còinnich* ▲ *; Beinn Dearg Mhòr* ▲
Terrain: *Hillwalk*
Distance: *6.5km; 4 miles*
Ascent & Descent: *780m; 2560ft*
Time: *3hrs 10mins–4hrs 10mins*
Start & Finish: *Large layby just east of Bealach Udal (NG 7554 2066)*

The shortest and fastest way to climb Beinn na Caillich and Sgùrr na Còinnich isn't a very inspiring route. The broad South Ridge of Sgùrr na Còinnich is rough and a bit dull (only equalled by the uninspiring view south to Ben Aslak) and having ascended Beinn na Caillich, the best return route to Bealach Udal involves climbing back over Sgùrr na Còinnich, the highest but least interesting of the two peaks.

Ascent

From the large layby, gain the hillside and follow it up and right over rather tedious tussocky grass and heather, to pass through the line of an old wall and gain the broad South Ridge. Ascend this weaving between scree and rocky outcrops to where the ground levels out at a large lochan. Final grassy and rocky slopes lead to the trig point on the summit.

Descend east to a broad ridge, then north-east to a saddle with a tiny lochan between two knolls. From here, continue down the grassy slopes of the broad East Ridge to Bealach nam Mulachag.

Ascend Beinn na Caillich via the lower of two stony ramplines on the right-hand side of the broad South Face (*see opposite*). From the right edge of the bealach overlooking the corrie, follow a stony path to the lowest rocks and skirt them on the right to gain the rampline. Ascend this on grass and scree runnels, to where the ramp breaks out onto the better defined South Ridge. Follow this, initially grassy then rockier, with great sea views to the summit.

Return to the bealach and climb back up Sgùrr na Còinnich's East Ridge to the summit.

Descent

Follow the line of ascent back down the South Ridge to Bealach Udal.

The stony ramp on Beinn na Caillich

Looking over Bealach na Cruinn-leum to Ben Aslak, from the flanks of Beinn Dubh a' Bhealaich

Beinn Dubh a' Bhealaich, Beinn na Seamraig, Ben Aslak & Round of Kylerhea Glen

*B*en Aslak and its two westerly neighbours are lower and less dramatic than the peaks on the north side of Bealach Udal, but offer an off the beaten track circuit with fine views of Sleat and Knoydart. Ben Aslak can also be combined with Beinn na Caillich and Sgùrr na Còinnich to the north, in a Round of Kylerhea Glen

Near the top of Beinn Dubh a' Bhealaich, looking north-east to Ben Aslak, right, and Sgùrr na Còinnich, left

Via Coire nan Cuilean

Summits: *Beinn Dubh a' Bhealach* ▲ *; Beinn na Seamraig* ▲ *; Ben Aslak* ▲ *; East Summit* ▲
Terrain: *Hillwalk*
Distance: *14.5km; 9 miles*
Ascent & Descent: *640m; 2100ft*
Time: *4 hrs 40mins–5hrs 40mins*
Start & Finish: *Laybys near the cattle grid in Glen Arroch (NG 7308 2168), 200m south-east of the bridge over the Allt Mòr*

The route starts with a 3.5km walk up a track, and ends with a 2.5km walk back down the road to the starting point. However, neither of these are quite as bad as they sound. The track allows you to avoid an otherwise tedious moorland trudge and the return along the single track road is downhill all the way and generally quiet. Most of the traffic comes from the Kyle

Rhea ferry which only carries a few cars at a time. A recent survey found Ben Aslak to be just 609m, removing its previous status as a Graham (see p10).

Approach
From the cattle grid, walk back down to the wooden bridge over the Allt Mòr. This usually has a locked barrier preventing vehicle access. Parking might be possible here, but space is tight. Cross the bridge, ascend the initial zigzags, then follow the track steadily south-east above the Allt Coire nan Cuilean. Although OS maps show the moorland to be heavily forested, this is not yet the case. The track ends at NG 7383 1906, just short of Bealach na Cruinn-leum.

Ascent
From the track end, an atv track leads almost directly to the North Ridge of Beinn Dubh a' Bhealaich (546m), which is climbed via slabby outcrops of red Torridonian sandstone to reach a small lochan. Skirt this to the east and continue to the undistinguished

239

The broad ridge of sandstone slabs leading to Beinn na Seamraig

summit and cairn.

Swing round to the right and follow a broad ridge of rocky slabs west, then ascend south-west to a high-point overlooking a lochan with the summit trig point of Beinn na Seamraig (561m) beyond. There are fine views across Sleat to Rùm and the Small Isles beyond.

Return to Beinn Dubh a' Bhealaich and descend the North Ridge to about the 450m contour mark (NG 7354 1863), from where a grassy burn leads north-east to Bealach na Cruinn-leum below Ben Aslak. Cross the bealach and ascend, initially hard going underfoot, towards a band of crags. Turn these easily on the left and ascend Ben Aslak's broad South-West

Ridge in a fine position to the summit, which is marked by a cairn on a slabby rock.

Descend to the lochan north-east of the summit, then east to the pointed but slightly lower East Summit, which gives a view over Kyle Rhea to Glenelg and the high peaks of Glen Shiel.

Descent

Return west to the lochan and descend north following the outflow. Pass to the east of the lochan beyond, then contour round the east side of Beinn Bheag and down to the aerial track before the Bealach Udal. Turn left and follow the road back to the start.

The trig point and cairn (centre) on Beinn na Seamraig, from the highpoint above the lochan

Round of Kylerhea Glen

Summits: *Beinn Bhuidhe* ▲ *; Beinn na Caillich* ▲ *;*
Sgùrr na Còinnich ▲ *; Ben Aslak* ▲ *; East*
Summit ▲
Terrain: *Hillwalk*
Distance: *15km; 9.25 miles*
Ascent & Descent: *1230m; 4035ft*
Time: *5hrs 30mins–6hrs 30 mins*
Start & Finish: *Kylerhea Otter Hide car park*
(NG 7866 2112)

Beinn na Caillich, Sgùrr na Còinnich and Ben Aslak
can also be climbed from Kylerhea in a round which
excludes Beinn Dubh a' Bhealaich and Beinn na
Seamraig.

It would also be possible to combine all five main
summits (Beinn na Caillich, Sgùrr na Còinnich, Beinn
Dubh a' Bhealach, Beinn na Seamraig and Ben
Aslak) in a single big round (22km/13.5 miles;
1550m/4900ft ascent & descent; 8–9hrs).

Approach

Start as for the ascent of Beinn na Caillich and Sgùrr
na Còinnich, climb up onto Beinn Bhuidhe (*see*
p235–6) and continue to Bealach nam Mulachag.

Ascent

Climb the lower of two stony ramplines on the right-
hand side of the broad South Ridge of Beinn na
Caillich and follow the better defined ridge to the top
(*diagram p236*). Return to the bealach, then ascend
the grassy East Face to the trig point on Sgùrr na Còinnich. Descend west past the lochan, then south-west
aiming for the aerial access track at Bealach Udal.

Ascend this track, then the open hillside contouring
below Beinn Bheag, aiming for a grassy gully between
craggy highpoints. At the lochan turn right (west) to
gain Ben Aslak's summit. Return to the lochan and
follow the flat summit ridge east, out to the pointed
East Summit which is lower by a few metres.

Descent

Descend the long East Ridge towards the sea. This
gives pleasant going until the end when the terrain
becomes much rougher and a tangle of dwarf birch
makes for tedious going. Keep descending, aiming for
a rusty metal shed by sheep pens, to pick up the
intermittent line of the old coast path. Follow this
north to grassy pasture, then swing inland to reach a
footbridge across the Kylerhea River. The bridge is at
NG 7845 2041 and totally hidden by trees.

Turn right onto a track and follow it round through
Kylerhea to the road. Turn left onto the main road,
then right to the Otter Hide access road and the start.

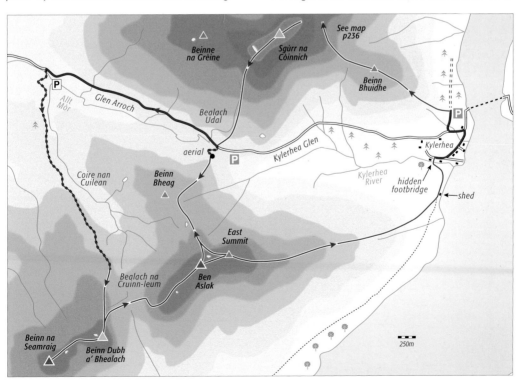

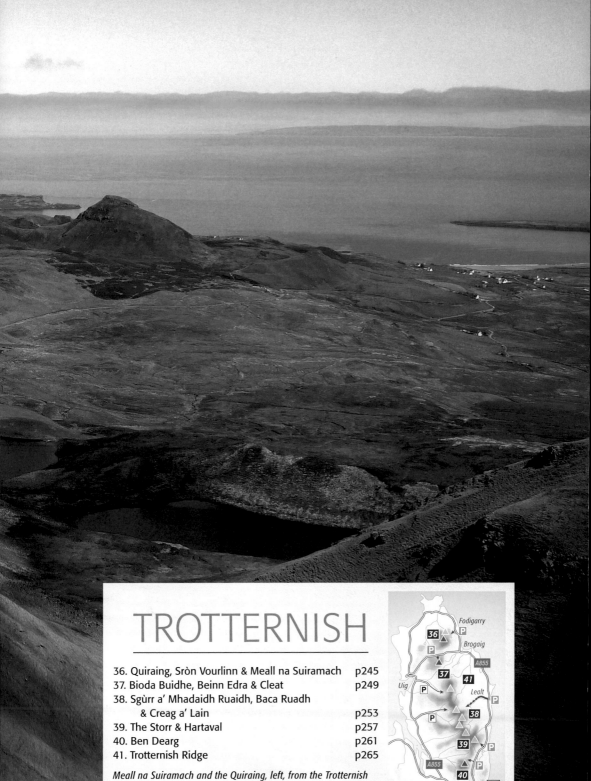

TROTTERNISH

Meall na Suiramach and the Quiraing, left, from the Trotternish Ridge. The village on the coast is Brogaig

The rounded summit of Meall na Suiramach, right, and the towers guarding the secret retreat of the Quiraing

Quiraing, Sròn Vourlinn & Meall na Suiramach

*T*he basalt cliffs of Meall na Suiramach lie above fossil rich sediments from the Jurassic period,175 million years ago. As the weight of the overlying basalt squeezes the beds of sediment eastwards, they have taken the leading edge of the escarpment with them, causing the jumbled landslips of towers and secret hideaways that are a characteristic of Skye's dramatic eastern seaboard

Sròn Vourlinn from the northern flanks of Meall na Suiramach

From Flodigarry

Summits: *Sròn Vourlinn* ▲ *; Meall na Suiramach* ▲
Terrain: *Hillwalk*
Distance: *13km; 8 miles*
Ascent & Descent: *675m; 2215ft*
Time: *4hrs 30mins–5hrs 30mins*
Start & Finish: *Car park in small quarry just north of gate and footpath signpost, on A855 south of Flodigarry (NG 4635 7103)*

The first question for any ascent of Meall na Suiramach (543m) and visit to the Quiraing, is where to start. The Uig road west from Brogaig is signposted 'Quiraing' and there's a large car park (NG 4396 6790) at the bealach, but it can be very busy in summer, as can the steep zigzag single track road leading to it. The bealach seems to be known as Bealach Ollasgairte, although the name does not appear on any map.

Parking is also possible in old quarry workings

(photo p242) below the bealach, about 1.3miles west from Brogaig at NG 4494 6807, NG 4487 6805 and in the layby opposite the cemetery car park at NG 4469 6808. From the layby, a path on the left side of the burn (marked on OS maps) leads north-east to join the path below the escarpment at about NG 4488 6881. Starting from the bealach reduces the day by about 1hr 30mins (8.5km/5.25 miles; ascent & descent 475m/1550ft) and from the cemetery by about 1hr (9.5km/6 miles; 595m/1950ft).

Approaching from Flodigarry via Loch Langaig and Loch Hasco probably offers the best day for hillwalkers and is the route described here. The second question is whether to do the round clockwise or anti-clockwise (the hillside of Maoladh Mòr is quite steep and probably pleasanter in descent – anti-clockwise), and whether to visit the Quiraing at the start or finish (The Table, the Quiraing's main feature, faces east and will lose the sun later in the day).

The route described here visits The Table first and proceeds anti-clockwise. This requires a backtrack

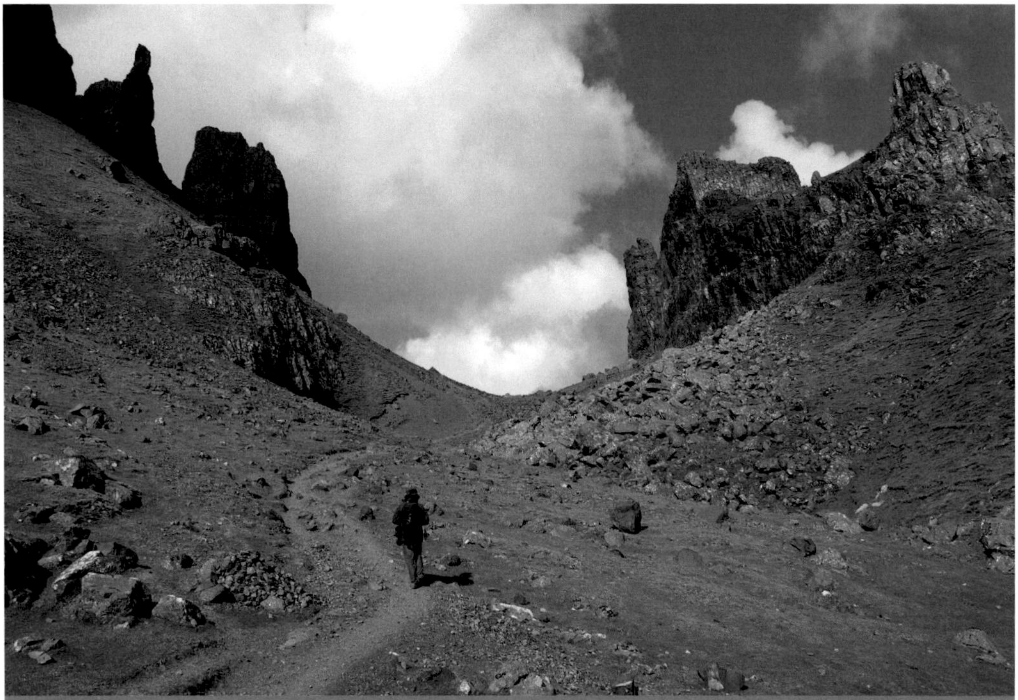

Approaching the col below The Prison, the rock formation on the right, and The Needle, the tower up on the left

and adds 2km to the route (as described). Visiting The Table at the end of the route removes the backtrack and reduces the total time by about 30mins (11km/6.75 miles; 675m/2215ft).

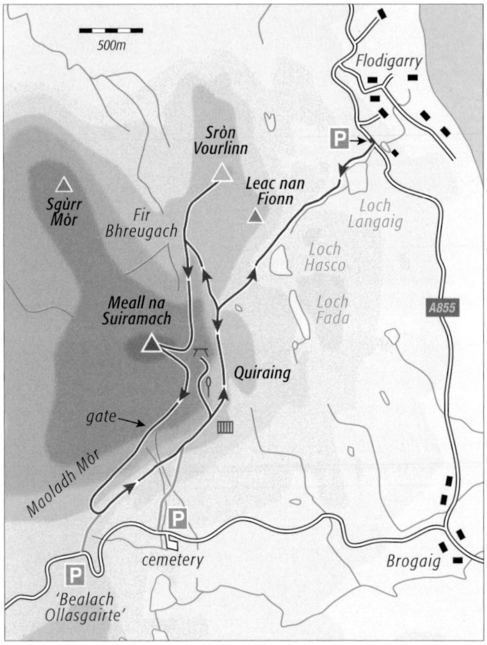

Approach

From the Flodigarry car park, walk south on the road for 600m to a gate and a track with a green Scottish Rights of Way Society sign, indicating the route to Maoladh Mòr via the Quiraing. Follow the track west past Loch Langaig and ascend past Loch Hasco and a lochan to reach the path which traverses in both directions below the cliffs of the main escarpment.

Ascent

Turn left and make a steady ascent southwards towards the Quiraing then turn west to reach a col sandwiched between the cliffs of The Prison to the south and the Quiraing and The Table to the north. Overlooking the col on the north side is the impressive rock tower of The Needle (*see map*). The Needle is an E2 Grade Rock Climb on worryingly loose and dangerous rock, characteristic of the whole Quiraing area.

Ascend the grass to the right of the mud and rubble slope left of The Needle to reach a well-defined path on The Needle's left side. Follow this round right to a narrow well-worn chimney and ascend it to reach the upper sanctuary below The Table. Turn round and mentally mark the top of the chimney because the terrain can be confusing on your return. Now follow the path as it weaves its way towards The Table below the main cliffs. The Table can be gained by assorted paths, but the one curving round to the left gains The Table from close to the back cliffs and probably offers the easiest ascent. The name Quiraing is thought to derive from the Old Norse *kvi rand* meaning 'round fold', as in the Gaelic *a' cuith-raing*. It is said that livestock were hidden in this inner sanctum in times of strife.

Retrace your steps to the col below The Needle ⸮ , then return north to the path junction above Loch Hasco. Continue north below the main escarpment, then ascend to a stile in the fence and a grassy col – Fir Bhreugach.

Cross over, turn right and follow the airy, pinnacled ridge north-east to the summit of Sròn Vourlinn (340m) and extensive views east over Flodigarry to the coast. Return to Fir Bhreugach and ascend the well-worn path up the northern flanks of Meall na Suiramach. Near the top the path curves round the top of a large grassy gully in the cliffs to reach a cairn. Shortly after this, there is a view down to The Table.

From the cairn (about NG 4492 6940), turn right away from the cliff-edge and head north-west over the moorland dome for about 350m to the summit trig point (NG 4461 6950) and views north and west to Lewis, Harris and the Uists.

Descent
Return in a south-easterly direction to the path along the escarpment and descend to a gate in a fence. Go through and continue down the steep side of the Maoladh Mòr towards the Bealach Ollasgairte car

The route to The Table from the col below The Prison

park. Short of the car park, swing round left to gain the path along the base of the main escarpment and follow it north to gain the col below the Quiraing, between The Prison ⁙ and The Needle ⸮ . Go through and swing north to reach the path above Loch Hasco and follow it back to the start.

Hiding in plain sight; the towers surrounding The Table, the Quiraing's inner sanctum

Druim an Ruma, left, and Dùn Dubh below the crumbling cliffs of Bioda Buidhe's East Face

Bioda Buidhe, Beinn Edra & Cleat

*E*asily accessed from the bealach on the hill road from Brogaig to Uig, these three summits make an enjoyable outing through dramatic scenery. The rolling grassy crest of the escarpment is easy to follow in good weather, but the lack of distinguishing features and paths makes for challenging navigation in poor visibility

The south side of Ben Edra from Bealach a' Mhòramhain

From Bealach Ollasgairte

Summits: Bioda Buidhe ▲; Druim na Coille ▲; Beinn Edra ▲; Optional – Cleat ▲

Terrain: Hillwalk
Distance: 12.5km; 7.75 miles
Ascent & Descent: 815m; 2670ft
Time: 4hrs 30mins–5hrs 30mins
Start & Finish: Car park at Bealach Ollasgairte on the Brogaig to Uig hill road (NG 4396 6790)

The escarpment below the East Face of Bioda Buidhe (466m) has some of the most impressive landslip towers in the area. The squat Dùn Dubh (black fort) probably gets its name from its resemblance to a hill-fort, rather than past occupation in the Iron Age – the rock is loose and the vegetation steep. Next door is the dramatic Druim an Ruma which is equally loose and vegetated. Both pinnacles are Difficult Grade Rock Climbs and not, in any way, recommended.

Some 5km along the escarpment to the south-east is Beinn Edra (611m). Given its surroundings it isn't a particularly distinguished mountain, although it has a trig point and is the highest point in the central section of the Trotternish Ridge.

In 1945 an American B-17 Flying Fortress crashed

into the North-East Face, with the death of all nine crew. In 2015, members of the Staffin community commemorated the 70th anniversary of the accident and unveiled a plaque to the crew's memory on the Staffin War Memorial.

Ascent

From the car park at Bealach Ollasgairte (unnamed on OS maps), ascend the path south along the edge of the escarpment, with good views east over the mini-mountain of Cleat, Dùn Dubh and Druim an Ruma, to gain the summit of Bioda Buidhe. The path, ill-defined in places, now swings round to the south-west, descends steadily above the cliffs of the escarpment, then more steeply south to Bealach nan Coisichean.

A more undulating route now leads beside the cliff-edge over Druim na Coille (321m) to Bealach Uige. From there it is a steady ascent to the trig point on Beinn Edra. Descend south for about 600m to Bealach a' Mhòramhain and drop down east then north above a small knoll, to below the North-East Face.

Engines, propeller machinery and undercarriage legs can be seen in the scree below the main gully on the face, along with scattered aluminium spars and fire-fused debris. Further debris can be found on the moor below in the vicinity of NG 4587 6329. Please 'take nothing but photos and leave nothing but bootprints'.

Looking north over Loch Corcasgil to Bioda Buidhe and Quiraing from the northern flanks of Beinn Edra

Continue north-west, contouring the hillside below Beinn Edra on assorted sheep paths to pass above Loch Corcasgil, then west through a rocky trough between the face and a knoll to below Bealach Uige,

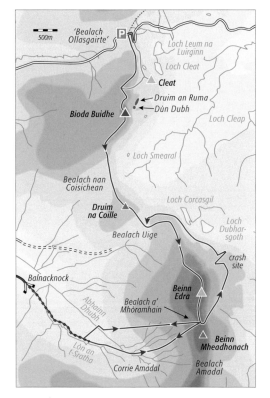

Unfortunately the continuation below the escarpment beyond the bealach is over very rough moorland, so it is easier to ascend steep grass to the bealach and rejoin the outward route.

Descent

Return over Bioda Buidhe back to the start. Cleat (336m) can be included at either the start or finish of the route as desired. It is easily accessed by going due south from the first big bend on the road east to Brogaig, or directly from the path on the escarpment,

Beinn Edra from Bealach Uige

by descending steep grass slopes at NG 4389 6700. Adding Cleat to the finish will increase the day's descent by 276m/905ft and ascent by 116m/380ft. Add Cleat at the start and the figures are reversed. Cleat adds about 1km to the total distance.

Via Fairy Glen

Summits: *Beinn Edra* ▲

Terrain: *Hillwalk*

Distance: *10.5km; 6.55 miles*

Ascent & Descent: *511m; 1676ft*

Time: *4–5hrs*

Start & Finish: *Access road to Fairy Glen*

Beinn Edra can also be approached from the west, starting from Balnaknock and the Fairy Glen in Glen Uig, gained from the A87, south of the Uig Hotel. The limitation of this route is that the popular Fairy Glen lies on a single track No Through Road which can be extremely busy in summer, with very limited parking.

Ascent

Park wherever possible and follow the road. When it ends at a barn, continue straight ahead on track to the right. This crosses the Lòn an t-Sratha burn and continues on its left (north) side up the glen for about 1.5km. Go through two gates and in about 200m the track ends.

There are **two options**: **(1)** Follow the fence at the second gate over the boggy moor to the Abhainn

The only remaining propeller blade from the B-17

Dhubh, cross over to an earth and stone dyke (NG 4352 6188) and ascend to Bealach a' Mhòramhain (the path marked on OS maps). **(2)** Alternatively, continue north beside the Lòn an t-Sratha on a vague path to reach the Abhainn Dhubh at about NG 4395 6150. Cross over and ascend to the bealach. From the bealach, climb grassy slopes north to Beinn Edra.

Descent

Return the same way.

Cleat can be accessed from the escarpment by descending steep grass slopes north of Bioda Buidhe

South-east from the flanks of Flasvein to the impressive cliffs of Sgùrr a' Mhadaidh Ruaidh, left, and Baca Ruadh

Sgùrr a' Mhadaidh Ruaidh, Baca Ruadh & Creag a' Lain

*T*he cliffs of Sgùrr a' Mhadaidh Ruaidh (Peak of the Red Fox) stand with Meall na Suiramach and The Storr as some of the most dramatic on the Trotternish Ridge. Most visitors only view them from the top of the escarpment; this route gets right in among the cliffs. The track approach over the moorland from Lealt is long, but keeps the bog-trotting to a minimum

Baca Ruadh from the flanks of Hartaval to the south

From Lealt

Summits: *Sgùrr a Mhadaidh Ruaidh* ▲ *;*
Baca Ruadh ▲ *; Creag a' Lain* ▲
Terrain: *Hillwalk*
Distance: *18km; 11.25miles*
Ascent & Descent: *710m; 2330ft*
Time: *5hrs 30mins–6hrs 30mins*
Start & Finish: *'Lealt Falls' car park on A855*
(NG 5166 6048) south of the turning to Lealt

The eastern approach from Lealt is long but makes for a more satisfactory hillwalk than coming in from the west. Parking is straightforward, the escarpment's impressive cliffs are revealed in all their glory from the start and it is easy to combine the summits into a satisfying round.

The approach track was used to extract diatomite, a silica rich marine sediment, from around Loch Cuithir in the 1950s and, at the time, was the "most expensive stretch of road built in the Highlands".

Approach
Start from the large layby car park on the east side of the A855, just south of the minor road signposted to Lealt. Follow the minor road to Lealt, then the track to its end, just west of Loch Cuithir. Alternatively, there is the possibility of limited parking at Lealt, just before the public road turns to track. This will save about 3km/1.75 miles and 40mins. The track can be driven all the way to Loch Cuithir, but it is rough in places and unsuitable for most cars.

Ascent
From the track end, cross the moorland due south towards the grassy scree slopes that flank the cliffs of Sgùrr a' Mhadaidh Ruaidh (593m) on their right

(north) side. Ascend in a rightwards arc below the cliffs to avoid the steepest ground, to arrive at a gully (NG 4702 5840). This cuts through the rocky escarpment to the right of Sgùrr a' Mhadaidh Ruaidh's North Face and is marked by a prominent pinnacle at its start.

Climb the gully, taking care of some loose rocks and earthy slopes at the top, to emerge on the escarpment at about 500m altitude, just south of the col between Creag a' Lain (609m) and Sgùrr a' Mhadaidh Ruaidh.

Follow the escarpment east, then turn north from the main path and along the elevated grassy spur leading out to the summit of Sgùrr a' Mhadaidh Ruaidh. Return south, then continue south-west round the head of Coire an t-Seasgaich to the col before Baca Ruadh (639m) and climb to that summit.

Return north-west along the path skirting below Sgùrr a' Mhadaidh Ruaidh to reach the col before Creag a' Lain and ascend steep grassy slopes to the summit.

Descent

Go north to pass through a wall and fence above Bealach na Leacaich between Flasvein and Creag a' Lain. Zigzag down right (east) through the escarpment below the bealach and contour north over a wide grassy shelf below the East Face of Flasvein to avoid the tier of broken cliffs that lie below (*see opposite*).

When clear of these, swing east down a broad grassy spur to reach the burn draining the corrie and follow it south-east down towards Loch Cuithir. Cross over a water channel and follow it to the track before the old sleeper bridge. Retrace the outward route to the start.

Sgùrr a' Mhadaidh Ruaidh

prominent pinnacle

Descending from Creag a' Lain towards the wall and fence across Bealach na Leacaich, with Flasvein beyond

Via Glenhinnisdal

Summits: *Creag a' Lain* ▲ ; *Sgùrr a Mhadaidh Ruaidh* ▲ ; *Baca Ruadh* ▲
Terrain: *Hillwalk*
Distance: *12.5km; 7.75miles*
Ascent & Descent: *790m; 2592ft*
Time: *4hrs 30mins–5hrs 30mins*
Start & Finish: *Glenhinnisdal road end (NG 4272 5862)*

The western approach, accessed from the A87 south of Uig, is more of an out and back moorland walk with little in the way of dramatic scenery until Bealach na Leacaich is reached. There is limited parking at the end of the public road through Glenhinnisdal

Ascent

From the last house, follow the continuation track to its end, beyond the Lòn Coire Chaiplin burn. If this proves awkward to cross, there is a small metal bridge about 150m further downstream. Ascend the left

Sgùrr a' Mhadaidh Ruaidh and the impressive escarpment above Loch Cuithir

(north) side of the Lòn Mhic Ibheir up Coire Iomhair, with a detour north then back south to avoid a line of crags, to reach Bealach na Leacaich. Higher up, a fence and wall run alongside the burn to the bealach.

From the bealach, go over Creag a' Lain and descend steeply to the col below Sgùrr a' Mhadaidh Ruaidh. Follow the escarpment east, then turn north from the main path and along the elevated grassy spur leading

out to the perched summit of Sgùrr a' Mhadaidh Ruaidh. Return south, then continue south-west round the head of Coire an t-Seasgaich to the col before Baca Ruadh (639m) and climb to that summit.

Descent

Retrace the outward route to Bealach na Leacaich and return down Coire Iomhair back to Glenhinnisdal.

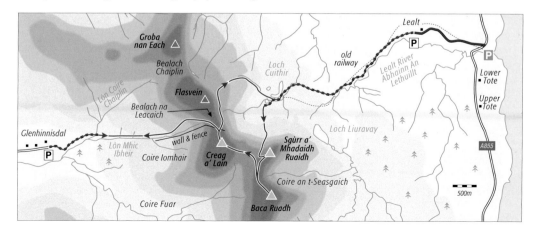

255

The South Ridge of The Storr gives a grandstand view of the Old Man of Storr and the pinnacles of Coire Faoin

The Storr & Hartaval

*A*long with the Basteir Tooth and the Inaccessible Pinnacle, the Old Man of Storr is a Skye landmark visible from unexpected locations all over the island, but unlike the other two, it's just an easy walk from the road. That makes it a prime target for thousands of summer tourists and walkers whose coaches and cars fill the car park and surrounding laybys and road verges. The first route described here largely avoids the crowds; the second embraces them. Take your pick...

The summit of Hartaval with The Storr behind

Via Bealach Beag

Summits: *The Storr* ▲ *; Hartaval* ▲
Terrain: *Hillwalk*
Distance: *11km; 6.57 miles*
Ascent & Descent: *840m; 2755ft*
Time: *4hrs 20mins–5hrs 20mins*
Start & Finish: *Parking beside a fenced water plant (NG 5012 5224) on the east side of the A855, towards the north end of Loch Leathan and below Bealach Beag (NG 5020 5242)*

The Storr (719m) and Hartaval (669m) can be ascended from a number of directions, depending on starting point and circuit direction. The Storr's South Ridge is furthest from the main car park and the least frequented route as a consequence. However, once Bealach Beag is gained, it is an easy route up grassy slopes with spectacular views across the cliffs to the Old Man and the coast. Like most of the Trotternish Ridge, The Storr can be very confusing in poor visibility and requires good navigation skills.

Approach
From the car park the driest route is to head up and right to reach a wall and fence marking the boundary of felled forestry. Ascend beside the wall to flatter, boulder-scattered ground below the main escarpment, where a path comes in from the right through a gap in the wall, and the fence surrounding the felled area turns right (NG 4983 5322). This path is the return

South Ridge of The Storr via Bealach Beag

The Old Man of Storr and surrounding pinnacles, with the Red Hills and the Cuillin in the distance. The hill between Loch Leathan and the sea is the fine Sithean a' Bhealaich Chumhaing (see Other Hills)

route. The wall itself continues up the steep hillside above, then stops. Go west below the cliffs from the gap in the wall to reach the large burn flowing from Bealach Beag, the obvious break at the lowest point in the cliffs above (*diagram p257*).

Ascent

Ascend the burn's right-hand bank on a well-defined path and scramble up through the break in the cliffs to a grassy bowl below the actual bealach. Turn right (east) on a path following a smaller burn. The path is ill-defined in places but traverses east above the cliffs, then ascends north-west up the broad South Ridge to a final east turn to arrive at The Storr's heavily eroded

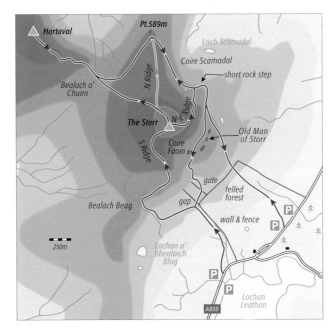

flatish summit and a disintegrating trig point. Go north for about 100m to reach the rim of the cliff-top on the upper North Ridge and descend it for about 200m, until a curving westerly line can be taken down an increasingly steep slope to Bealach a' Chuirn below Hartaval. Zigzag up the steep slope above the bealach to the rounded top and follow it to the summit.

Descent

Return to the bealach. The next section requires good navigation in poor visibility. Ascend directly, then contour leftwards (north-east) above small crags, onto the broad lower slopes of the North Ridge. Pass to the right of a small, rocky tor (NG 4934 5498), shown on the OS 1:25k map as a tiny 590m contour (*see opposite*), and drop down right (east) at a small cairn, to join a well-trodden path.

Contour south round the top of Coire Scamadal to reach cairns and an old fence at the base of the North-East Ridge (*see opposite*). Scramble down the escarpment via a short rock step to a path leading to a col crossed by a fence.

Cross over and continue south towards the Old Man of Storr and The Sanctuary; the maze of landslip towers and hollows in Coire Faoin below the main cliffs of the East Face. Take a diagonal south-west line through the towers to emerge above the felled forest.

Zigzag down grassy slopes to a metal gate in a fence above the felled forest, then straight ahead to the gap in the wall passed on the ascent. Turn left and follow the wall back to the start.

Via North-East or North Ridge

Summits: *The Storr* ▲ *; Hartaval* ▲
Terrain: *Hillwalk*
Distance: *10km; 6.25 miles*
Ascent & Descent: *840m; 2755ft*
Time: *4hrs 10mins–5hrs 10mins*
Start & Finish: *Old Man of Storr car park on A855 (NG 5090 5290)*

The North-East Ridge of The Storr gives a dramatic route, but it is exposed in places and there is also a lot of unpleasant basalt gravel and loose rock. A longer, safer, but less dramatic alternative is to continue round Coire Scamadal and ascend the broad North Ridge.

Approach

From the car park, ascend the new path and go through a gate at the top. Continue past the Old Man of Storr to a col and cross over a fence. Swing round left (west) and ascend to the escarpment and a scramble up a short rock step to old fence posts leading up the North-East Ridge.

Ascent

Climb the North-East Ridge over grass, scree and broken rocks on an ill-defined path near to the cliff edge, with breathtaking views down through the impressive gullies splitting the cliffs. Scramble up through the broken lower tier of the upper cliffs, then traverse right and ascend a grassy break in the escarpment to the summit just beyond. It is also possible to ascend more directly to the grassy break, avoiding most of the rubble, but missing the dramatic views.

Alternatively, continue round the top of Coire

Welcome to The Storr

Scamadal, then ascend to reach the North Ridge and follow that to the summit.

From the summit, return north to the cliff-top rim of the North Ridge and descend it for about 200m until a curving westerly line can be taken down an increasingly steep slope to Bealach a' Chuirn below Hartaval. Zigzag up the steep slope above the bealach to the rounded top and follow it to the summit.

Descent

Return to Bealach a' Chuirn. The next section requires good navigation in poor visibility. Ascend directly then contour leftwards (north-east) above small crags, onto the broad lower slopes of the North Ridge. Pass to the right of a small, rocky tor (NG 4934 5498), shown on the OS 1:25k map as a tiny 590m contour, then drop down right (east) at a small cairn to join a well-trodden path. Contour south round the top of Coire Scamadal on this path to reach cairns and the old fence at the base of the North-East Ridge. From there, reverse the ascent route back to the start.

Looking east from Hartaval across Bealach a' Chuirn to the 590m rocky tor and the summit of The Storr

The traverse round the top of Coire Scamadal to the base of the North Ridge and the 590m rocky tor

Ascending the escarpment edge towards Ben Dearg. The final gravel slope can be seen at the top

Ben Dearg

L *ying at the very southern end of the Trotternish Ridge, Ben Dearg sees fewer visitors than the other peaks. Walkers on the Syke Trail leave the ridge at The Storr as do many parties making a traverse of the ridge. This is a pity as Ben Dearg is a fine peak with some interesting castle-like towers and a hidden, grassy, landslip-created hollow below the summit*

The Quiraing-like landslide hollow below Ben Dearg; The Storr and Hartaval in the distance

Via Bealach Mòr

Summits: *Ben Dearg* ▲
Terrain: *Hillwalk*
Distance: *6km; 5 miles*
Ascent & Descent: *415m; 13610ft*
Time: *2hrs 30mins–3hrs 30mins*
Start & Finish: *Car park below 'Bride's Veil Falls' on A855 (marked Waterfall on OS 1:25k) opposite Storr Lochs (NG 4951 5097)*

Approaching Bealach Mòr requires care to make sure the best line is taken, as anything too direct will land you in deep bog. A more circumspect route gains the better drained grassy strip below the escarpment, by the shortest route and follows that round to the bealach.

Approach
The small car park by the waterfall, the so called Bride's Veil Falls, is a stop-off for tourist buses, so

arriving early pays dividends. However, few stay long, so a parking place usually opens up if you wait. Alternatively, there is a small pull-off on the right, 460m further north (NG 4978 5134) and a larger layby on the right, a further 250m beyond.

Go through the gate, turn right onto a grassy atv track, go past two electricity poles and head north to reach a burn after about 220m. Cross over and follow the grassy right (north) bank of the burn upstream to reach rough grassy pasture below the escarpment.

Contour west for about 650m, following sheep tracks and sticking to the grassy sections as much as possible to below Bealach Mòr (NG 4863 5112), a small grassy saddle at the low point of the craggy escarpment projecting from Ben Dearg (552m). Work up the steep grass to gain the bealach on the escarpment. The escarpment continues north-east to Bealach Beag and The Storr (*see photo above*).

Ascent
Turn left and ascend the cliff-edge towards Ben Dearg, following old fence posts and with increasingly good

views of the hill's towers and landslips.

Towards the top the ground steepens significantly and grass gives way to clumps of moss, black basalt gravel and earth. Weave up this between craggy bits to where the grass returns. The ground stays steep and the terrain is quite exposed, but the angle soon eases and the summit reached. The gravel slope isn't as steep as it looks from below, but it is unstable and requires careful footwork, especially in poor weather. If this line doesn't appeal then it can be avoided by climbing steep grassy slopes about 120m further right (west).

From the summit, descend south following the old fence round the top of grassy slopes to the cliffs at Ben Dearg's south-eastern highpoint, which offers good views south to Ben Tianavaig, Portree and the Cuillin. The grassy slopes between the highpoints lead down to a hollow hidden from below by the castellated towers seen on the approach. Like the Quiraing, this has been created by this whole section of the hillside collapsing in a massive landslide.

Descent

Return to the col between the highpoints, descend steep grass into the hidden hollow below and follow it left to the prominent tower at the hollow's northern end. A strip of grass leads down between the tower and the long, eroded gully that is a prominent feature on the eastern side of the hill (*photo p260*).

Descend beside the gully to where the ground levels out, cross over the gully and continue to a dip containing pools, which can grow to form a lochan when rainfall is high. Go round this area on the left to gain the bottom of the slope leading to Bealach Mòr and follow the approach route back to the start.

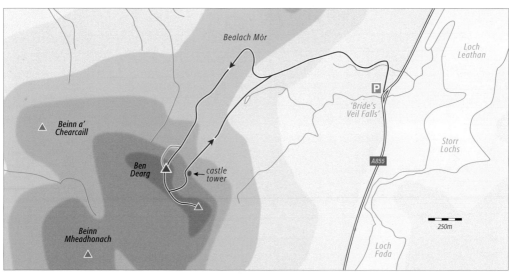

Descending beside the long, eroded gully that is a prominent feature on the eastern side of hill

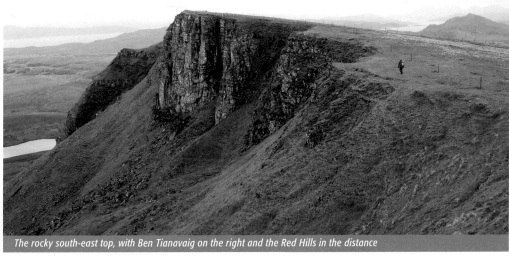

The rocky south-east top, with Ben Tianavaig on the right and the Red Hills in the distance

Sgùrr a' Mhadaidh Ruaidh, Beinn Edra, Meall na Suiramach and The Quiraing from Baca Ruadh

Trotternish Ridge

F or most parties a complete traverse of the 36km (22 mile) Trotternish Ridge from Flodigarry to Portree will be a two-day expedition with a night on the ridge. However, long single-day traverses are also possible depending on start and finish points. Many parties use two cars, as public transport is limited, but hitching is also an option. However tackled, the Trotternish Ridge is a route for a long, sunny summer day; the views are everything, while the rolling, featureless terrain can make navigation a challenge in poor visibility

Looking south over Sgùrr a' Mhalaidh to the snow-topped Cuillin

Bealach Ollasgairte to The Storr

Summits: *Bioda Buidhe* ▲ *; Druim na Coille* ▲ *; Beinn Edra* ▲ *; Beinn Mheadhonach* ▲ *; Groba nan Each* ▲ *; Flasvein* ▲ *; Creag a' Lain* ▲ *; Sgùrr a Mhadaidh Ruaidh* ▲ *; Baca Ruadh* ▲ *; Sgùrr a' Mhalaidh* ▲ *; Hartaval* ▲ *; The Storr* ▲ *; Optional – Meall na Suiramach* ▲ *; Ben Dearg* ▲ *; A' Chorra-Beinn* ▲ *; Pein a' Chlèibh* ▲
Terrain: *Hillwalk*
Distance: *22km; 13.5miles*
Ascent: *1480m; 4855ft*
Descent: *1570m; 5151ft*
Time: *8hrs 30mins–9hrs 30mins*
Start & Finish: *Car park at Bealach Ollasgairte on the Brogaig to Uig hill road (NG 4396 6790), & Old Man of Storr car park on A855 (NG 5090 5290)*

A long linear route with a significant total height gain and loss. Bioda Buidhe, Beinn Edra, Hartaval and

The Storr have the greatest gain and loss, but much of the ridge in between is less demanding. There are few easy options for retreat until The Storr is reached. The terrain is mostly grassy until The Storr, but can be boggy underfoot. Alternative start and finishing points are listed at the end of the route description. The ridge is an excellent location for seeing Golden Eagles.

Ascent

From the car park at Bealach Ollasgairte (unnamed on OS maps), ascend the path south along the edge of the escarpment with good views east over the mini-mountain of Cleat, to gain the summit of Bioda Buidhe. After this the path is only intermittent.

Swing round to the south-west making the most of the grassier ground, trying not to lose too much height and staying above the cliffs of the escarpment, until it is possible to descend south to Bealach nan Coisichean.

More undulating terrain now leads beside the cliff-edge over Druim na Coille (321m) to Bealach Uige, from where the longest ascent on the route gains the trig point on Beinn Edra (611m). Beyond the

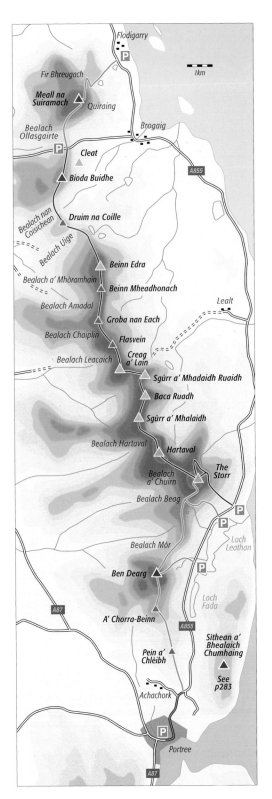

terrain is a series of highpoints separated by bealachs until the impressive cliffs and corries of flat-topped Creag a' Lain (609m) and Sgùrr a' Mhadaidh Ruaidh (593m) are reached. It is worth walking out to the isolated summit of the latter. Baca Ruadh (639m) and Sgùrr a' Mhalaidh (615m), are followed by an initially steep ascent to Hartaval (669m). A steep descent gains Bealach a' Chuirn and the second largest ascent to the summit of The Storr *(19.5km/12 miles; 1480m/4855ft ascent; 1020m/ 3345ft descent; 7hrs 30mins)* from Bealach Ollasgairte to The Storr summit.

Descent
Go north for about 100m to reach the rim of the cliff-top on the upper North Ridge. There are now **two options**: (1) Descend the top of a grassy break in the cliffs and traverse right (east) towards the cliff edge to gain the North-East Ridge. A loose, unpleasant and ill-defined path leads down through scree, rocks and grass, with breathtaking views through the impressive gullies splitting the cliffs, to reach cairns and old fence posts at the foot of the North-East Ridge.

(2) The alternative is nicer, but less dramatic and 1km longer. Continue north down the North Ridge *(see map & diagrams p258–9)*. Pass to the right of a small rocky tor (NG 4934 5498), shown on the OS 1:25k map as a tiny 590m contour, then drop down right (east) at a small cairn to join a well-trodden path. Contour south round the top of Coire Scamadal to reach cairns and the old fence at the foot of the North-East Ridge.

From the foot of the North-East Ridge, scramble down the escarpment via a short rock step to a path leading to a col crossed by a fence. Cross over and continue south past the Old Man of Storr. Go through the gate in the fence surrounding the felled forestry and descend the new path to the car park *(2.5km/ 1.5 miles; 550m/1805ft descent; 1hr)* from The Storr summit to Storr car park.

Alternatives
Approach from Flodigarry: This gives a more aesthetic traverse, but will mean viewing the Quiraing *(see p245–7)* on another day. Start from a small car park just north of a gate and footpath signpost, on the A855 south of Flodigarry (NG 4635 7103). Walk south on the road for 600m, go through the gate and follow the track west past Loch Langaig, Loch Hasco and a tiny lochan to meet a path, which traverses in both directions below the main escarpment. Turn right, traverse below the main escarpment, then ascend to a stile in the fence and a grassy col; Fir Bhreugach. Turn left and ascend a well-worn path up the northern flanks of Meall na Suiramach. Near the top, the path curves round above a large grassy gully in the cliffs to

North to Baca Ruadh and flat-topped Creag a' Lain

reach a cairn. Shortly after this, there is a view down to the Quiraing below. From the cairn (about NG 4492 6940), turn right away from the cliff edge and head north-west over the moorland dome for about 350m to the summit trig point (NG 4461 6950). Return in a south-easterly direction to the path along the escarpment and descend to a gate in a fence. Go through and continue down the steep side of the Maoladh Mòr to the car park at Bealach Ollasgairte *(5.5km/3.5 miles; 450m/1475ft ascent; 295m/ 970ft descent; 2hrs 10mins)* from Flodigarry to Bealach Ollasgairte.

Descent via Bealach Beag: If the main Storr car park is very busy then a car can be left on the A855 in the parking area or one of the laybys (NG 5020 5242) below Bealach Beag *(see p257–8)*. From the summit of The Storr, turn west then south down the steep grass of the South Ridge to gain a path contouring west to the grassy bowl below Bealach Beag. Follow the path down the left (east) side of the burn then swing left over grass to the wall and fence enclosing the felled forestry. Descend beside this to the road, swinging south-west at the end to the parking *(3km/1.75 miles; 570m/1870ft descent; 1hr)* from The Storr summit via Bealach Beag to parking on A855.

Descent via Ben Dearg: Descend as above but continue past Bealach Beag, over two highpoints above Lochan a' Bhealaich Bhig, then west to Bealach Mòr. Ascend the cliff-edge towards Ben Dearg, following old fence posts. Towards the top the ground steepens significantly and the grass gives way to clumps of moss, black basalt gravel and earth. Weave up this to where the grass returns. The gravel slope isn't as steep as it looks from below, but it is unstable and requires

careful footwork, especially in poor weather. If this line doesn't appeal then it can be avoided by climbing steep grassy slopes about 120m further right (west).

From the summit, descend south following the old fence round the top of steep grassy slopes, then zigzag down into a Quiraing-like landslide hollow surrounded by castellated rock towers. Follow the hollow left to where a strip of grass leads down between a large rock tower and the long, eroded gully that is a prominent feature on this eastern side of the hill.

Descend beside the gully to where the ground levels out, cross over and continue to a dip containing pools, which can grow to form a lochan when rainfall is high. Pass this area on the left to a grassy slope below Bealach Mòr.

Sticking to sheep tracks through the grass below the escarpment, go roughly north-east, then east for about 700m to meet a burn at NG 4922 5119. Follow the grassy left (north) bank of the burn south and east towards the A855. Leave the burn at about NG 4943 5117 to gain an atv track and follow it to parking at the so called Bride's Veil Falls (NG 4951 5097), marked Waterfall on OS 1:25k and opposite Storr Lochs. *(7km/4.25 miles; 250m/820ft ascent; 820m/ 2690ft descent; 2hrs 25mins)* from The Storr summit to Ben Dearg parking.

Descent to Portree: From Ben Dearg continue south-east over a rocky top, then south round A' Chorra-Bheinn and Peinn a' Chlèibh on increasingly boggy and tiring ground to reach a track leading to the A855 and a final walk down into Portree. This finish will only appeal to purists. *(12.5km/7.75miles; 330m/1083ft ascent; 1010m/3314ft descent; 4hrs)* from The Storr summit to Portree.

OTHER HILLS

The summit of Ben Tianavaig, looking north to Sithean a' Bhealaich Chumhaing (see Assorted Other Hills) and on the skyline, The Storr

Looking south from Healabhal Mhòr to Healabhal Bheag. The turreted hill behind is Beinn na Boineid, with Rùm in the distance

Healabhal Bheag, Healabhal Mhòr (MacLeod's Tables) & Beinn Bhac-ghlais

*T*he flat-topped summits of MacLeod's Tables dominate Duirinish in the north-west corner of Skye and are prominent landmarks, visible from much of the island's high ground. Like most of northern Skye, the landscape is characterised by horizontal basalt lavas topped by grassy plateaux and surrounded by tussocky heather moorland

The bulky southern flanks of Healabhal Mhòr

From Orbost

Summits: *Healabhal Bheag* ▲ ;
Beinn Bhac-ghlais ▲ ; *Healabhal Mhòr* ▲
Terrain: *Hillwalk*
Distance: *15km; 9.25 miles*
Ascent & Descent: *855m; 2810ft*
Time: *5hrs 30mins–6hrs 30mins*
Start & Finish: *Gated track entrance before left-hand bend on road to Orbost (NG 2562 4449)*

Despite what might be presumed from the Gaelic, *mhòr* meaning big and *bheag* meaning small, Healabhal Mhòr is actually 18m lower than its southerly sibling, 489m Healabhal Bheag.
 This may be due to its proximity to Dunvegan

Castle, seat of Clan MacLeod and the understand-able lack of sophisticated surveying equipment in 13th century Scotland. Nevertheless, Healabhal Mhòr is a significantly bulkier hill than Healabhal Bheag, so whoever named these hills was actually spot on.
 There are two starting points for this circular route; Osdale, north of the East Ridge of Healabhal Mhòr and near Orbost, east of the East Ridge of Healabhal Bheag. Both routes have to cross a barbed wire fence beside the Osdale River, but parking is probably easier at the Orbost approach and that is the route described here.
 Beinn Bhac-ghlais (409m) lies to the south of MacLeod's Tables. It is the lesser of the three hills both in terms of stature and interest, however it is also a Sub-2000ft Marilyn (see p10) and worth climbing at the same time as the two Tables.

The Cuillin and the Western Red Hills from the trig point on Healabhal Bheag

Approach

From the A863, follow the B844 road signposted to Glendale and continue straight on for Orbost where the B844 turns sharply to the right. After nearly 1 mile (1.8km), at a sweeping left-hand bend, a gated track leads off to the right. Park here.

Ascent

Go through the gate, walk up the track, turn left and follow the fence west until clear of the small wooded gorge carrying the Allt na Glas Bhuaile. Gain the high ground on the left and ascend south towards Beinn Bhuidhe. Go around this on its right side and continue ascending towards An Cruachan.

Skirt this to its right to regain the broad crest and follow it towards the steep and rocky slopes guarding the summit of Healabhal Bheag. Climb these fairly directly over grass and boulders to reach the trig point and spectacular views south-east over Loch Bracadale and its islands; from Askival and Ainshval on Rùm to The Cuillin, Blàbheinn, Garbh-bheinn, Glamaig and the Western Red Hills. The highest point (by 1m) is about 140m south-west of the trig point.

From this highpoint, descend the South Ridge to Bealach Bharcasaig, cross a barbed wire fence and climb to the summit of Beinn Bhac-ghlais. The highest point (by 1m) is 60m south of the cairn. Return to the bealach, ascend a short distance, then contour north round the left side of Healabhal Bheag to reach the

col between it and Beinn na h-Uamha. Leaving Beinn Bhac-ghlais out of the round reduces the total distance by about 4km and the time by about 1hr 30mins.

From the col, pass to the right of Beinn na h-Uamha and to the left of An Sgùrran to reach the grassy slopes of Healabhal Mhòr and follow them to the

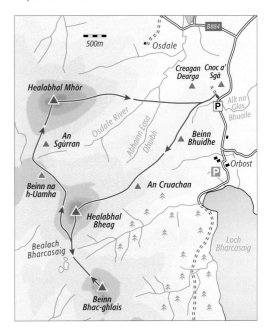

The steep frontal prow of Healabhal Bheag

summit. The highest point (by 2m) is 30m north-west of the large cairn. The summit plateau is even bigger than Healabhal Bheag's. There are fine views north and west to the Outer Hebrides and the mountains of Harris and the Uists.

Descent

The East Ridge makes for a slightly steeper descent on grassy slopes scattered with boulders, to reach the Osdale River, about 400m above the point where it joins the Abhainn Easa Dhuibh. The next section can be very boggy in wet conditions. Cross over a barbed wire fence, then continue east across the Abhainn Easa Dhuibh and ascend to the broad col between Creagan Dearga and Beinn Bhuidhe, to gain the outward route and follow it back to the start.

Healabhal Mhòr from the flanks of Healabhal Bheag

The South Ridge of Ben Tianavaig and rock towers above Mc Queen's Loch from Gedintailor to the south

Ben Tianavaig

*C*lose proximity to Portree and easy access makes Ben Tianavaig (413m) one of Skye's most popular small hills. Thankfully though, it is still mostly frequented by hillwalkers, rather than the bus loads of tourists that blight The Storr and The Quiraing. And what a great hillwalk it is; an elevated grassy summit with breathtaking views, gained via an airy cliff-top ridge. The easiest and most frequented route is from Camustianavaig to the south

Approaching the final section of the South Ridge below the summit

South Ridge from Camustianavaig

Summits: *Ben Tianavaig* ▲
Terrain: *Hillwalk*
Distance: *7.5km, 4.5 miles*
Ascent & Descent: *430m; 1410ft*
Time: *2hrs 40mins–3hrs 40mins*
Start & Finish: *Camustianavaig – small car park on Tianavaig Bay (NG 5085 3889)*

The long South Ridge is ascended over heather and grass on a well-worn path. The finest route is to descend the An Ceam Dubh to the coast and follow it back to Camustianavaig.

Approach
From the parking, follow the road north and uphill for about 170m to the first house on the right, which has a gated access track to its left. The signposted path starts immediately left of the metal gate across the track.

Ascent
Follow the path onto the open hillside keeping right where it divides and contour east round the high ground above the coast, with views over to Raasay and the truncated cone of Dùn Cana.

Gain Ben Tianavaig's South Ridge and follow the crest above the cliffs to the summit trig point, turning back occasionally to appreciate the view south to the Western and Eastern Red Hills. There is also a path below the crest, should the wind be strong.

Descent
The easiest descent is to return down the South Ridge, but this makes for a very short day. A more interesting route is to explore the cliffs and towers below Ben Tianavaig's East Face, before descending south-east to the coast.

From the summit, descend the grassy North Ridge then swing right (east) round a crag to a col and ascend to the crest of the small cliff enclosing the north end of the shallow grassy corrie below

Looking down the South Ridge to the Western and Eastern Red Hills

Tianavaig's East Face. This corrie has been formed by landslips and displays the characteristic grassy hollows rock towers and lochans found throughout the Trotternish Ridge to the north. The cliff-top gives an uninterrupted view across to Raasay and the coastline more than 300m below.

Return to the col and descend grassy slopes into the shallow corrie. Continue east below the small cliff at the northern end to reach an isolated diamond-shaped rock pinnacle, from where a further descent on grass and heather leads to the crown-like pinnacles marking the top of the cliffs of the eastern escarpment, overlooking Mc Queen's Loch. While it is possible to descend to the loch and the coast, the route is rough going through thick and pathless heather.

A much better option is to turn south, keeping right of the pinnacles, before picking the line of least resistance, steeply down An Ceum Dubh (The Black Step) through grass and scattered heather to the coast.

Follow the shingle beach south-west round the coast to where it fades and a path continues round the headland above the sea. Follow this to where it finally drops back down to the beach at Tianavaig Bay and traverse the fore-shore back to the start.

North Ridge from Penifiler

Summits: *Ben Tianavaig* ▲
Terrain: *Hillwalk*
Distance: *7.5km, 4.5 miles*
Ascent & Descent: *390m; 1280ft*
Time: *2hrs 30mins–3hrs 30mins*
Start & Finish: *Good verge parking on the left, before the last houses at Penifiler (NG 4888 4163)*

The abandoned settlement of Scorr

The northern approach from Penifiler is a much wilder outing than the route from Camustianavaig. The heather moorland is rough and wet in places, but the coastline gives varied walking and the abandoned settlement at Scorr adds interest. There are fine views north to Portree and Trotternish.

Approach

At the end of the road there is a pedestrian gate beside the gated track leading down to Inveralivaig.

Ascent

Go through the pedestrian gate onto open moorland. Turn left beside the fence and pass under powerlines, then go right to gain a shallow open glen with a small burn in it, down which the powerlines run. Follow the right (east) side of the burn down the glen to reach a larger burn.

Cross over, ascend to an overgrown wall and follow it over moorland and rock slabs to the coast over-looking Camas Bàn bay. The grey sand is probably due to the coal deposits at the bay's northern end.

About 50m left (west) from the wall a steep path descends to the bay. Go down this to reach the coast and follow the bay east to the grassy coastal flats leading to the deserted settlement of Scorr.

Ascend south-east beside the Scorr Burn on grass then heather to gain Ben Tianavaig's tussocky North Ridge and follow it to the summit.

Descent

From the summit, descend west aiming for Druim Loch, the furthest of the two lochans, and the aerial above Penifiler. Weave down through small crags to an area of scrub bushes and bracken and cross over the Lòn Bàn burn at NG 5013 4117.

Ascend to gain the high ground and follow its right edge overlooking Loch Meallachan, before descending west to pass to the south of Druim Loch. Continue in the same line to reach the shallow open glen with the powerlines, then cross over the small burn to rejoin the outward route.

Portree, Sithean a' Bhealaich Chumhaing (see Assorted Other Hills), far right, and The Storr, beyond, from the North Ridge

277

The distinctive summit cone of Dùn Cana, from the red rocky pavement south of Bealach Ruadh

Dùn Cana & Meall Daimh

*W*hat's in a name? Dùn Caan or Dùn Cana? Maps have Dùn Caan, but Sorley MacLean, celebrated Gaelic poet and son of Raasay names it Dùn Cana (Dhùn Cana in fact!) in his meditation on the deserted village of Hallaig below the peak. Raasay isn't Skye of course, but excluding such a prominent and enjoyable mountain, that is both easily and almost always accessed from Skye, seems pedantic; you get to ride on a ferry too!

Boarding the Raasay ferry at Sconsor

Via Inverarish Burn

Summits: Dùn Cana ▲; Meall Daimh ▲
Terrain: Hillwalk
Distance: 17.5km; 11 miles
Ascent & Descent: 585m; 1920ft
Time: 5hrs 11mins–6hrs 11mins
Start & Finish: Raasay Ferry Terminal. (There is free parking at the Sconsor Terminal)

The distinctive flat-topped summit of Dùn Cana (444m) is a prominent landmark off Skye's eastern seaboard and is easily combined with Meall Daimh (393m) to the north, to give an interesting and enjoyable round of Raasay's two highest mountains.

The route can be linked with the network of paths through the forestry above Raasay House and accomplished in a day on foot from the ferry.

Approach
There is a regular service to Raasay from the ferry terminal at Sconsor on Skye *www.calmac.co.uk*

Ascent
From the pier, follow the road past the terminal building (toilets) and ascend slightly to a Y-junction in front of the old stable block. Go right here past a turning on the left (signposted cemetery) and the new distillery to reach another Y-junction, where you keep left on the higher main road. A long straight leads to another junction (NG 5562 3612) and a signpost to

Descending from the summit of Dùn Cana. Meall Daimh is the prominent hill above Loch na Meilich to the left

the Temptation Hill path. This hill is at NG 5495 3708 and unnamed on OS maps. Ignore the path, but turn diagonally left and ascend the twisting narrow road to reach a track turning on the right, signposted Burma

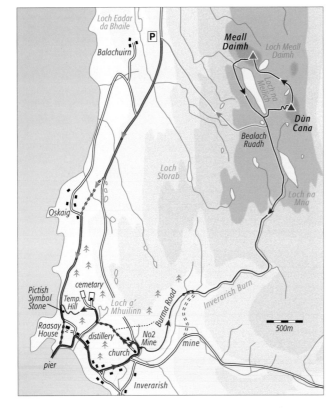

Path. This leads to a small car park surrounded by forestry. The buildings mark the site of the old No2 Ironstone Mine which closed in 1918. Follow the Burma Road Path, built by foresters in the 1950s and clearly a tough job. Ascend through forestry and rhododendrons to exit the trees at an area of felling. Continue to where the path becomes a better defined track and cross a bridge. Where the track bends sharply south, a path signposted 'Dun Cana 3.8km' branches off left. An initial ascent through trees leads to a deer gate, open hillside and a path beside the Inverarish Burn.

As height is gained the heather moor-land gives rougher going and the path fades in places, but the route sticks to the left (west) side of the burn all the way to Loch na Mna. The OS map shows the path following the west shore of the loch, but the most prominent path climbs the front of the escarpment west of the loch and passes over rocky slabs to reach a round lochan above Bealach Ruadh at the south end of Loch na Meilich.

Descend to Loch na Meilich, ascend a path up the western flanks of Dùn Cana and scramble through the crags ringing the summit to the cylindrical trig point.

To continue to Meall Daimh, descend steeply north from the summit and cross moorland, passing right of an island studded lochan, to reach Loch Meall

Daimh. This can be skirted to its right or left to gain steep grassy slopes leading to the summit of Meall Daimh; at 393m the second highest point on the island.

From the summit, head west and descend to the northern outflow of Loch na Meilich. Cross over the burn, gain the northern end of the escarpment enclosing the west side of Loch na Meilich and follow it back to the round lochan above Bealach Ruadh.

Descent

From Bealach Ruadh there are **three options**:

(1) Return beside the Inverarish Burn to No2 Mine. Exit to the road and turn right, then left to the Manse and follow the track round left towards the church. Turn right at the T-junction and ascend the track past a sign to Dùn Borodale, then round and down through felled forestry to Loch a' Mhuilinn and the road.

Turn right here and ascend to where the road leads straight ahead to a house and left to the old cemetery. Go left, then break off left over open ground to gain a path which leads round Temptation Hill above Raasay House with fine views north to The Cuillin, then drops down to the road. Turn left and pass the Pictish symbol stone on the left, to reach the entrance to Raasay House. Go down the drive and through the grounds on a track, to arrive back at the pier.

The distance and timings for this route are as detailed in the Via Inverarish Burn information panel on *p279*.

(2) Leaving out Temptation Hill and returning totally by the outward route involves some 50m less ascent and 500m less distance and is about 15mins quicker.

Pictish Symbol Stone by the road north of Raasay House

(3) Turn right (west) at the round lochan above Bealach Ruadh and descend the moorland path west then north-west to reach the road. Turn left and follow the road south for about 1.2km to a Y-junction on the right leading to Balachuirn. Ignore this and continue on the road for a further 1km, to a gate on the right at the start of a track. Descend the track to emerge on the lower road just south of Oskaig.

Turn left and follow the road south past the Pictish symbol stone on the left, to the entrance to Raasay House. Go down the drive and through the grounds on a track to arrive back at the pier. This option also involves some 50m less ascent and 500m less distance and is about 15mins quicker.

Looking south towards Dùn Cana from the flanks of Meall Daimh. The prominent cone-shaped peak in the distance is Beinn na Crò – one of Skye's most distinctive summits when viewed from the Applecross mainland to the north-east

Assorted Other Hills

L ow-level hills can save the day when cloud, wind or rain make the high tops unattractive. All of the hills described here are below 609.6m (2000ft) and receive fairly frequent ascents, although there may be no evidence of a path on the ground

Approaching the trig point on Beinn na h-Iolaire, Raasay, with the island of Rona beyond

Most of the hills in this section are Sub-2000ft Marilyns (see Using this Guide p10) and as such they see a modest, but steady stream of ascents from hillwalkers ticking the Marilyns list.

All are worth considering for 'off' days, although some are significantly better and more interesting than others. The Other Fine Hills listed here are all worth an ascent.

[45] Ben Geary 284m ▲ (NG 25363 61463)
Easily climbed to its trig point, via the aerial access track at NG 2612 6015 (verge parking), W of Knockbreck Primary School. Extensive views over the wild bogs of Waternish.

[46] Biod an Athair 314m ▲ (NG 15832 54936)
From the road-end at Galtrigill, S of Dunvegan Head, follow the track SW to its end. Cross open moorland and bog NW making the best of green grassy areas to the summit trig point above impressive sea-cliffs.

[47] Beinn Bhreac 329m ▲ (NG 25365 53070)
A rolling heather and bog hill with fine sea views,

easily climbed from the busy but limited Coral Beaches car park at Claigan NG 2318 5372. Follow the track past the Souterrain (marked on maps) then a grassy track to about 230m. Ascend about 750m NE to a small summit cairn among peat hags. The trig point 1.5km to the NW, is lower at 314m. For a circuit, follow a heather-covered dyke (see OS 1:25k) to the 314m trig point, then descend heather and rough grass to Lovaig Bay and round to the Coral Beaches.

[48] Beinn Chreagach 326m ▲ (NG 28911 53428)
Easily climbed from the B886 to Waternish, N of the old Fairy Bridge. Verge parking with care in the vicinity of the milestone marked on maps. Follow the N side of Allt na Beinne Creagaich (see OS 1:25k) over rough heather to the summit cairn.

[49] Cruachan-Glen Vic Askill 295m ▲ (NG 35758 46047). Easily climbed from Edinbane Power Station NG 3505 4404 beyond Balmeanach (reached by a minor road from the A863 north of Bracadale), via the wind turbine access track, then rough grass and heather to the summit cairn.

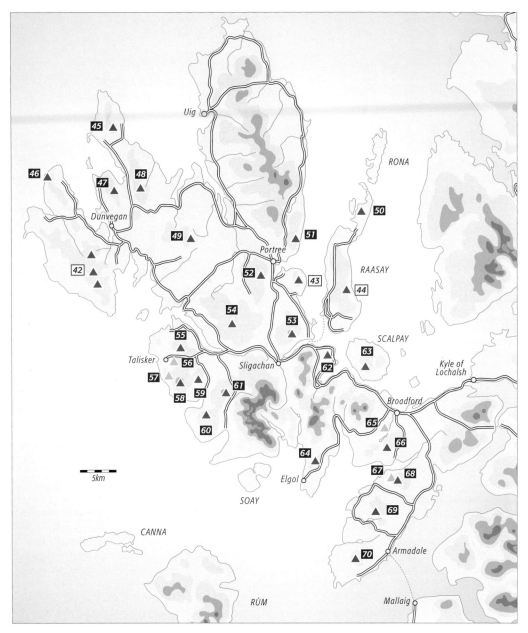

[50] **Beinn na h-Iolaire** 254m ▲ (NG 59988 50248)
Fine rocky hill at the northern tip of Raasay, with
extensive sea views. Follow the public road to its end
at a small car park before Arnish. Follow the LH track
to the Mission House at Torran, then right on a path
signed to Rona and pass below Meall Dearg (see OS
1:25k). Turn right beyond this on the Rona path, leaving
it near the col to climb N to the trig point. Return to
the last junction and descend W to Eilean Fladday,
from where a good path and track lead back to Torran.

[51] **Sithean a' Bhealaich Chumhaing** 393m ▲ (NG
50897 46616). This dramatic 'mini Ben Tianavaig', is
easily climbed from Portree. From a small car park
on the E side of Portree Bay below the Cuillin Hills
Hotel, follow the coast path to where it turns steeply
N. Go through a wall on the right, continue NE
through fields and gates and rise up to a burn.
Ascend beside the burn, cross the fence on the right,
then climb up and right to the cliff-top. Contour round
above Rubha na h-Àirde Glaise to the trig point (*see
also map p266*).

[52] **Beinn na Greine** 417m ▲ (NG 45966 41612)
Park (NG 4340 4124) at foot of the access road to the
aerials on ▲ **Skriaig** (396m), approached from B885 W

283

North to the summit of Sithean a' Bhealaich Chumhaing above Portree, Trotternish

of Portree and a minor road to Glenmore. Cross peat hags and some bog to reach the summit knoll, trig point and walled shelter and views down Glen Sligachan.

[53] Ben Lee 444m ▲ (NG 50251 33615)
Good views of Sgùrr nan Gillean and Am Bàsteir enhance this moorland round, which can include ▲ **Meall Odhar Beag** and ▲ **Meall Odhar Mòr** (335m). Follow the coast path NE from Sligachan Campsite to the prominent waterfall and ascend on its right side over Cnoc an t-Sìthein to the summit cairn.

[54] Roineval 439m ▲ (NG 41845 35047)
Easily climbed from the A863 overlooking Loch Harport. Park at NG 3912 3484, walk 150m W on the road to a track on the right and follow it 2.5km to Bealach Mòr. Cross marshy ground S to a fence, then climb SE to the trig point.

[55] Arnaval 369m ▲ (NG 34535 31659)
Highpoint of craggy escarpment topped by undulating terrain of rocky knolls and lochans (tricky in poor visibility), easily climbed from the road to Talisker Bay. Verge parking where the Allt a' Bhàthaich crosses the road (NG 3423 3057). Follow the burn N, then continue N to the summit.

[56] Preshal More 324m ▲ (NG 33307 29995)

Fantastic rocky fortress with views over Talisker Bay. Park on the right just before the bridge over the River Talisker (NG 3324 3070). Cross the bridge and cattle grid, then go left onto a track and ascend it to a gate. Continue round the S side of the hill, ascending to below the cliffs. Where they reduce in height ascend a rocky gully with a grassy tongue at its base and a pinnacle at its start, to gain the top.

From the summit cairn, head NW to a large cairn (317m) and fine views. Return to the summit, then descend E with care to a grassy and heather col with old sheep pens. Descend steep grass N through the crags then NW to regain the track. It is easy to extend the route to ▲ **Stockval** (416m) sticking to the high ground.

[57] Preshal Beg 345m ▲ (NG 32950 27866)
Despite the name, this is higher than Preshal More. A rather dull moorland walk S above the Sleadale Burn is lifted by the impressive Dùn Sleadale broch at NG 3238 2920 and the basalt columns on Preshal Beg. The summit can be gained via the E face. The parking at Talisker is busy and very limited.

[58] Beinn Bhreac 448m ▲ (NG 34482 26723)
Easily climbed with **Biod Mòr** from the Glen Eynort road (see below). Highest points are 100m E and 240m NNE of the trig point (see OS 1:25k).

[59] Biod Mòr 384m ▲ (NG 37066 27384)
Park at the highpoint in Glen Eynort. Descend the road 1.8km to a bridge over the Eynort River (NG 3811 2822). Cross this, skirt fenced pasture N then W to gain hillside and ascend to Loch Bioda Mòr and the summit cairn. Descend SW, cross Clachan Gorma to Beinn na Cuinneig and skirt crags to a lochan and the summit of **Beinn Bhreac** to its W. Descend the broad spur N then E past Cearra to a track from the old shielings, which leads north of the felled forestry back to the start.

[60] An Cruachan ▲ (435m NG 38177 22503)
Easily gained from Glen Brittle via the forest track (NG 4192 2504), 500m N of the road bridge over the River Brittle. Ascend the track to Bealach Brittle then W on an atv track to a gate. Guala a' Choire Mhòir leads to the summit trig point and good views of The Cuillin. An Cruachan and **Beinn a' Bhraghad** (see below) can also be climbed from Eynort via Beinn Staic utilising forestry tracks, either to the N end of Beinn a' Bhraghad or to Bealach Eadar dà Bheinn.

[61] Beinn a' Bhràghad 461m ▲ (NG 40976 25408)
Park in Glen Brittle at the start of a track NG 4160 2747, signposted Bealach Brittle. Follow the track over a slight ridge and descend to a clearing through the forest, with a deep-cut burn (NG 4071 2723). Ascend this south to open hillside and the trig point. The summit is 210m to the SW (see OS 1:25k). Superb views of The Cuillin.

[62] Meall a' Mhaoil 284m ▲ (NG 55388 30765)
A rounded heather and grass clad hill significantly enhanced by fine views west to the Western Red Hills and N to Raasay. Park at the track N of Moll (NG 5598 3037). Follow it for about 850m, then ascend N to gain the broad SW ridge leading to the trig point.

[63] Mullach na Càrn 396m ▲ (NG 60582 29226)
There is no public boat service to Scalpay, however the Skye Boat Centre boatyard at Dunan is worth investigating. Once on the island, follow the Allt na Criche above Loch na Cairidh and E of the forestry (NG 5950 2851), to pass through a deer fence and gain the lochan, then ascend N to the summit cairn (*see map p217*).

[64] Ben Meabost 345m ▲ (NG 53661 15941)
Easily climbed from the B8083 Elgol road. Park just south of the turning to Drinan. From opposite the junction follow a path up onto the southern flanks and ascend through the crags to the summit cairn. It can also be combined from Elgol with ▲ **Ben Cleat** (277m), ▲ **Ben Leacach** (272m) and the Camasunary path. Stunning views to Sgùrr na Stri and Blàbheinn.

[65] Beinn Shuardail 281m ▲ (NG 63066 20639)
Interesting limestone hill and the first recorded ascent of a Skye mountain in 1772 by Rev Mr John Lightfoot and Rev Mr John Stuart, Thomas Pennant's travel companions: see Pennant's *A Tour in Scotland and Voyage to the Hebrides p327*. This pre-dates by a few days, Pennant's ascent of Beinn na Caillich recorded on *p329*. Easy access from the parking by the chambered cairn (NG 6272 2206). Ascend via Bealach a' Ghlinne and return via the old marble quarries to the S and the track through Strath Suardal (*see map p217*).

[66] Beinn nan Càrn 301m ▲ (NG 63599 18075)
Park on the minor road to Hesta, south of Broadford, by sheep pens just before the village (NG 6504 1788), or at a small quarry (NG 6529 1822). Either way, it is a relentless moorland trek NW through undulating heather and rough grass, to pass S of Loch an Eilein and ascend the E flank to the summit. The track from the Heasta Road to Loch Buidhe might offer another route (see OS 1:25k).

[67] Sgiath-bheinn an Uird 294m ▲ (NG 64287 13806). The highest point of the distinctive 'white' quartzite mountains forming the W side of the Sleat peninsula and easily identified from Strathaird and Boraig. Usually combined with the slightly higher, but less interesting **Sgòrach Breac** (see below).

[68] Sgòrach Breac 299m ▲ (NG 65172 13195)
An enjoyable, rocky circuit including **Sgiath-bheinn an Uird** starts from the minor road to Ord, off the A851 to Armadale. Park at sheep pens (NG 6308 1241) and ascend NW, crossing extensive quartzite slabs to reach Sgiath-bheinn an Uird. Descend SE, cross lower-lying ground and ascend to the trig point of Sgòrach Breac atop a small red sandstone crag. Return to the road via Locha Fada Ghasgain and Allt Dearg (see OS 1:25k).

[69] Sgùrr na h-Iolaire 292m ▲ (NG 61716 09051)
Undistinguished hill, easily ascended to the trig point over heather and rough grass from the western outflow of Loch Dhùghaill on the minor road to Tarskavaig, off the A851 to Armadale. If the water is high, then park at the road's highpoint overlooking Loch Dhùghaill and traverse above the loch's east side.

[70] Sgùrr nan Caorach 281m ▲ (NG 59378 02999). Start from the end of the road at Aird, where the footpath continues to Point of Sleat, the most southerly point on Skye. Go through a gate, then head N to cross a fence and reach the trig point. However, the highest point by 100m, lies 650m to the E, beyond a lochan and is marked 280m on OS 1:25k.